Second Edition

Assistive Technology for People with Disabilities

Diane Pedrotty Bryant
The University of Texas at Austin

Brian R. Bryant
Psycho-Educational Services

Boston Columbus Indianapolis New York San Francisco Upper Saddle River
Amsterdam Cape Town Dubai London Madrid Milan Munich Paris Montreal Toronto
Delhi Mexico City Sao Paulo Sydney Hong Kong Seoul Singapore Taipei Tokyo

KH

Vice President and Editor in Chief: Jeffery W. Johnston
Executive Editor and Publisher: Stephen D. Dragin
Editorial Assistant: Jamie Bushell
Vice President, Director of Marketing: Margaret Waples
Marketing Manager: Weslie Sellinger
Senior Managing Editor: Pamela D. Bennett
Production Manager: Susan Hannahs
Senior Art Director: Jayne Conte
Cover Designer: Suzanne Behnke
Cover Art: Fotosearch
Full-Service Project Management: Niraj Bhatt/Aptara®, Inc.
Composition: Aptara®, Inc.
Text and Printer/Bindery: Courier/Westford
Text Font: Times

Credits and acknowledgments for material borrowed from other sources and reproduced, with permission, in this textbook appear on the appropriate page within the text.

Every effort has been made to provide accurate and current Internet information in this book. However, the Internet and information posted on it are constantly changing, so it is inevitable that some of the Internet addresses listed in this textbook will change.

Library of Congress Cataloging-in-Publication Data
Bryant, Diane Pedrotty.
Assistive technology for people with disabilities / Diane Pedrotty Bryant.—2nd ed.
p. cm.
ISBN-13: 978-0-13-705009-3
ISBN-10: 0-13-705009-7
1. Self-help devices for people with disabilities. 2. Rehabilitation technology. I. Title.
RM950.B79 2012
617′.033—dc22
2011010234

10 9 8 7 6 5 4 3 2 1

www.pearsonhighered.com

ISBN 10: 0-13-705009-7
ISBN 13: 978-0-13-705009-3

2/28/12

Dedication

This book is dedicated to those individuals who use assistive technology to help them become independent members of society and better able to access all of the environments in which we live, work, enjoy leisure and recreational activities, and learn. We also dedicate this book to the many professionals and family members who work tirelessly to ensure that assistive technology devices and services are accessible for users. Finally, we dedicate this book to our brother/brother-in-law, Paul, who taught us so many valuable lessons about the liberating potential of assistive technology, and our mother/mother-in-law Adeline, who advocated for Paul in the public schools years before such advocacy became the norm.

PREFACE

This textbook is intended to provide readers with a wide range of information about assistive technology adaptations with an emphasis on devices and services. Assistive technology (AT) is an area that is characterized by rapid development and innovation as a result of work done by researchers, engineers, educators, users and families, therapists, and rehabilitation specialists to inform and provide better and more promising devices to meet the needs of technology users. We know more than ever about the benefits of assistive technology to enhance the lives of individuals with disabilities to promote independence, access, and equity.

NEW TO THIS EDITION

The intent of this second edition is to provide readers and instructors with updated information about assistive technology devices and services. We paid careful attention to the reviewers' comments and suggestions to revise the content by including current ideas and trends in the field of AT and incorporating many of the "new technologies" that are benefiting all individuals. We live in a remarkable electronic age that brings social and educational networks rapidly together. More and more devices are emerging that make these connections possible for all individuals. In addition, the improved capacity of devices to recognize speech and read text and the incorporation of accessibility features in computers has tremendous potential to promote independence in the disability community. With this in mind, this revision includes the following changes, many of which reflect the reviewers' input, that we believe significantly improve the content:

- Assistive technology devices have been updated throughout the book to reflect more current applications in the field. This change should greatly help readers better understand more current technologies.
- Although we continued to include pictures of devices, we have included URLs of vendors for readers to review online the features of software and devices. We believe the inclusion of these URLs is a particular solution for including sources for pictures and descriptions of devices. It is important to note that we do not endorse any specific vendor, product, or software; rather, we included examples of current technologies for readers to review with their instructors. For example, the *Journal of Special Education Technology* is one source for readers to refer to for research that is being done on current devices in the AT field. It is important that readers identify and review the evidence that supports various devices and software. Additionally, we have added a few URLs of advocacy groups and institutions that support efforts to make the public aware of issues pertaining to AT.
- We have placed the Personal Perspectives strategically within the chapters so that they set the tone for the chapter or for a section of the chapter. We also deleted Chapter 8 from the first edition; although the content was educationally significant, the reviewers did not think it fit as well with the rest of the chapters. We also deleted the Focus activities within each chapter to help make chapters flow better.
- We added Scenario Applications to provide readers with opportunities to apply the content in each chapter in a practical situation. We included some reference back to the Adaptations Framework (Chapter 2) so that readers could apply some of the information back to the educational setting and the needs of their students with disabilities. We also included For Discussion questions for class activities. Finally, references have been updated.

- We included a case study in Chapter 3 to help the reader learn about the application of the assessment process to the identification and evaluation of assistive technology devices for individual users.
- We added newer concepts such as universal design, information about the Independent Living Movement, information about efficacy, and vocabulary.

PURPOSE AND AUDIENCE

This textbook presents information about assistive technology adaptations to educators, therapists, users and families, and rehabilitation specialists. By providing information that is grounded in research and supported by individuals who use technology, decision makers, users, and their families will obtain information to better inform choices made about technology and individual needs. This book is intended for undergraduate and graduate students who are taking an assistive technology course and for individuals who are working in the rehabilitation and therapy fields. The focus of the book is on the lifespan, various disabilities, and the environments in which all individuals function as a part of life. Assistive technology makes activities possible for many people, and, as our colleague Dr. Peg Nosek noted, it is liberating! It is this message of possibility, liberation, access, and independence that we hope serves as an underpinning theme throughout the chapters.

FEATURES

There are several noteworthy features that are intended to enrich the content and assist readers in learning about assistive technology adaptations. First, we have included instructional features such as Objectives, Making Connections, Scenario Applications, and Discussion Questions to help readers think about the content before and after reading each chapter. Second, we have included Personal Perspectives that highlight the viewpoints of individuals who use technology, have children who use technology, provide professional development, and/or serve as advocates for assistive technology. We think this feature helps to personalize the information presented in the chapters and illustrate the impact of assistive technology on the lives of individuals who benefit most. Third, we have included updated pictures of devices and URLs to help readers go online to see and read about new technologies. We think providing URLs is a good way to help readers stay apprised of current and new technologies. We hope these features will promote reader activity and connections with the content.

CONTENT AND ORGANIZATION

The eight chapters in the book address a variety of topics related to assistive technology devices and services. Topics include an introduction to assistive technology, the Adaptations Framework, assessment, mobility, communication, access to information, academic instruction, and independent living. Each topic was chosen because of its contribution to assistive technology and the effects of AT on the lives of individuals with disabilities across the lifespan.

The first three chapters of the book provide introductory material and assessment information about assistive technology. The Adaptations Framework is introduced and is applied throughout the book as a means of considering assistive technology and matching adaptations, such as AT devices, with individuals' needs in various settings. Next, we provide chapters on mobility, communication, and access to the information pervasive in our society—these are basic life requirements. We provide a chapter that focuses on assistive technology during the school years because of the importance of ensuring that all students have access to the curriculum and that teachers examine ways to make instruction more meaningful for learning. Finally, we conclude the book with a chapter on independent living. We think this represents a good culminating chapter that focuses on how assistive technology is applicable across all environments. We hope you enjoy the book!

ACKNOWLEDGMENTS

When we started revising our book on assistive technology, we were struck by the considerable amount of "new technologies" that have emerged for all consumers and more specifically for individuals with disabilities. One of the biggest challenges with this revision was to identify content that would not be outdated immediately. We hope that we have captured the "big ideas" in assistive technology and that the examples we provided will illustrate the ideas successfully. Throughout this book, you will read Personal Perspectives and references to a number of our colleagues whom we have met and worked with over the years. Their perspectives, we believe, enrich the content of this text, because they speak to the issues, challenges, and "new technologies" from their vantage point, whether an educator, a parent, a researcher, and most importantly as a user of AT. We acknowledge and thank our Personal Perspective authors: Diana Carl, Anne Corn, Lewis Golinker, Mike Haynes, Tony "Mac" McGregor, Robin Lock, Peg Nosek, Bonnie O'Reilly, Mark O'Reilly, Penny Reed, Sam, and Jamie Judd-Wall. We believe that the reflections offered in the Personal Perspectives will help readers understand the application of assistive technology from different viewpoints.

We also acknowledge our coauthors in several of the chapters. Their assistance in revising the content is deeply appreciated, and their work strengthens the book. We thank Guliz Kraft, Robin Lock, and Minyi Shih. In addition, we recognize Joy Zabala, Tricia Legler, and Marshall Raskind, three friends, who have taught us much about assistive technology from their professional and personal experiences working with AT users and their families. Much of what we know has come from working closely with these three professionals.

We also express our appreciation to our editor, Ann Davis, and Penny Burleson, editorial assistant, for their assistance, support, and patience. We acknowledge and thank our reviewers, whose insight and helpful feedback strengthened the content of this book. They offered many thoughtful comments, suggestions, and feedback that addressed the areas that required attention in this revision. We are deeply indebted to them for their time and expertise. Thank you to Emily C. Bouck, Purdue University; Kristy K. Ehlers, Oklahoma State University; Linda Mechling, University of North Carolina—Wilmington; and James Stachowiak, University of Iowa. We hope that the combined efforts of all we have mentioned have made this book an informative and pleasant reading experience for you.

Finally, we would like to acknowledge the students and parents with whom we have worked over the years. They are the people who are most affected by AT's promise. They have taught us much over the years, and we hope that, for them, AT eventually fulfills its potential as a tool for accessibility and full participation in all of life's activities.

CONTENTS

1 INTRODUCTION TO ASSISTIVE TECHNOLOGY DEVICES AND SERVICES

Objectives

1. Examine definitions of key assistive technology terms.
2. Demonstrate knowledge concerning the history of assistive technology.
3. Identify key professionals involved in assistive technology service delivery.

MAKING CONNECTIONS

Think about how inventions have changed people's lives over the past 100 years. Some inventions, such as automobiles, computers, the Internet, microwaves, televisions, refrigerators, and airplanes, have dramatically altered our way of life. Others, such as remote control units and electric devices, ATMs, and digital networks, have certainly made our lives easier on a daily basis. Now, think about people you know with disabilities that could be developmental, acquired, or part of the aging process. What special needs do these people have, and what devices do they use to access various environmental contexts? Think about inventions that make things possible for people with disabilities—for example, think about an aging grandparent who might use a remote control to turn on the lights because of difficulty with standing and walking. Consider the ramifications to access and independence if those inventions did not exist for people with disabilities. Now, recall legislation that has been passed to help secure people's civil rights. How might these laws apply to people with disabilities? What laws are specifically designed for people with disabilities?

In this chapter, we provide background information that sets the stage for the central themes (i.e., access and independence) that run throughout this text. In this chapter, we (a) introduce and discuss the concepts of access and independence; (b) define *assistive technology* (more specifically, *AT device*, *AT service*, and *instructional technology*); (c) provide a historical overview of AT development; and (d) discuss the multidisciplinary nature of AT service delivery.

ACCESS AND INDEPENDENCE

About 20 years ago, International Business Machines (IBM, 1991) provided a training package for assistive technology (AT) in which they noted, "For people without disabilities, technology makes things easier; for people with disabilities, technology makes things possible" (p. 2). Of all we have read concerning AT and its application, this statement seems to be the most succinct. There is no doubt that technological advances have made most people's lives considerably easier in the past 40 years or so. The first commercial pocket calculators in the 1970s sold for several hundred dollars. Seemingly overnight these minicomputers were being offered free of charge to car owners who purchased at least eight gallons of gasoline. Presto—balancing a checkbook, or at least attempting to do so, became that much easier. For people with math disabilities, balancing a checkbook became possible, because their computational weaknesses make such a task nearly impossible to perform independently. This is but one example of the "easier . . . possible" comparison. We might also recall how speaking into a computer's microphone and having the words magically appear on paper was once a pipedream for those of us who labored at typing a term paper. Thanks to voice-to-text technology, such a task is accomplished simply by using a computer and specialized software. For most of us, writing was made easier; for a person with a severe motor or vision difficulty who would otherwise struggle with inputting text into a computer, writing became not only possible but somewhat simple to perform (if writing is ever simple). Advances in technology have benefited most of society, but it could be argued that for people with disabilities, technology has provided a means to an end, which is independence. That is, AT devices serve as a vehicle to help individuals with disabilities do what they want to do, when they want to do it, thereby reducing the need to depend on others to do things for them. To accentuate the importance of access and independence facilitated by AT across all environments, including the classroom, we provide the perspective of a leader in AT who is also the parent of an AT user; this perspective also sets the stage for the remaining content in this chapter (see Personal Perspective 1.1).

PERSONAL PERSPECTIVE 1.1

Diana Carl is a parent of an assistive technology user. As the former Director of Special Education Services at Region 4 Education Service Center (ESC) in Houston, Texas, Diana was the lead facilitator of the Texas Assistive Technology Network (TATN) for 11 years. TATN is the statewide leadership function designated by the Texas Education Agency; Region 4 provides leadership for this collaborative project between the 20 ESCs in Texas. She is a nationally recognized leader in AT and the education of students with disabilities.

Tell our readers a little bit about your daughter.

My daughter had a cerebral hemorrhage when she was born and was in the hospital in high-intensity care units for three months. We were told by the doctors that the odds were that Dana would have severe and profound disabilities. She was being fed by tube and the doctors did not anticipate that she would be able to suck a bottle or that we would be able to care for her at home. We were asked to plan our next step and decide whether we would take her home or place her in an institution. After considerable reflection and discussions with our doctors, family, and friends, my husband and I decided that we would never know if we could care for her at home unless we tried. That decision was made some 37 years ago and was the best decision of our lives. During her first year, every cold would send her back to the hospital so we could not take her out in public and had to screen everyone's health that came over to the house. Today, Dana uses a power wheelchair for mobility; she has cerebral palsy, seizures, and her right arm doesn't work well for her. However, what one will quickly discover is that her speech is not involved; and when you talk with her, you will find out she does not consider herself "disabled." She does not like to be defined by her disability or categorized as disabled. Dana is very much a self-confident individual with her own mind. One of Dana's primary characteristics is that she is quite social and makes friends easily. She has physical challenges but actually lives a physically active and independent lifestyle. Swimming is her passion and her outlet from the wheelchair. Year round she swims about 30 to 50 laps usually six days a week. Many people that we meet, particularly at the health club, say that Dana has been an inspiration to them and they often nickname her the "Energizer Bunny."

How has being a parent of a child with a disability influenced your professional life?

Prior to Dana's birth, I worked in the public schools in special education and in the medical center in Houston for a prominent medical school. I have a Master of Arts degree in psychology and spent many years as an associate school psychologist providing the psycho-educational testing to determine if a student is eligible for special education services. You would think that I, who was not a novice to the educational system, would have a handle on how to navigate the system for my child with disabilities. What I can tell you is that having the experience I had as a professional did not prepare me for the experience of having a child with a disability. It is entirely different when it is your own child and you are walking the walk and not talking the talk. As an outcome of my experience, I have chosen the path to work from inside the system to promote systemic change that will improve the educational outcomes for children with disabilities.

In searching for and investigating methods of therapy for Dana's cerebral palsy, a friend told me about a neuro-developmental treatment (NDT) opportunity. Dana and I spent six weeks for two consecutive summers living in a dorm situation with other parents and their children with disabilities, many with severe to profound disabilities. In the mornings, the kids received therapy and in the afternoons the therapists were in classes to earn NDT certification. It was a life-changing experience for me to live on a daily basis with these parents and children. I learned about living, loving, and caring for children that previously I had almost seen as unresponsive. Career-wise I soon made a change and became the evaluation specialist at a separate campus for students with severe and profound disabilities in one of Houston's larger suburban public school districts. In this position, I was supported in learning about and using AT to facilitate student access to curricular and daily activities.

Later it all seemed natural to combine what I had learned as a parent, as an associate school psychologist, and an AT specialist to take a position in AT at our regional ESC. Region 4 provides professional development and technical assistance to the public schools that provide education to almost a quarter of the school children in the state of Texas. My interests focused on systemic change and building the capacity of public school personnel to provide quality services in the area of AT. The vision is that students with disabilities receive appropriate AT devices and quality services when needed to access the curriculum and succeed academically.

(continued)

After 30 years in special education, I retired from Region 4. I continue to serve on national, state, and local advisory boards and frequently present at conferences. As a consultant, I have been contracting with the Center for Applied Special Technology (CAST) and working as the Special Project Coordinator of the AIM [Accessible Instructional Materials] Consortium. I am a founding member of the Quality Indicators in Assistive Technology (QIAT) Consortium and have served on the QIAT Leadership Team for the past 10 years. Recently, I have been working with the National Assistive Technology Technical Assistance Project at RESNA [Rehabilitation Engineering and Assistive Technology Society of North America] to develop quality indicators for service provision for the Assistive Technology Act state programs. As it turns out, I am not really retired, just repurposed.

You have worked in assistive technology for much of your career. What changes have you seen that can be directly attributed to legislation?

The most profound changes in AT have occurred as a result of the Individuals with Disabilities Education Act (IDEA) and its subsequent reauthorizations. My colleagues and I often talk about the "legal evolution of access." From the passage of the Education for All Handicapped Children Act (EHA), Public Law 94-142, in 1975 to the present, public schools have been responsible for providing each student with a disability a free, appropriate public education (FAPE). In 1975, EHA provided **"access to schools,"** as prior to that time, many children with disabilities were not permitted to attend schools. In 1990, EHA was reauthorized as the Individuals with Disabilities Education Act (IDEA). At that time, although students with disabilities routinely attended school, they were mostly educated in separate classrooms and facilities. IDEA (1990) provided **"access to classrooms"** as it required students with disabilities to be educated with their general education peers. By the reauthorization of IDEA in 1997, Congress was dissatisfied with the limited academic progress of students with disabilities. Although students were largely being educated in the same schools and same classrooms as their peers without disabilities, their educational programs were designed specifically to meet their individual needs and generally were not correlated with the general education curriculum. Therefore, IDEA (1997) emphasized **"access to the general education curriculum,"** which may necessitate AT devices and services. As the perception of what constitutes FAPE continues to evolve, in the reauthorization of IDEA in 2004, emphasis was placed on **"access to instructional materials."** This emphasis provides students who are unable to read or use information through the use of traditional print materials with accessible instructional materials appropriate to their individual needs. IDEA (2004) includes requirements for state and local educational agencies to ensure that, when needed, textbooks and related core instructional materials are provided to students with print disabilities in specialized formats in a timely manner. The four specialized formats are Braille, audio, large print, and digital text. In most instances, assistive technologies are needed for students to be able to use the materials in the specialized formats. For example, digital text can be used on the computer with various reading programs that allow the student to manipulate features and functions such as text size, text and background colors, text-to-speech, and learning supports.

As we look forward to the future for today's students with disabilities, we can be greatly encouraged by the opportunities available to them through access to the schools, the classrooms, the general education curriculum, and instructional materials. I am hopeful that Congress will continue to provide legislation that strengthens the rights of students with disabilities to the same education the other students receive and the provision of quality AT devices and services that are needed to support them.

What are the most critical issues that will be faced by AT providers in the near future?

Accountability continues to be a critical issue. Educators are increasingly being held accountable to ensure that all students are learning. How to effectively include students with disabilities in the accountability system continues to be a challenge. Many states limit the allowable accommodations that can be used on the tests, and frequently AT is not allowed. It is often perceived as being an unfair advantage. The definition of an accommodation is that it does not invalidate the nature of the task or the construct that is being measured. It stands to reason that if the AT is truly an accommodation, then its use should be allowed.

Another issue focuses on when AT is included in the IEP [Individualized Education Program], the effectiveness of its use must be evaluated on a trial basis before adoption is recommended. Prior to the use of an AT device, the team supporting that student will need to determine how they will know if the trial is successful. Then, with clearly defined roles and responsibilities, the team members will want to collect implementation data.

Yet another issue relates to the increasing national emphasis on universal design and universal design for learning, which may blur the lines between what is instructional technology (used in general education) and AT (specifically required for a special education student). As classrooms increasingly incorporate universally designed technology, many of the features needed to support learning will be available to all with the result that more students, who would otherwise struggle and go through a cycle of failure, are successful at the outset and fewer will be referred to special education services. It is important to remember that universally designed technology meets the needs of many but does not meet the needs of all. There will continue to be a need for AT for the specific needs of some of the students. For example, a student who is blind may need a Braille note-taker with a refreshable Braille display, which would not be included in the classroom technology infrastructure.

Finally, the connection between AT and the Response to Intervention (RtI) initiative, which was spurred by IDEA (2004) as a means for identifying students with learning disabilities, remains relatively unexplored and a challenging issue for educators. The critical question that needs to be addressed by national, state, and local education agencies is the role of AT in the RtI process, which includes prevention and intervention practices.

Describe the changes you have seen in AT service delivery in the past 20 years.

In the federal legislation that builds the foundation for the provision of AT, there is an important hallmark that should be noted for its impact on service delivery. IDEA (1997) mandated that in the development of the Individualized Education Program (IEP), each IEP team must consider whether or not the student needs AT to receive FAPE. Previously, AT was generally either not considered at all or was the responsibility of small, expert district level AT teams. As a result of IDEA (1997), responsibility for decision-making about AT shifted to campus-based IEP teams. Thus, districts have become increasingly aware that IEP team members need knowledge and skills to make informed AT decisions and are increasingly seeking professional development opportunities.

Professional development methods of delivery have been widely expanded with the use of new technologies and the Internet. Many of the school districts use their internal networks for communication, resources, and training. Most vendors make excellent use of Web sites with resources and training materials including videos and webinars. There are numerous national centers funded by the U.S. Department of Education with vast amounts of resources, products, and training materials. Professionals and families have many available resources and opportunities from which to choose to expand their knowledge about AT. Furthermore, the growth of the social networking technologies including wikis and blogs and the ubiquitous use of cell phones and MP3 players will surely play an ever-increasing role in the near future.

Source: Reprinted with permission from Psycho-Educational Services.

ASSISTIVE TECHNOLOGY DEFINED

Interestingly, the term *assistive technology* is not defined in any dictionary we could find. But the term *assist* is defined in *Webster's New World Compact Desk Dictionary and Style Guide*, 2nd ed. (2002) as "to help; aid" (p. 29), and *technology* is defined by the same source as "1. the science of the practical or industrial arts. 2. applied science" (p. 495). Thus, we are relatively safe in stating that AT is "the application of practical or industrial arts that help people with disabilities." We have added "people with disabilities" to tie AT specifically to disabilities and to differentiate helpful technology from assistive technology, in keeping with the IBM reference earlier. We realize that some may disagree somewhat with this definition, but the key point is that AT is really a concept, a perspective as it were, that leads one down the road to making practical decisions about specific devices, services, and adaptations that can be used by people with disabilities, their advocates, and their family members to make independence possible. With this in mind, it would be helpful to examine the definitions of *assistive technology device*, *assistive technology service*, *instructional technology*, and *adaptations*, because they are the primary focus of this text.

Assistive Technology Device

Assistive technology device was defined first in the Technology-Related Assistance for Individuals with Disabilities Act of 1988 (PL 100-407; replaced by the Assistive Technology Act of 1998, PL 105-394). The definition was included later in the 1990 reauthorization of the Individuals with Disabilities Education Act and has remained in subsequent versions of IDEA, including IDEA 2004. According to IDEA 2004, an assistive technology device refers to "any item, piece of equipment, or product system, whether acquired commercially off the shelf, modified, or customized, that is used to increase, maintain or improve the functional capabilities of a child with a disability" (Section 602[1]). Note that in this definition, and later in the definition of AT service, the terms *child* and *children* are used. In the original 1988 definition, this was not the case, and *individual* was used. Because we discuss AT devices and services in this text as being used throughout the lifespan, it is important to think in terms of AT use for youths and adults.

The federal definition is sufficiently broad to include just about any item or system, from electronic wheelchairs for people with mobility impairments to remedial reading software programs for children with dyslexia. We discuss three components of the AT device definition: *What* it is, *how* it is made, and its *use*.

The *what* obviously refers to the unit itself, which can be an item (e.g., a Hoover cane to help a person who is blind move about), a piece of equipment (e.g., a corner chair that supports a child's torso in extension, which helps the shoulders and arms to move freely), or a product system (e.g., a computer with speech recognition software and a microphone attachment that allows a person to speak into the computer and have the spoken words translated to text in a word processing program).

The *how* refers to whether the device is purchased as an "as-is" item in a store (e.g., a motorized wheelchair from a mobility vendor), modified (e.g., the same chair, but with "special features," such as balloon tires for beach access), or customized (e.g., the same type of chair but one that is created specially for a person with very specific needs). The key ingredient to this section of the definition is that the device can be bought from an available vendor, adapted from another device to tailor it to specific customer features, or made from scratch.

Finally, the *use* deals with the purpose of the device as it pertains to the user. The device has to be able to be used either to enhance a person's functioning or to maintain functioning at its current level, that is, to prevent a condition from worsening. This means that the device allows a person with a disability either to do something that he or she could not do without the device or to keep doing what is currently being done. A practical interpretation of the federal definition could be as follows: An AT device is anything that is bought or made that helps a person with a disability accomplish tasks that would otherwise be difficult or impossible to perform. We hope that this simpler description captures the essence of the term *assistive technology device*.

Just what types of devices are used? This is perhaps debatable, but for our purposes, we group AT devices into seven categories: positioning, mobility, augmentative and alternative communication, computer access, adaptive toys and games, adaptive environments, and instructional aids. Considerable space is devoted to each AT category throughout this text; here, we introduce the concepts inherent in each category.

Positioning refers to finding the best posture for a person to be in for a particular function. This function might entail moving about from one place to another, sitting during conversation, eating, sleeping, and so on. Because some people with disabilities have idiosyncratic physical conditions, their specific body features must be adapted to allow for maximum efficiency and comfort during typical functioning. Physical and occupational therapists are key professional contacts who deal with positioning issues.

Mobility refers literally to the act of movement. Humans are active creatures, and mobility allows us to do everything from flipping the pages of a book to boarding an airplane. Thus, AT devices that facilitate mobility help people move about in various environments. When most people think of mobility AT devices, they think of wheelchairs, but mobility devices also include children's scooter boards, vehicular modifications, white canes, electronic direction-finding/mobility aids, and other adaptations and devices. Rehabilitation engineers, physical therapists, orientation and mobility specialists, and engineers are vital team members when mobility issues are discussed.

Augmentative and alternative communication (AAC) devices help people to communicate with each other, even if they have speech difficulties. Professionals once used the term *nonverbal* to describe individuals who could not speak. Thanks to AAC devices, use of *nonverbal* is antiquated and largely inappropriate today. Stories of people's use of AAC devices to communicate with one another are sometimes profound and inspiring. We have heard several accounts of a child and a parent verbally communicating their love for each other for the first time; it is not difficult to see the power of augmentative and alternative communication when used for this and many other purposes.

Computer access devices are those that allow people to use the computer, even if their disability inhibits typical access. For example, instead of using a conventional keyboard to input information into a computer, people with physical impairments can use beams of light to activate or simulate a terminal. Or they can speak into a microphone and tell the computer what functions to employ. Or a stick can be held in one's mouth and a key depressed on the keyboard by applying pressure. People who are blind require alternative output methodologies for computer use, and text to speech offers a critical access feature. Access to computers allows for all sorts of uses, from general word processing to data analysis to communication with people in other countries. Educators and rehabilitation specialists typically are called on to assist in this area.

It is usually agreed that early cognitive development occurs as children play. ***Adaptive toys and games*** is an area of assistive technology that provides children with disabilities the opportunity to play with toys, games, and one another, thus allowing children to develop cognitive skills associated with these activities. Anyone who has seen groups of children playing while a child with a disability sits or stands excluded from the activities is well aware of the social and cognitive repercussions of such exclusion. Conversely, children playing together, despite physical or sensory differences, are a joyous sight to behold. (Note: We recognize that some readers may find our use of the term "joyous sight to behold" a bit of an overstatement; we would challenge those readers to watch children at play, especially those children who have been typically excluded from such an activity, and arrive at another conclusion.)

Aids to daily living refers to the use of devices and approaches that allow a person to manipulate the environment to allow for daily living, working, schooling, playing, and so forth. For instance, most people use remote control units to change channels on their television sets without having to get up from the couch. People with disabilities can do the same thing and also can use the same units to turn lights on and off, respond to a ring of the doorbell, adjust their beds, and carry on a number of other activities in the home, school, or workplace. We typically consider "gadgets" as helpful toys; in reality, these "toys" become AT devices when they help a person with a disability "increase, maintain, or improve" capabilities in various environments.

Instructional aids help educate a person in school or during employment training. Instructional aids also can be used during functional living skills training in an adult's new home. Whatever the application, this broad category involves devices and adaptations that help facilitate learning in one way or another. Instructional aids include technology that is used to compensate for a person's functional limitations (e.g., screen reader programs that allow for information access) or technology that is used for remediation purposes (e.g., math or reading instructional programs).

It is important to note that the types of AT devices often overlap. For example, positioning is closely intertwined with mobility, and adaptive toys and games with instructional aids. We categorized the devices to aid in discussion, but one must always maintain a broad perspective when considering AT devices, whether discussing categories or seeking alternative adaptations.

It is also important to realize that assistive technology devices fall along a continuum that ranges from low tech (or light or "lite" tech as it is sometimes called) to high tech. Johnston, Beard, and Carpenter (2007, p. 20) presented a continuum that includes no tech (where no aids are required), to light tech (which includes devices such as pencil grips, highlight tape, and standard wheelchairs), to high tech (which includes devices such as computer access, electronic devices, and electric wheelchairs). The Johnston et al. continuum helps remind us that AT devices are not always needed or prescribed, but the low-tech to high-tech continuum suits our purposes because we are talking about AT devices throughout this text.

Low-tech solutions are usually the easiest and least expensive to prescribe. As discussed in the next section on AT services, sometimes we have limited resources. This should not be used as an excuse for avoiding high-tech solutions when they are most appropriate, but the fact remains that at times, low-tech solutions are sufficient for helping a person compensate for disability-related struggles. Throughout this text, we present solutions that range along the low-tech to high-tech continuum. For now, it is important to recognize that the continuum exists and that AT solutions should be examined with the continuum in mind.

Assistive Technology Service

Assistive technology service is also a term that has been defined in federal legislation. According to IDEA 2004 (Section 602[2]),

> (2) Assistive technology service.—The term 'assistive technology service' means any service that directly assists a child with a disability in the selection, acquisition, or use of an assistive technology device. Such term includes—

(A) the evaluation of the needs of such child, including a functional evaluation of the child in the child's customary environment;
(B) purchasing, leasing, or otherwise providing for the acquisition of assistive technology devices by such child;
(C) selecting, designing, fitting, customizing, adapting, applying, maintaining, repairing, or replacing assistive technology devices;
(D) coordinating and using other therapies, interventions, or services with assistive technology devices, such as those associated with existing education and rehabilitation plans and programs;
(E) training or technical assistance for such child, or, where appropriate, the family of such child; and
(F) training or technical assistance for professionals (including individuals providing education and rehabilitation services), employers, or other individuals who provide services to, employ, or are otherwise substantially involved in the major life functions of such child.

When considering AT services, it is best to think in terms of devices existing outside of a vacuum. That is, devices are simply "things" that are available for use; the use is an important aspect. Without AT services, these devices would exist on catalogue pages only, with no apparent use or even any ability for people to acquire the devices, in many instances. The phrase "means any service that directly assists 'an individual' [sic] with a disability in the selection, acquisition, or use of an assistive technology device" provides the essence of the definition. The services are provided to decide what device to select, how to get the device, and how to use it; or how a person can use the device so that his or her goals can be met though the device's use. We discuss briefly the elements included in the definition. Many of the definition's elements are discussed in detail elsewhere in the text; so this section is intended as an overview of each definitional element.

The phrase "a functional evaluation of the child in the child's customary environment" refers to what is commonly considered the "person–technology match." Assistive technology devices are not "one size fits all"; that is, one specific device is not appropriate for everyone, and each must be matched with a person for correct application. You do not enter a shoe store and immediately buy a pair of shoes because you like how they look on another person. You try on the shoes. Do the shoes fit? Are they comfortable? Do they give you freedom of movement so that you can do what you want while the shoes are on your feet? Do they look good on you? Analogously, AT evaluations are conducted so that people can be reasonably sure that the devices match the user's needs and attributes and the tasks to be done. The phrase "individual's customary environment" merits particular attention. Back to the shoe analogy: If you live on a ranch with rocky terrain and you are looking for a good work boot, the store's cushiony carpet will tell little about how the shoe will feel in your normal workplace. So it would be best to try the shoe in your customary environment. Although the shoe store is unlikely to give you that luxury, AT evaluators should consider such a factor; in fact, this element of the definition mandates such a consideration. It should be added that "environments" may be more appropriate for this element of the definition, given that people function in multiple environments, and AT devices are usually used across these multiple environments.

The "purchasing, leasing, or otherwise providing for the acquisition of assistive technology devices" phrase of the definition is critical. There is an old saying that goes something like, "Given unlimited resources, we can do anything." Well, resources for purchasing or leasing AT devices are typically limited. Usually, there are several devices that can be useful to an individual.

Identifying ways to secure funding for the devices is critical if these device are to be acquired (i.e., bought or leased). Personal health insurance benefits, special education funds, and Medicaid are but three of a variety of options that can be used, but knowing about and accessing these options requires expertise. Social workers are particularly adept in this area, as are rehabilitation counselors and special education personnel; thus, decisions about purchasing and/or leasing should be made after close consultation with these or other knowledgeable professionals.

Once the need for AT devices has been determined, the "selecting, designing, fitting, customizing, adapting, applying, maintaining, repairing, or replacing" element of the definition comes into play. Clearly, this element coincides with the AT evaluation because the words describe important features of the evaluation process. A device might have to be designed from scratch, or a design modification might have to be identified for an intact unit. In a broad sense, the "person-technology match" is an effort to identify the perfect "fitting" of a device to an individual; but in a more restrictive sense, positioning also would fall into this category.

We mentioned earlier that AT devices do not exist in a vacuum. This is the predominant issue when considering the "coordinating and using other therapies, interventions, or services" element of the definition. When a child is matched with an AAC device, for example, the device becomes a tool that can be used by the child and his or her speech-language pathologist as part of a speech-language therapy program. As another example, using voice-to-text as a means to access a computer would be only one part of an effort to enhance a student's writing skills. Instructional intervention on idea generation, syntax, vocabulary selection, and editing must incorporate the device—the device itself cannot be expected to "teach" these writing skills. Voice-to-text technology allows for access to writing instruction, but it does not replace writing instruction.

Some AT devices are simple to use and some are complicated, but *all* devices require the user to be trained in order to maximize use. This is the basic notion behind the "training or technical assistance for such child, or, where appropriate, the family of such child" element. Anyone who has bought a digital video recorder and has tried to program the device, or worse yet, has tried to set an automatic lawn sprinkler system, knows that some devices are complicated and are difficult to learn to use without special training. Most AT practitioners can recount stories in which AT users were inept with a device, which therefore did not get used or was used inefficiently or ineffectively. To prevent or reduce such occurrences, training must be done on the device. Preferably this training occurs during the AT evaluation and is supplemented once the device is selected.

In addition to training the AT user, training also should be conducted for family members, who generally serve as the primary support system for the user. When the user has difficulties with the device, family members step in to assist, but they can do so only if they know how the device operates. Also, because the device is a tool for independence and the family is critical to fostering independence, it is vital that members know how the device is used to facilitate integration into family and community activities. Without such training, full implementation of the device is unlikely.

The final element of the definition, "training or technical assistance for professionals," is particularly challenging. As educators, we have walked into many classrooms where a device is left sitting on a counter because the teacher has not received training on how the device can be used in the classroom. Contrast this scenario with one in which the teacher is knowledgeable about the AT device and integrates the device, and therefore the student, into curricular activities. But education is only one setting where training is needed. Employers and fellow employees require device training for maximum workplace efficiency. Further, speech-language pathologists require training on the latest AAC devices, and social workers, rehabilitation counselors, and other professionals who work in disability-related fields must receive ongoing training on devices. Training in the benefits of AT should be offered, and when a person with an AT device participates in a program or activity, significant participants in that program/activity should have specialized training in the use and integration of the devices being utilized.

If all AT services are implemented, there is greater likelihood for success, no matter what the context of the device's use. In particular, it should be noted that AT services are ongoing, with periodic training updates, evaluations, and monitoring to ensure that the device is being used appropriately. Although AT service implementation cannot guarantee success, such implementation makes success possible.

Instructional Technology

Instructional technology refers to any technology that is used as part of the education of an individual. The term includes presentation hardware and software used by teachers and students, including overhead transparencies and projectors; multimedia software and tools; Internet technology for watching real-time activities; and the like. The term also includes instructional software that is used to *remediate* academic weaknesses. Although we stated earlier that, in its broadest sense, the term *AT device* could include instructional software, generally instructional software is classified with instructional technology. Our point that instructional technology can be considered AT is illustrated by the case of two students, Maria and Phil, who use a reading instructional software program. Phil has no reading difficulties and uses the instructional software to improve his skills. Maria, on the other hand, has dyslexia and uses the instructional software and hardware (a computer) to "increase her functional (reading) capabilities." For Phil, the technology is helpful; for Maria, the software is assistive, that is, an AT device.

Instructional technology also can include such techniques as anchoring instruction, when the technique involves the use of CD-ROMs, video, or some other technology. This and other instructional approaches and devices provide the educator with innovative ways to instruct, whether that instruction occurs in a classroom, a workplace, at home, or elsewhere.

Adaptations

In the next chapter, we argue that AT is but one of many adaptations that are available to help a person with a disability accomplish a task. For our purposes, adaptations are *alterations that are made so that a person who does not possess the requisite abilities needed for task completion can accomplish a task.* In this way, adaptations are access vehicles that facilitate participation and inclusion in everyday activities. As described in the next chapter, not every adaptation requires AT devices. Yet, a mind-set for making adaptations is necessary for anyone who interacts with people who have disabilities. Otherwise, people with disabilities are destined to be excluded from activities in which they could otherwise participate.

It is also important to understand that adaptations can be either remedial or compensatory. Our earlier example of the instructional program being used by Maria and Phil to improve their reading skills would be considered a remedial adaptation. But if Maria uses a screen reader program to access her e-mail by bypassing her area of weakness (i.e., reading), then the adaptation would be compensatory. Many of the devices and approaches discussed in these chapters are compensatory in scope, but it should not be assumed that remediation and compensation are mutually exclusive concepts. For instance, one never gives up trying to teach a nonreader how to read, so AT devices can be used for remediation purposes throughout the lifespan. But it is also important that a person have access to print, so the use of a compensatory strategy concurrently with remedial efforts is reasonable.

HISTORICAL OVERVIEW OF ASSISTIVE TECHNOLOGY

Like all fields of study, AT has a history from which it has evolved, and the field changes dramatically, seemingly on a daily basis. For the sake of chronological convenience, we look at the history of AT in three periods: (a) before 1900, which we call the Foundation Period; (b) from 1900 through 1972, which we term the Establishment Period; and (c) from 1973 to the present, which we call the Empowerment Period. Some of the information, such as the invention of a particular AT device, has a direct connection for AT use. Other significant events, such as the opening of special schools or the first publication of a periodical, have an indirect connection to AT, either as a venue or an opportunity for AT service delivery or as a means to disseminate information pertaining to AT use. (Note: We have not included litigation in our history section, choosing instead to include Personal Perspective 1.2, which features Lewis Golinker, a lawyer and leading disability advocate, who presents significant cases that have affected AT acquisition and use.)

Foundation Period: Pre-1900s

In their excellent text entitled *Assistive Technologies: Principles and Practice*, Cook and Hussey (2002) recount the fictional case of Borg, a Stone Age resident who broke his leg on a hunting trip. The authors make the point that, for all intents and purposes, AT began with humans' attempts to "make do" after a debilitating injury, whether temporary or permanent. In Borg's case, his leg healed improperly, leaving him with a noticeable limp. Reaching down, he found a stick, which he cut to the proper length and used to help himself walk more easily. Certainly the stick fits the definition of an AT device in that it is an *item* that was *customized* and that helped him *maintain* one of his functional capabilities. One can easily agree with Cook and Hussey's assertion that AT devices existed as soon as human beings began making "things" to help them adapt to the functional limitations imposed by disabilities, whether those disabilities were acquired or congenital.

If one assumes that AT development paralleled the disability field, then one can look to history to see indications that adaptations of some kind were needed as far back as 1000 B.C., when speech and language difficulties were first recorded. One of the earliest incidences of acquired learning disabilities can be traced to A.D. 33, when Mecurial reported the case of a man losing his memory for letters after being hit on the head with an axe during a skirmish (Wiederholt & Bryant, 1987). We also know that the first recorded spinal surgery occurred around A.D. 600, providing evidence that individuals existed with acquired physical conditions that undoubtedly required postsurgical adaptations for remaining functional limitations. Those may have been as simple as special feeding utensils and techniques or as complex as specially designed wheeled mobility mechanisms. Further examination of historical accounts shows autopsies being performed on deceased veterans in the 1600s and 1700s to examine causal factors for physical and mental conditions (Cook & Hussey, 2002). And, of course, there are literary accounts of seafarers with wooden legs and hooks continuing to go to sea long after injuries caused the loss of their extremities. There is little doubt that human ingenuity helped such people perform their tasks in a way that would maintain their value to their crewmates. At the end of the 18th century, special education began with Dr. Jean-Marc-Gaspard Itard's efforts to teach Victor, nicknamed "The Wild Boy of Aveyron" because of his early years spent in seclusion in the woods of France.

PERSONAL PERSPECTIVE 1.2

Lewis Golinker is an attorney at law in New York state. Lew is a leading advocate for people with disabilities, especially those who benefit from AAC devices. He has a long history of helping people with disabilities acquire AT devices. We wanted our readers to recognize the importance of litigation in helping people secure the timely acquisition and use of AT devices and services. So we asked Lew to answer one question for us: "Lew, thank you for your work on behalf of people with disabilities. Please share with our readers five or six key court cases that have made a difference with regard to assistive technology."

Here is Lew's response.

> The cases that follow were selected because they establish decision-making rules for similar cases, rather than just a result for a specific item for a particular individual. Medicaid cases are most frequently listed because Medicaid has been the most important funding source (but clearly not the only source) for assistive devices for people with severe disabilities. The list does not rank the cases by importance. Rather, they start from the narrowest premise regarding coverage and expand to the broadest rules.

1. *Rush v. Parham*, 625 F.2d 1150 (5th Cir. 1980). The plaintiff in this case was a Georgia Medicaid recipient who sought trans-sexual surgery. The Georgia Medicaid agency denied the request, claiming the surgery was experimental. The Court of Appeals remanded the case to the district court for further proceedings to clarify the state's rationale to deny the service. Of greatest importance is that the Court of Appeals stated plainly that Medicaid coverage exclusions *had to have a legitimate basis. A state could not "just refuse," as an exercise of its "discretion," to cover an item or service or procedure.* More specifically, the Medicaid "amount, duration and scope" rule 42 C.F.R. § 440.230(b) and (c) prohibited such exclusions. The key statement by the Court of Appeals on this point was: "We caution, however, that if defendants simply denied payment for the proposed surgery because it was transsexual surgery, Georgia should now be required to pay for the operation, since a 'state may not arbitrarily deny or reduce the amount, duration, or scope of a required service . . . solely because of the diagnosis, type of illness, or condition.' 42 C.F.R. s 440.230(c)(1), as corrected by 43 Fed.Reg. 57253 (Dec. 7, 1978)."

2. *Fred C. v. Texas Health & Human Services Commission*, 988 F.Supp. 1032 (W.D.Tex. 1997), affirmed per curiam, 167 F.3d 537 (5th Cir. 1998); prior proceedings, 924 F.Supp. 788 (W.D. Tex. 1996), vacated, 117 F.3d 1416, 1997 WL 335781 (5th Cir. 1997). The plaintiff in this case sought a speech-generating device [SGD], which Texas Medicaid agreed to cover for children, but not adults. Texas Medicaid claimed it had the discretion not to cover SGDs for adults, but cited to no factual reason why SGDs should not be covered. It was admitted that SGDs were durable medical equipment [DME] for children, and DME was covered for adults and they were equally effective for treatment of severe communication impairments in children as well as adults. *The District Court ruled that a Medicaid program's "discretion" did not extend to refusals to cover specific items for adults when the item fit within one or more covered benefits categories available for adults, and there was no medical evidence to support non-coverage.*

In addition, *Fred C.* is very important because it establishes a general rule of decision for a court to determine whether an item or service must be covered. The rule consists of 4 questions: (1) is the person eligible for the program from which funding is being sought; (2) does the thing being sought—item, service, procedure—"fit" within the definition of one or more covered benefits categories; (3) is the thing being sought "medically necessary;" and (4) are there any special rules or limitations (such as experimental care exclusions) that apply to the thing being sought? If the first 3 questions are answered "yes," and the last one "no," the

(*continued*)

thing being sought must be covered. This decision-making framework is very valuable to ensure that consistent decisions will be issued across time, across courts and states, and across specific items and services in dispute.

Viewed together, *Rush* holds that a state lacks total discretion over what to cover at the treatment, device or procedure level: it cannot "just refuse" to cover something. *Fred C.* expands that holding to specify that to justify non-coverage on the basis of age, Medicaid must be able to point to medical evidence to show the treatment, device or procedure is not effective [in] the specific age groups for which coverage will be denied.

The holding in *Fred C.* was copied by the District Court in *Hunter v. Chiles*, 944 F.Supp 914 (S.D. Fl. 1996), an SGD coverage case involving Florida Medicaid.

3. *Esteban v. Cook*, 77 F.Supp. 2d 1256 (S.D.Fl. 1999). The plaintiff in this case sought a wheelchair, which Florida Medicaid conceded was covered. However, Florida Medicaid imposed a coverage cap for wheelchairs at a rate far below the cost of the needed wheelchair, in effect, making it non-covered. The District Court directed Florida to eliminate the rate cap. The Medicaid program lacked the discretion to set rates at levels that make otherwise covered services or devices unavailable.

Esteban further clarifies the scope of Medicaid "discretion" such that a state may not use Medicaid payment rates as a surrogate basis for excluding items or services Medicaid may not want to cover.

4. *DeSario v. Thomas*, 963 F.Supp. 120 (D.Conn. 1997), reversed, 139 F.2d 80 (2nd Cir. 1998), cert. granted, vacated, and remanded on basis of September 4, 1998 "Dear State Medicaid Director" Letter, 525 U.S. 1098 (1999). *DeSario* is perhaps the single most important Medicaid durable medical equipment decision. It arose from Connecticut Medicaid's recognition that when it and other Medicaid programs denied a Medicaid funding request for items of medical equipment by claiming they were not covered, the decisions all but uniformly supported the Medicaid recipient and ordered coverage. Court rejected Medicaid's claim that such coverage exclusions were within the state's discretion. Connecticut Medicaid concluded that the *ad hoc* application of its discretion will be insufficient to withstand judicial review, so it redesigned its decision making process to appear as if it was not relying on its discretion. Instead, it created an exclusive list of items that it stated were covered; if an item was not on the state's list, requests would be denied. Medicaid's reliance on its exclusive list was challenged because it represents no more than a change in time for the application of the state's discretion. Medicaid was not claiming the list was based on greater or even different information to justify the non-coverage decision; just that the list existed and controlled the outcome of the funding request. The District Court rejected this argument in total, but the Court of Appeals reversed. It said the state could create an exclusive list, and could categorically deny coverage to anything not on the list, even if it met Connecticut Medicaid's definition of durable medical equipment. Indeed, it could be denied even if non-coverage had life or death consequences. The language used by the Court of Appeals decision, as well as its conclusion causes *DeSario* to be considered one of if not the single worst Medicaid decision ever issued. It was so inconsistent with the fundamental goals of the Medicaid program that the Department of Health & Human Services [HHS], which is responsible for Medicaid program administration, issued an opinion letter rejecting the Court of Appeals' analysis and conclusion. In a "Dear State Medicaid Director" letter dated September 4, 1998, HHS expressly prohibited Medicaid programs from employing exclusive lists of DME items. It stated that any item of equipment sought by a recipient had to be reviewed for compliance with the state Medicaid program's definition of DME, and if it met those criteria had to be covered. In addition, once it was determined to be covered, the Medicaid program had to offer a procedure to allow the recipient to show the item of equipment was medically necessary. If both were satisfied, Medicaid had to provide the item. Exclusive lists of covered items and lists of "non-covered" items were both prohibited by this letter. The September 4, 1998 SMD Letter was issued while *DeSario's* Court of Appeals decision was being appealed to the Supreme Court. The Supreme Court thereafter vacated the Court of Appeals decision on the basis of the SMD letter and remanded the case to the Second Circuit. The effect of that action was to remove all force and effect to the Second Circuit decision. Since it was issued, the SMD Letter has been relied on several times by other courts to support coverage of DME items over Medicaid program objections.

DeSario further limits Medicaid program discretion to refuse coverage of DME items: it is not total; it cannot be age-based without medical facts; it cannot be rate-based; and it cannot be based on the existence of state coverage lists or other similar guidance that make categorical conclusions about coverage. The state must have a process for any item of equipment to be reviewed under the criteria of the state's DME definition.

5. *Lankford v. Sherman*, 451 F.3d 496 (8th Cir. 2006). The plaintiffs in this case challenged an attempt by Missouri Medicaid to limit the items of equipment that will be covered for adults. The Court rejected the Missouri proposal and set forth a clear rule for the analysis of DME coverage disputes: "While a state has discretion to determine the optional services in its Medicaid plan, a state's failure to provide Medicaid coverage for non-experimental, medically necessary services within a covered Medicaid category is both per se unreasonable and inconsistent with the stated goals of Medicaid." This is a rule that applies beyond DME to any Medicaid service. It states a conclusion that is consistent with Medicaid decisions issued throughout the history of the program, across many items and services, and in many different federal and state courts. A compilation of decisions stating this principle first was prepared for the Court of Appeals in *Fred C.* 10 years earlier. In *Lankford*, this analysis finally became the official rule stated by the Court.

From *Rush,* to *Fred C.,* to *Esteban*, to *DeSario,* to *Lankford*, the scope of state discretion to limit coverage of specific items has been steadily eroded. Now, there are 2 Courts of Appeals that have adopted the same decision making framework for Medicaid coverage and funding of medical equipment. *Fred C.* was the first to state the framework. *Lankford* re-stated it 10 years later: (1) is the person eligible for the program from which funding is being sought; (2) does the thing being sought—item, service, procedure—"fit" within the definition of one or more covered benefits categories; (3) is the thing being sought "medically necessary;" and (4) are there any special rules or limitations (such as experimental care exclusions) that apply to the thing being sought? If the first 3 questions are answered "yes," and the last one "no," the thing being sought must be covered.

6. SGD Decisions: There have been several SGD decisions that establish a firm foundation for SGD coverage and funding by every state Medicaid program. The earliest decision is *Meyers v. Reagen,* 776 F.2d 241 (8th Cir. 1985). Other decisions include *Myers v. State of Mississippi,* 3:94 CV 185 (LN) (S.D. Miss. 1995); *Fred C. v. Texas Health & Human Services Commission,* 988 F.Supp. 1032 (W.D.Tex. 1997), affirmed per curiam, 167 F.3d 537 (5th Cir. 1998); prior proceedings, 924 F.Supp. 788 (W.D. Tex. 1996), vacated, 117 F.3d 1416, 1997 WL 335781 (5th Cir. 1997); *Hunter v. Chiles*, 944 F.Supp. 914 (S.D.Fl. 1996); *Will T. v. Taylor*, 465 F.Supp. 2d 1267 (N.D.Ga. 2000); and *Lankford v. Sherman*, 451 F.3d 496 (8th Cir. 2006). These cases establish that SGDs "fit" within several Medicaid covered services: DME; prosthetic devices; and as necessary equipment within the speech-language pathology benefit. As a result of these decisions and approximately a dozen more that settled, all Medicaid programs cover and provide SGDs to recipients of all ages, and all SGDs are covered, with no limitations based on health condition.

Source: Reprinted with permission from Psycho-Educational Services.

The 1800s began a period of service for individuals with disabilities that has continued to this day and laid the foundation for disability services as we know it. During that century, in 1817, Thomas Hopkins Gallaudet opened his school for students who were deaf. The name of the school, the American Asylum for Education of the Deaf and Dumb (later, the American School for the Deaf), provides an indication of how terminology has changed over the past 200 years. Twelve years later, a Frenchman by the familiar name of Louis Braille introduced an adaptation of Barbier's "Ecriture Nocturne" (night writing, originally developed for the French military) embossed code so that people who were blind could decode the printed word. In 1834, he perfected the literary code that bears his name.

At about the same time, Dr. J. G. Blomer established an institute for people with physical disabilities where he maintained a workroom for devising apparatus, bandages, and artificial limbs—early AT devices (McMurtrie, 1980). Samuel Gridley Howe started the New England Asylum for the Blind (later the Perkins School for the Blind) in 1832, providing educational services that utilized a variety of techniques specially tailored to the students' visual needs. In 1836, Taylor devised what was thought to be the first tangible math apparatus that could be used by individuals who were blind. The *American Annals of the Deaf* was first published in 1847, followed a year later by the opening of the first residential institution for people with mental retardation (the Perkins Institution in Boston).

The latter half of the 19th century found several significant events that indirectly affected AT by benefiting individuals with disabilities. The first occurred in 1855, when Kentucky set up a printing house for people who were blind, which several years later was incorporated as the American Printing House for the Blind. In 1860, the *Gallaudet Guide and Deaf Mute's Companion* became the first publication written especially for people with disabilities. Four years later, in 1864, Gallaudet University was founded as the National Deaf Mute College (Smith & Tyler, 2010).

In 1869, a patent was filed for the basic design for the manual wheelchair in use to this day (Pelka, 1997). The wheelchair had been introduced in the United States during the Civil War, when wooden chairs and wooden wheels provided mobility for soldiers whose legs had been amputated. In 1877, Thomas Edison invented the phonograph, a significant event for those who would later benefit from learning through listening to material on recordings. A short two years later, Public Law 45-186 provided a subsidy to provide books in Braille; the same law also funded the American Printing House for the Blind. Then, in 1884, the Home of the Merciful Savior opened its doors in Philadelphia to children with physical disabilities. Finally, in 1892, Frank Hall invented the Braille typewriter.

To summarize the Foundation Period from the perspective of the 21st century, one sees seemingly small steps occurring in the disabilities field that led the way for major breakthroughs in the 20th century. But the steps taken up to 1900 were anything but minor. Rather, the dedicated leaders of their time (a) worked to ensure that people with sustained injuries survived those injuries; (b) studied the relationships or resulting limitations to neurological damage; and (c) developed programs to teach academics and life skills to people with cognitive, sensory, and motor limitations. No doubt some of the programs involved what could be now termed AT devices.

Establishment Period: 1900–1972

We label the 72-year period from 1900 through 1972 the Establishment Period because these years established the disability disciplines as specific entities, and the policies, laws, and litigation that emerged during this time ushered in an era of unprecedented gains for people with disabilities, their families, and their advocates. Throughout this period, educational, scientific, and psychological advances were made concerning the causes, preventions, and ramifications of disabilities. In addition, people's viewpoints concerning disabilities and the capabilities of people with disabilities changed dramatically. Devices and techniques were devised to help people with disabilities utilize their strengths to compensate for their limitations. In addition, legal and procedural barriers that discriminated against people seen as "different" were addressed. Finally, organizations such as the currently named Council for Exceptional Children, American Speech-Language-Hearing Association, American Association on Intellectual and Developmental Disabilities, Easter Seals, United Cerebral Palsy, the ARC, and the Learning Disabilities Association of America, to name but a few, were formed to advocate for people with disabilities and the professionals and families associated with the disability movement. Our discussion here is intended to introduce readers to events that led to a rapid development of AT devices and services, years before those terms officially existed.

We mentioned in the Foundation Period the impact of war on disabilities—that is, battles led to injuries that led to physical, language, sensory, and cognitive conditions. Shortly after World War I, the U.S. Congress recognized the results of battle-caused disabilities when it passed the Soldier Rehabilitation Act (also known as the Smith-Sears Veterans Rehabilitation Act) in 1918. This significant legislation was intended to help veterans with disabilities resume life, postdisability, and included the first vocational rehabilitation provision. The work of people such as Kurt Goldstein and other injured veterans stimulated service delivery and enhancement and brought a focus on people who had served their country and who now needed their fellow citizens' assistance to reenter American life. Two years later, the Smith-Fess Civilian Vocational Rehabilitation Act was passed, extending vocational rehabilitation services to nonveterans whose challenges were similar to those of their military counterparts. Funds were provided for vocational guidance, training, job adjustment, prostheses, and placement services (Bryant, 1996). Clearly, recognition of functional capabilities and people's assets became the rule rather than the exception; rehabilitation professionals focused on using techniques and devices to help people compensate for their functional limitations. Not surprisingly, this new focus brought about a new emphasis on compensatory strategies and equipment that would change the face of disabilities forever.

In 1920 Barr, Stroud, and Fournier d'Albe patented the first reading machine, the Optophone, for use by people who were blind. Three years later, Barr and colleagues expanded their apparatus facilities to deal with the increased demands for their services.

By the end of the decade, guide dogs had been introduced to America, providing mobility independence potential to people who were blind. Breakthroughs in blindness continued, including the National Institute for the Blind's introduction of a high-speed rotary press for embossed type and the Library of Congress's 1931 decision to distribute Braille reading materials under its auspices. The next year, long-standing debate as to the "preferred" Braille style partially was settled when British and American committees adopted Standard English Braille as uniform type. In 1933, the American Printing House for the Blind adopted Standard English Braille Grade 2 for junior and senior high school textbooks. A few years later, the first talking books on long-playing records were produced and disseminated. By 1936, the American Printing House for the Blind had produced and disseminated its first recorded materials. On another front, in 1932, an engineer named Harry Jennings ushered in a new era in mobility enhancements when he built the first folding, tubular steel wheelchair.

The passage of the Social Security Act in 1935 provided, among other things, grants to states for assisting (a) individuals who were blind and (b) children with disabilities. The decade of the 1930s also produced the Coyne Voice Pitch Indicator, which allowed people's speech patterns to appear as visual images. The year 1937 brought a patent for the X-frame folding wheelchair by Herbert A. Everest and Harry C. Jennings. In 1939, Lowenfeld began his six-year exploration of the educational role of talking books, which resulted in the demonstrated value of these tools in the teaching-learning process. Also in 1939, Homer Dudley presented the VODER, which produced electrically generated synthesized speech sounds at the World Fair. Although the VODER required a very long training time for successful use, it ushered an era of increased attention to speech synthesis (History of Speech Synthesis, 2000).

The 1940s continued to see service delivery breakthroughs, as the United States military began providing its members with speech and hearing services. The Barden-LaFollette Act, also known as the Rehabilitation Act of 1943, introduced training funds for physicians, nurses, rehabilitation counselors, physical therapists, occupational therapists, social workers, psychologists, and other rehabilitation specialists. The year 1947 brought about the introduction of the Hoover cane, which was developed as part of a comprehensive approach to orientation and mobility training that was known as the "touch cane technique" and was designed in part to assist veterans who became blind during World War II (Sauberger, 1996). World War II provided the impetus for the foundation of Recording for the Blind (later called Recording for the Blind and Dyslexic) in 1948. Annie T. McDonald established the organization to help veterans who had lost their sight during the war obtain an education under the G.I. Bill of Rights. World War II also saw the development of battery-operated hearing aids, but their bulk presented great difficulty in their use.

In the latter part of 1940, Sir Ludwig Guttman, a German-born neurologist, first came up with the idea of creating a separate Olympic competition for World War II veterans with spinal fractures. His efforts led to the Paralympic Games, which were first held in 1960 in Rome and have immediately followed the Olympic Games ever since.

Several events of the 1950s assisted communication and educational skills for people who were blind. The initial contribution occurred in 1951 with the availability of the Perkins Brailler, a device still in use today. The year 1952 saw the introduction of the Tellatouch communication device for people who were both deaf and blind. The following year the Megascope was invented and the Nemeth Braille Mathematics Code was introduced.

Computerized Braille was first demonstrated in 1955, and the following year the American Printing House for the Blind first made materials available for day school students. By 1957, the Visotonor and Visotactor were available; the first device transformed musical sounds to letters, and the second was a reading machine that produced vibrations that could be felt by the fingers in order to facilitate decoding.

The end of the 1950s introduced Public Law 85-905, which allowed funding for captioned films, and 1958 saw its first application in a motion picture film (Hardman, Drew, & Egan, 2007). The 1960s saw legislation intended for students who were bilingual (the Bilingual Education Act of 1968) and who had learning disabilities (the Children with Specific Learning Disabilities Act of 1969). South Carolina passed the nation's first statewide architectural access code in 1963.

On the athletic front, the first Olympic-style games for athletes with disabilities were held in Rome, Italy, in 1960. This event marked the fulfillment of the efforts of Sir Ludwig Guttman, who felt that sports could be a therapeutic method to enhance physical strength and self-respect (Wikipedia contributors, 2009).

The year 1965 saw the establishment of the National Commission on Architectural Barriers to Rehabilitation of the Handicapped, which led to the passage of the Architectural Barriers Act of 1968. The lasercane, which emitted beams of light to detect objects deterring unobstructed movement, was invented in 1966 and helped people receive advance notice of obstacles and detect items that were not detected by a traditional white cane (e.g., things that would hit above the elbow). Shortly thereafter, in 1971, the Optacon was marketed as another tool to allow people who were blind to read text. In that same year, the first Braille Vision Books were produced, which contained one page for Braille next to a page of print.

One cannot discuss the Establishment Period without some mention of the landmark U.S. Supreme Court decision in *Brown v. Board of Education* in 1954. The renunciation of the "separate but equal" constitutional concept not only served as a catalyst for the African-American civil rights movement, but it became an inspiration to the disability rights movement that has allowed for the proliferation of AT device creation and use.

Our final entry during this period involves the formation of Prentke Romich, a company that was established to help people with communication challenges. This commercialization of augmentative and alternative communication devices would lead to ongoing refinements and developments of electronic communication systems that continue to this day.

To summarize the Establishment Period, it was a time of action on behalf of people with disabilities. World Wars I and II, Korea, and Vietnam had created a new group of Americans with disabilities who were reentering the postwar society with special needs. Advances in medicine were allowing children to live through disease and birth difficulties at a rate unimagined at the turn of the century. People with disabilities were becoming a larger percentage of the U.S. population, and they had as much of a right to live the American Dream as their nondisabled fellow citizens. Inventions and innovations were helping people use their functional strengths to reduce the impact of their functional weaknesses, and people with disabilities were entering the workforce in record numbers. The disability rights movement was beginning to be recognized as a social and political force. Organizations had been established that pressed for new legislation and policies in education and employment. Assistive technology devices and services were being devised and utilized at an unprecedented rate, and companies were being formed to spearhead the development of more sophisticated products. It was truly an exciting time, but to paraphrase a familiar quote, "We hadn't seen anything yet." Beginning in 1973, the disability rights movement was to begin an unprecedented run that continues to this day—a span we refer to as the Empowerment Period.

Empowerment Period: 1973 to Present

Webster's Universal College Dictionary (1997) defines empower(ment) as "1. giv(ing) official or legal power or authority to. 2. . . . endow[ing] with an ability" (p. 263). Thus, we can describe the Empowerment Period as one that has given, and is giving, people with disabilities and their supporters the ability and legal authority to continue their legitimate pursuit of the American Dream; however, they choose to define and operationalize that dream.

The year 1973 was selected because that was the year the Rehabilitation Act was revised to include Section 504, which for the first time made it formal United States policy that discrimination against people with disabilities would not be tolerated. Specifically, Section 504 stated that anyone receiving federal dollars could not discriminate against individuals because of their disabilities. Sadly, this landmark legislation was not implemented until 1977, after a sit-in at the Secretary of State's office several years after its passage. Partially as a result of this activism, disability rights was recognized as a civil rights issue, a distinction that has remained to this day the driving force behind disability advocacy in education, housing, employment, and all other facets of life. Thus, Section 504 is considered as significant civil rights legislation that ushered in the Empowerment Period.

With regard to assistive technology, Title II of Section 504 referred to auxiliary aids, which must be provided when necessary to ensure that a person with a disability has an equal opportunity to benefit from programs and services provided by a public entity. The law further states that auxiliary aids need not produce the identical result or level of achievement for people with and without disabilities. Rather, such aids simply provide a level playing field in which all people have the same opportunity to succeed. The U.S. Department of Education's Office for Civil Rights (OCR) is the enforcement agency for Section 504 and responds to students and others who question their university's or college's adherence to the auxiliary aid provision. Even though legislation technically allowed a college or university to avoid providing auxiliary aids if such provision caused undue hardships, such instances were rare, because OCR dictated that auxiliary aids could be excluded based on lack of funding.

The year 1974 introduced the development of the closed-circuit television (CCTV) for the electronic magnification of print, and the first compact Braille electronic calculator was developed. In the following year, an early version of the speech synthesizer was developed and the first talking calculator with audio and visual output was introduced. Also in 1975, special education law was enacted with the passage of PL 94-142, later named the Education for All Handicapped Children Act (EHA). Education for students with disabilities was now protected in public schools and at publicly supported institutions of higher learning. A period of extraordinary AT development to support educational activities and posteducational employment and living was about to begin.

In 1976, the Kurzweil Reading Machine gave people who were blind the opportunity to access text, but it was so costly that few could afford the technology at the time. During the four years between 1976 and 1979, the Optacon Dissemination project saw that device used with increasing frequency. Grants became available to provide adaptive equipment to classrooms and concurrent training to classroom teachers.

In 1976, Sweden became the first official host of the Paralympic Winter Games. Several years later, following the Seoul 1998 Paralympic Games and the Albertville 1992 Winter Paralympic Games, a formal agreement was signed by the governing bodies of both governing organizations (International Olympic Committee and International Paralympic Committee) that future games would be held in the same year and the same city.

Also in 1976, Pialoux, Chouard and McLeod published a paper in the journal *Acta Oto-Laryngologica* reporting that they had implanted eight-channel cochlear implants in seven patients, and that the recipients had understood about 50% of ordinary words without lip-reading. This was the first such audiological data to be reported in the literature.

VersaBraille was introduced in 1978, followed by the View Scan. The first Braille embosser connected to a microcomputer was introduced in the late 1970s, increasing dramatically the availability of Braille text to children and adults. At the same time, IBM operated its special needs unit, which led the way in developing and adapting technology for people with disabilities.

The Education for All Handicapped Children Act (EHA) was passed in 1975 and implemented in 1978. For the first time, a federal law mandated that all children with disabilities would receive a free, appropriate public education.

EHA was modified in 1985 and made its first provisions for AT. The reauthorization of the law in 1997 went so far as to mandate the consideration of assistive technology for all students with disabilities (see Personal Perspective 1.1). The passage of the Americans with Disabilities Act (ADA) in 1990 continued the string of legislation passed on behalf of people with disabilities by extending the principles of Section 504 to all sectors of the United States, public and private.

One important component of the ADA was the institution of curb cuts so that all public locations would be accessible to all people. Although curb cuts had been in place in previous years, for the first time they had to be placed in spots where wheelchair users could move along sidewalks without endangering themselves (Roberts, n.d.). Thus, a common barrier for wheelchair users was required by law to be removed. Curb cuts not only helped wheelchair users move about their environment with fewer obstacles, they also proved useful for people with baby carriages, luggage, carts, and any other items with wheels. Curb cuts are a good example of universal design, which we discuss more fully in Chapter 2. According to Connell et al. (1997), *universal design* refers to ensuring that products and environments by the nature of their design are usable for all individuals as much as possible without having to make adaptations. Thus, removing barriers for individuals with disabilities through careful universally designed environments and products can also help people without disabilities.

The last law to be discussed here is the Technology-Related Assistance for Individuals with Disabilities Act of 1988 (commonly called the Tech Act) and its reauthorizations of 1992 and 1998. For the first time, in passing this act, Congress acknowledged the potential of AT to assist persons with disabilities to access the American Dream (Bryant & Seay, 1998). The overall purpose of the Tech Act was to provide financial assistance to states to help them develop consumer-responsive, cross-age, and cross-disability programs of technology-related assistance (Rehabilitation Engineering and Assistive Technology Society of North America [RESNA], 1992). Although assistive technology has been viewed historically as beneficial to individuals with physical and sensory impairments, over time there has been an increased focus on technology for people with all types of disabilities (Bryant & Bryant, 1998; Bryant & O'Connell, 1998; Wise & Olson, 1994).

In the mid-1980s, Congress recognized that technological advances were providing an opportunity for Americans with disabilities to realize the potential that the laws were designed to ensure. Thus, the passage of the Tech Act in 1988 reflected:

> Congress' sense that the [Tech] Act promotes values inherent in the ADA. . . . By stating that disability is a natural part of the human experience and in no way diminishes the right of individuals with disabilities to live independently, enjoy self-determination, make choices, contribute to society, pursue meaningful careers, and enjoy full inclusion and integration in the economic, political, social, cultural, and educational mainstream of American society, the [Tech] Act incorporates one of the fundamental concepts of the ADA—that individuals with disabilities are able to pursue the "American dream." (*Source:* U.S. House of Representatives Report 103–208, 1993, p. 6)

When Congress passed the 1994 amendments in Public Law 103-218, it intentionally shifted the purposes of the Tech Act from those relating to public awareness of AT benefits to those that focused on systems change and advocacy (L. Golinker, personal communication, April 1994).

The Tech Act's reauthorization mandated that state Tech Act projects identify and eliminate systemic barriers that impede the timely acquisition and use of AT devices and services. As a result, the Tech Act has profound implications for members of the disability community. Because many children and adults with disabilities can benefit from AT devices and services in school and in the workplace, it is critical that barriers to AT access be eliminated. Tech Act state project efforts work on behalf of individuals with all disabilities to assist in the identification and elimination of AT-related barriers.

Throughout the 1990s, several lawsuits were filed on behalf of people with communication disorders to have Medicaid fund the purchase of AAC devices as durable medical equipment (see Personal Perspective 1.2). These cases demonstrate the dual importance of legislation and litigation for securing not only the civil rights of people with disabilities, but access to AT devices and services to help some members of society obtain the "American Dream."

In 1997 Dragon Systems published Dragon NaturallySpeaking, Personal Edition, V1.0, the first continuous-speech, general-purpose, large-vocabulary speech recognition system (Fishman, 1997). In the years since, voice recognition programs have become more proficient and their cost has decreased dramatically. Efficiency, in terms of both effectiveness and cost, has been the word that best describes assistive technology development in the past 10 years or so. Recent developments in speech synthesis, graphics magnification, Braille printers, augmentative communication devices, wheelchair production, hearing magnification, environmental control units, AAC devices, and so forth have increased the proficiency of the technology and, for the most part, driven costs down to an affordable level for most consumers. And funding for AT devices, although still not what we would like, has become much easier to come by, with Medicaid and special education dollars being utilized as never before.

Innovations for all technology users, such as wireless Internet, e-text, and cell phones, provide almost limitless information accessibility for people with disabilities. CD-ROMS and e-books help make widespread access to text that students with disabilities (and those who read for enjoyment) only dreamed of 10 years ago. Perhaps universal design (see Chapter 2) for classrooms, homes, and businesses has yet to become pervasive, but its applications have proven to be successful in the past 10 years or so, and it is only a matter of time before these applications are commonplace. Colleges and universities throughout the United States are reconfiguring old buildings to allow access for all students, and schools are providing AT devices and services to their students with disabilities in unprecedented numbers.

Accessibility is now also extended to print materials in public schools. State education agencies (SEAs) and local education agencies (LEAs) are required to ensure that textbooks and related core instructional materials are provided to students with print disabilities in specialized formats in a timely manner (Section 300.172, Final Regulations of IDEA 2004). Print disabilities include visual impairments, physical limitations, and organic dysfunction, including students who cannot see print, turn pages in books, and/or read print (e.g., students with reading disabilities/dyslexia). Thus, SEAs and LEAs are required to ensure that students with print disabilities have accessible instructional materials. Furthermore, SEAs must adopt the National Instructional Materials Accessibility Standard (NIMAS) and must include in all purchasing contracts the requirement to produce a NIMAS-compliant file. NIMAS is a standard file format for developing electronic files of print instructional materials. This standard file format then can more readily be converted into accessible formats. The intent is to reduce barriers to print by standardizing the format in which text is made accessible. The Child Study Team (e.g., the IEP team) is responsible for determining whether a student needs accessible instructional materials, which is documented in the IEP. It is then up to the SEA/LEA to ensure that these materials are ordered in a timely manner (Texas Assistive Technology Network, 2008). For additional information about NIMAS and the technical standard for producing materials, see http://aim.cast.org.

As we proceed through the 21st century, litigation against insurance companies will doubtless have an effect in providing additional funding for AT devices. As regulations and systems

Table 1.1 Selected Events Along the Assistive Technology Timeline

Foundation Period (Pre-1900s)	Establishment Period (1900–1972)	Empowerment Period (1973–Present)
1817 Gallaudet opens first school for deaf students ***1834*** Braille code perfected ***1836*** Math apparatus created for people who are blind ***1869*** Patent filed for basic design of wheelchair ***1892*** Braille typewriter invented	***1920*** Optophone invented ***1920s*** Guide dogs utilized ***1932*** First folding, tubular steel wheelchair built ***1939*** VODER introduced ***1947*** Hoover cane ***1948*** RFB&D established ***1954*** *Brown v. Board of Education* ***1966*** Lasercane ***1966*** Prentke-Romich founded (AAC devices)	***1973*** Section 504 of Rehabilitation Act ***1974*** CCTVs developed ***1976*** EHA passed ***1978*** VersaBraille introduced ***1985*** EHA provides for AT ***1986*** Architectural Barriers Act ***1988*** Tech Act passed ***1990*** Americans with Disabilities Act ***1990s*** Various court cases provide for Medicaid funding of AAC devices ***2004*** Individuals with Disabilities Education Improvement Act—National Instructional Materials Accessibility Standard

are developed for accessing AT devices and services via public and private funding, AT assessments will play an even larger role in providing evidence for the person–technology match that is and will be required by the funding agencies. Researchers will focus on the efficacy of AT devices and provide a corpus of evidence-based practices that will grow and help refine the way in which we acquire and use the devices. Whatever happens, we are deeply indebted to the people and events listed in this history, and to the countless others who made contributions that we have failed to note in this brief overview. Table 1.1 provides key chronological events in the field of AT across the three time periods.

MULTIDISCIPLINARY NATURE OF ASSISTIVE TECHNOLOGY SERVICE PROVISION

It is the nature of assistive technology to be multidisciplinary in that professionals involved in AT come from education, medicine, speech-language pathology, occupational therapy, physical therapy, social work, rehabilitation counseling, and engineering, among other fields. This was evidenced in the previous section as we discussed laws passed to provide training of disability specialists in a variety of disciplines.

Terms such as *AT* are synonymous with adaptive technology, adaptive aids, auxiliary aids, rehabilitation technology, prostheses, and other such terms that make the field somewhat confusing at times. In addition, there has traditionally been a knowledge gap among professionals; between professionals and consumers; and among professionals, consumers, and vendors. For example, a consumer or family member may hear of an AT device that seems the perfect answer to the person's difficulties. In some instances, professionals may never have heard of the device, or perhaps the reality of the device is not what the consumer or family member had perceived. And vendors may be quick to point out the virtues of a device without mentioning potential drawbacks. Added to this may be the "this is what we have, so take it or leave it" mentality, which results from having a library of devices from which people are expected to choose. The reality of AT is that it is a constantly evolving field, with new devices being created and improvements made in existing devices seemingly on a daily basis. A quick tour of the Exhibits Hall at Closing the Gap or CSUN leaves the attendees with their heads spinning from the myriad of devices, all with advantages and potential problems.

Without doubt, knowledgeable leadership and participation in the AT evaluation and implementation processes is critical to successful AT use. Further, interdisciplinary knowledge (i.e., knowledge of how all professionals contribute to the process by bringing specific skills to the table and shared knowledge about devices and services among professionals) promotes dialogue and eventual integration of the devices into the consumer's daily life. Augmentative communication is not strictly the responsibility of speech-language pathologists, nor are positioning and mobility issues restricted to physical and occupational therapists. In the same way, if only educators or rehabilitation specialists know computer access issues, the picture is destined to be incomplete.

That said, there is a growing awareness that professionals need to work together and cross disciplinary boundaries for the good of the user. The degree to which that awareness translates to actual practice will dramatically affect the ability to acquire and use AT devices and services in a timely fashion.

SUMMARY

Assistive technology has had a tremendous impact on the lives of individuals with disabilities as demonstrated in this chapter, with the numerous developments in the field inspired by influential people who had the insight to see the potential of devices and services. We introduced important concepts, such as AT devices and services, instructional technology, and adaptations, which will be explained in more detail throughout the book. A historical overview of key events during the Foundation, Establishment, and Empowerment Periods that influenced developments in AT should provide readers with a sense of the leaders and important events that have shaped AT benefits as we know them today. Finally, the multidisciplinary approach to AT evaluation and intervention—including professionals, families, and users—was emphasized as a critical component of AT service.

SCENARIO APPLICATIONS

Scenario 1.1

Visit a school or interview a teacher to identify AT devices that are used at the school. What categories (e.g., augmentative and alternative communication, computer access) of AT are represented? Are some categories more represented than others? Is there a relationship between the disabilities (e.g., visual impairments, learning disabilities) students have and the categories of AT that are used?

Scenario 1.2

Conduct an online search for "assistive technology" and "assistive technology vendors." Start a list of important URLs that you can access for future information about AT and about products that are available. Add the URLs that are presented in other chapters to this list. Refer to the URLs to find picture examples of AT devices described in the chapters. Do a final online search for research that has been conducted on the use of the devices with individuals with disabilities.

For Discussion

1. What is the definition of *AT device*? Describe the definition's key components and their importance to independent functioning.
2. Create a timeline depicting key events in the history of assistive technology. Divide the timeline according to devices, services, and legislation.
3. Who are the key professionals who are involved in assistive technology service delivery, and what are their roles?
4. From all the historical events described in this chapter, create a top 10 list of significant happenings across the three periods.
5. Pick a significant person in AT history. Conduct a mock interview with the individual and write it up as part of a mock Internet biography.
6. Assistive technology has a variety of applications for all types of people. Who might benefit from AT use? Why might some people be better candidates for AT use than others?
7. How are the events discussed by Diana Carl in Personal Perspective 1.1 similar to some of the historical events presented in this chapter?
8. Summarize key results from the cases presented by Lewis Golinker in Personal Perspective 1.2 and their impact on the field of AT.

References

Bryant, B. R., & O'Connell, M. (1998). The impact of the collaboration among tech act projects and protection and advocacy systems. *Intervention in School and Clinic, 33*(5), 309–312.

Bryant, B. R., & Seay, P. C. (1998). The Technology-Related Assistance to Individuals with Disabilities Act: Relevance to individuals with learning disabilities and their advocates. *Journal of Learning Disabilities, 31*(1), 4–15.

Bryant, D. P., & Bryant, B. R. (1998). Using assistive technology adaptations to include students with learning disabilities in cooperative learning activities. *Journal of Learning Disabilities, 31*(1), 41–54.

Bryant, W. V. (1996). *In search of freedom: How persons with disabilities have been disenfranchised from the mainstream of American Society.* Springfield, IL: Charles C Thomas.

Connell, B. R., Jones, M., Mace, R., Mueller, J., Mullick, A., Ostroff, E., et al. (1997). *The principles of universal design.* Retrieved March 19, 2011, from http://www.design.ncsu.edu/cud/about_ud/udprincipleshtmlformat.html

Cook, A. M., & Hussey, S. M. (2002). *Assistive technologies: Principles and practice* (2nd ed.). St. Louis: Mosby.

Hardman, M. L., Drew, C. J., & Egan, M. W. (2007). *Human exceptionality: School, community, and family* (9th ed.). Boston: Allyn & Bacon/Pearson Education.

History of speech synthesis, 1770–1970. (2000). Retrieved March 4, 2011, from http://www.ling.su.se/staff/hartmut/kemplne.htm

IBM (International Business Machines). (1991). *Technology and persons with disabilities.* Atlanta: IBM Corporate Support Programs.

The Individuals with Disabilities Education Improvement Act of 2004. Pub. L. No. 108-446: IDEA 2004.

Johnson, L., Beard, L., & Carpenter, L. B. (2007). *Assistive technology: Access for all students.* Upper Saddle River, NJ: Prentice Hall.

McMurtrie, D. C. (1980). Notes on the early history of care for cripples. In William R. F. Phillips & J. Rosenberg (Eds.), *The origins of modern treatment and education of physically handicapped children* (pp. 27–41). New York: ARNO Press. (Reprinted from Early history of the care and treatment of cripples, in *Johns Hopkins Hospital Bulletin*, pp. xxv, 57–62, 1914, Baltimore.)

Pelka, F. (1997). *The disability rights movement.* Santa Barbara, CA: ANC:CLIO.

Rehabilitation Engineering and Assistive Technology Society of North America (RESNA). (1992). *Project director's handbook.* Arlington, VA: Author.

Roberts, S. (n.d.). Instructional design and accessibility: Cognitive curb cuts. Retrieved March 4, 2011, from http://www.aect.org/Divisions/roberts.htm

Sauberger, D. (1996). *O&M living history: Where did our O&M techniques come from?* Retrieved March 19 from http://www.sauerburger.org/dona/omhistory.htm

Smith, D. D., & Tyler, N. C. (2010). *Introduction to special education: Making a difference* (7th ed.). Upper Saddle River, NJ: Merrill/Pearson Education.

Texas Assistive Technology Network. (2008). *Making decisions about Accessible Instructional Materials: What ARD committees need to know.* Retrieved March 4, 2011, from http://www.texasat.net/default.aspx?name=resources.aim

U.S. House of Representatives. (1993). House of Representative Report 103–208. Washington, DC: Author.

Webster's New World Compact Desk Dictionary and Style Guide (2nd ed.). (2002). Cleveland, OH: Wiley.

Webster's Universal College Dictionary. (1997). New York: Gramercy Books.

Wiederholt, J. L., & Bryant, B. R. (1987). *Assessing the reading abilities and instructional needs of students.* Austin, TX: Pro-Ed.

Wikipedia contributors. (2009). Ludwig Guttmann. Retrieved March 4, 2011, from http://en.wikipedia.org/wiki/Ludwig_Guttmann

Wise, B. W., & Olson, R. K. (1994). Computer speech and the remediation of reading and spelling problems. *Journal of Special Education Technology, 12*(3), 207–220.

2 CONSIDERING, SELECTING, AND EVALUATING ASSISTIVE TECHNOLOGY

Chapter at a Glance

Objectives

1. Describe how considering assistive technology is included in the 2004 IDEA and the Rehabilitation Act Amendments of 1998.
2. Explain the four components of the Adaptations Framework.

MAKING CONNECTIONS

Refer back to Chapter 1 to review the definitions of assistive technology, and assistive technology devices and services. These definitions provide a fundamental understanding of AT that will be integrated into discussions throughout this book. Now, identify and describe the seven categories of AT devices also described in Chapter 1. As you read the chapters in this book, you will learn about many devices and issues that apply to these seven categories. The purpose of this chapter is to (a) provide a brief introduction to using AT; (b) describe universal design, which is a critical concept for understanding technology; (c) describe AT adaptations; and (d) explain ways to select and evaluate the use of AT adaptations.

USING ASSISTIVE TECHNOLOGY

According to legislation such as ADA (1991) and IDEA (2004), individuals with disabilities have the right to be able to access environments that are available to all people. Environments include but are not limited to public school classrooms and curriculum, recreational and leisure activities, daily living activities (e.g., public transportation, access to buildings), and vocational and postsecondary settings. Simply, assistive technology (AT) adaptations (or accommodations as stipulated in IDEA 2004) are changes to conditions that facilitate access to those environments. AT devices are examples of adaptations that may be necessary for individuals with disabilities to circumvent disability-related barriers (Bryant, Smith, & Bryant, 2008; MacArthur & Haynes, 1995; McGregor & Pachuski, 1996).

The use of AT adaptations to promote access across environments is evident throughout life. In the classroom, AT adaptations are common components of the delivery of special education services for assisting school-aged students to compensate for challenges associated with various disabilities (McGregor & Pachuski, 1996; Okolo, Cavalier, Ferretti, & MacArthur, 2000). For example, a student with a severe reading disability who struggles with decoding could use electronic text to access print. The recognition of the instructional capabilities of assistive technologies has prompted an array of AT adaptation solutions (e.g., word prediction software, electronic spell checkers) to help students who have academic goals on their Individualized Education Programs (IEPs) and to facilitate progress in the general education or functional life skills curriculum.

On the other hand, in the home or other environments where eating occurs, eating utensils can be adapted (e.g., built-up handles) to enable individuals with motor problems to grasp the handle and feed themselves independently. A liquid indicator can be attached to a cup to signal to an individual who is blind the level of liquid in relation to the top of the drinking utensil. Public transportation, such as the city bus, is required to have wheelchair accessibility to provide equal access for individuals who use wheelchairs. Advances in computer-based technology, such as voice recognition and text-to-speech software, have allowed individuals with sensory disabilities, for example, access to computers across environments such as home, school, and work.

Thus, key pieces of legislation along with advances in technology have helped individuals with disabilities across the lifespan achieve more of the freedom and independence with all environments that many of us take for granted.

UNIVERSAL DESIGN

Universal design (UD) is the design of products and environments that can be used by all individuals as much as possible without having to make adaptations (Connell et al., 1997). UD then promotes accessibility for as many people as possible across environments. UD stems from efforts to make environments "barrier free" and assistive technology, which creates access to environments, that might not otherwise be possible for individuals with disabilities. Removing barriers allows people with disabilities to participate in events and activities of daily life, but removing those barriers also helps people without disabilities (Center for Applied Special Technology [CAST], 2004). For instance, curb cuts or wheelchair ramps allow people who use wheelchairs to use sidewalks, cross streets, have access to buildings, and be free to move independently as they shop, go to restaurants, or go to the movies. But, curb cuts and wheel chair ramps also help parents with strollers and people with shopping carts as they shop and walk through neighborhoods or shopping centers. So, the universal design feature of curbs and ramps benefits many individuals in society.

Universal design can also be applied to education and is called universal design for learning (UDL) (CAST, 2004). UDL focuses on the design of curricula and instruction that helps teachers be responsive to the individual differences of their students with disabilities while also being beneficial for students without disabilities. Orkwis and McLane (1998) describe universal design as how materials and instruction are designed so that all students with a variety of differences in learning, seeing, hearing, moving, and understanding English can access and benefit from instruction.

Universal design of curricula and instruction means that adaptations are incorporated into the materials and instruction during development. The intent is that the materials be flexible enough to accommodate the diverse learning needs evident in most classrooms.

There are three features of universally designed curricula and instruction (Bryant et al., 2008; Miller, 2002; Orkwis & McLane, 1998). First, there are multiple means of representation, which means that information is presented in various formats to reduce sensory and cognitive barriers. For example, written text can be accompanied by audio for students who are blind, and graphics can be used to enhance the content for students who are deaf or have learning problems. Closed captions on video are another example of ways information is represented. The second feature, multiple means of expression, refers to the ability of students to respond in a variety of ways. For example, voice recognition software, scanning devices, and switches help students with physical disabilities access the computer to complete computer-based activities. The third feature, multiple means of engagement, refers to actively involving students in activities and matching the mode of representation and expression with their needs and interests. For example, changing how information is presented and how students are to respond, such as in small groups or in partners using the computer, provides different ways to engage students in the learning process.

Digital media is an excellent example of how universal design features promote access for students with different needs such as learning, seeing, hearing, moving, and understanding English (Miller, 2002; Orkwis & McLane, 1998). For example, current technology and partnerships with textbook publishers now make electronic versions of texts readily available. Thus, print is not the only way to access books. For the student with learning disabilities who has difficulty reading, the computer can be used to immediately translate visual access (print) to the curriculum materials to an auditory means (listening to the text) of gaining information. A social studies text can be "heard" instead of "read." By using the same electronic version of the book, the computer can convert print to Braille for the student with severe visual disabilities. In this case, the blind student who uses a tactile means of accessing print can read the social studies text. Universal design allows the broadest spectrum of learners to access the curriculum: students with varying learning needs, those with disabilities, and those with other special needs.

ASSISTIVE TECHNOLOGY ADAPTATIONS

Adaptations become "assistive technology" when they conform to the definition of such technology (see Chapter 1) and help individuals "improve functional capabilities." Thus, if a person with a disability uses a device, it becomes assistive when it is "used to increase, maintain or improve the functional capabilities of individuals with disabilities." Bryant, Seay, and Bryant (1999) noted that AT, in some instances, is simply technology that becomes assistive when its use satisfies the criteria found in the AT definition. For example, a calculator is "helpful" technology to many people but can be considered AT when used to perform basic calculations by an individual with a mathematics disability. Similarly, a doctor might dictate her findings about a patient into a handheld recording device. For someone with traumatic brain injury or a learning disability who needs assistance to remember items and appointments, a personal handheld device may be crucial in helping the individual with daily living skills; thus, the device becomes a type of assistive technology. Finally, a person might enjoy listening to a favorite novel on a CD, whereas, for a person with a print disability (blindness, visual impairment, physical limitations, organic dysfunction such as a learning disability in reading/dyslexia), an electronic novel might be the best way to access the book and thus becomes assistive technology for that individual. AT adaptations can also be thought of in terms of their features, thus ranging from simple to complex.

Simple-to-Complex Adaptation Features

AT adaptations range on a continuum from simple to complex (McGregor & Pachuski, 1996), depending on features such as types of AT (e.g., technological: hardware platform specifications, electronic capabilities; and nontechnological: enlarged print, writing template, adaptive eating utensil); ease of implementation; maintenance demands; environmental needs; and user, family, and teacher/caregiver training requirements. For example, a calculator with large keys might be considered a relatively simple adaptation because the technology components are quite simple, it is fairly simple to use, maintenance costs are restricted primarily to battery replacement, it can be used and stored in a small space, and only limited training is necessary. On the other hand, an augmentative communication piece of software, such as Speaking Dynamically Pro (software that speaks what is displayed on the screen), would be an example of a complex AT adaptation. This software requires training for the user, family, and teacher on the technological features such as graphics, buttons, digitized speech, scanning and printing capabilities, word processing abilities, and various access method capabilities. Although these are excellent features in terms of providing communication options for the user, the software is complex to use, at least initially, would require an upgrade as needed, and must be compatible with available computer platforms.

TYPES OF AT ADAPTATIONS

AT adaptations vary considerably depending on the no-, lower-, or higher-tech nature of the device or software. An AT adaptation does not have to have all of the "bells and whistles" to be considered as AT. "No-tech" adaptations can be quite simple and appropriate for the user. A universal cuff to help the user hold something (e.g., crayon or cup); a grab bar in a bathtub to provide an individual with a physical disability much-needed support; a toothbrush with a built-up handle to help the person with fine motor problems hold the device; a key guard to limit random, erroneous keystrokes often caused by limited fine motor coordination; and enlarged print for someone with a print disability are examples of no-tech adaptations. Lower-tech adaptations might include page turners for books to enable a person with limited use of upper extremities to have access to print, a talking watch to help an individual who has a visual impairment tell time, a simple voice output device to aid communication, and a signaling device to alert someone with a hearing impairment that the doorbell is ringing. Finally, a powered wheelchair for an individual with a mobility impairment, a voice output device with speech synthesis to facilitate communication, and an interface and switch to turn electrical appliances on and off as part of environmental control are examples of higher-tech adaptations. Obviously, the more technology that is required to operate a device or to use software (e.g., graphics, voice output), the farther along the AT adaptation is situated on the continuum.

It is important to keep in mind that the selection of the AT adaptation depends on the needs of the user and the benefits of the adaptation in promoting access and independence. Decision makers must carefully analyze the needs of the user and the components of the device or software that might help the user to be successful with environmental demands (Todis, 1996). Information about components can be obtained from vendors, users, and professionals across disciplines (e.g., assistive technology specialists, occupational therapists, speech and language therapists) and organizations that are designed to provide consumer information (e.g., Alliance for Technology Access, 2001).

EASE OF USE

The use of the AT adaptation should be evaluated carefully by professionals, family members, and users by examining several factors. First, it should be noted how easy it is for the AT adaptation to be used and whether further training is required. For example, an electronic device may overwhelm the family and user, thus limiting the possibility that the device will be used. More training may be required for successful implementation (Lemons, 2000).

Second, users should note their ability to keep pace with their peers or colleagues to complete the tasks of the setting demands (e.g., taking notes in class). Practice using various types of AT adaptations (technological in particular) may be needed to maximize their effectiveness. For instance, Anderson-Inman and colleagues (Anderson-Inman, Knox-Quinn, & Horney, 1996) found that secondary school students with learning disabilities expressed a need to develop fluent keyboarding skills so that they could use specialized software for studying.

Finally, user fatigue should be monitored to determine if the use of the adaptation proves tiring and thus hinders productivity. Observations of the user in action may also result in optimized patterns of technology use or the development of new techniques that prove more effective.

MAINTENANCE DEMANDS

The performance (i.e., reliability and durability) of technological adaptations should be monitored carefully (Bowser & Reed, 1995). If the performance of the adaptation necessitates frequent repairs, and thus interferes with the user's success, then the AT adaptation may need to be reconsidered. Devices that are frequently broken or that need parts, which take time to order and receive, are quickly abandoned; thus, the potential of AT is lost needlessly. Finally, the availability of technical support is critical. Users and service providers must have access to support by technology experts when problems are encountered with the AT.

ENVIRONMENTAL NEEDS

Environments must be examined to ensure that individuals can use the AT adaptation as needed. Any AT adaptation that involves hardware and software should be examined to determine specific environmental needs (e.g., space, electricity) (Raskind & Shaw, 1996). Some devices will necessitate environmental accommodations. Devices that produce sound, such as talking calculators, speech synthesizers, and tape recorders, may need to be used in a location that does not distract others; headphones are an alternative to segregation. The location of electrical outlets will dictate where devices that require electricity can be set up; other devices may require batteries—battery-operated versions are often preferable when mobile environments are part of the setting. Physical space may need to be analyzed if it impedes cross-environmental use. For example, if an individual uses a wheelchair, then access to all environments (e.g., classroom, corridors, and doorways) must be ensured. Finally, professionals, family members, and users should note the versatility of AT devices across environments, such as classroom to dorm room/home, home to community, and class to class, to ensure that devices can be easily used or adapted to be used across environments (e.g., transporting the device, ability to use device across setting demands).

TRAINING FOR ASSISTIVE TECHNOLOGY

Training, which is considered to be an AT service, is critical to ensure that AT adaptations are used and maintained rather than abandoned (Parette, Brotherson, Hourcade, & Bradley, 1996). Not surprisingly, training in the use of specific AT adaptations is one of the top-ranked issues for the successful implementation of the devices (Wehmeyer, 1999). For instance, Todis (1996) noted that specialists were frustrated by the limited use of AT adaptations because classroom teachers had difficulty coming up with solutions to problems with technology devices that were not working properly. Unfortunately, Todis (1996) found that devices were left unused and students were left without the support they needed.

The need for training applies to any individual who works with the user, such as classroom teachers, instructional assistants, specialized professionals (e.g., speech/language therapists), family members, and the user (Todis, 1996). Because teachers are usually the first people with whom families discuss school issues, teachers should have a good working knowledge of AT adaptations (Parette, Brotherson, & Huer, 2000). Professional development workshops can provide both low- and high-intensity training, coupled with follow-up support that focuses on practical application and troubleshooting implementation problems (Derer, Polsgrove, & Rieth, 1996). Also, because instructional assistants may be the primary caregivers in different environments, they must be included in workshops so that they, too, can become competent in the use of AT adaptations (Todis, 1996).

Because of the transportability of AT across environments, including the home, family members must be trained in the use of adaptations (Bryant & Bryant, 1998). For instance, Lemons (2000), in a survey of parents whose children used augmentative communication devices, found a need to know more about these devices. Specific training procedures should focus on handling, care, and storage of devices to ensure proper treatment of expensive hardware. Also, families should be aware of the outcomes associated with the use of AT devices; these outcomes should reflect the needs of the family in promoting their child's independence. Support services, such as training and funding options, should be available to families as they adjust to the adaptations their children require as part of appropriate educational programming (Bryant & Bryant, 1998).

Training for the user is critical because, without training, the adaptation may not be used consistently or properly and so may be abandoned. Several topics and procedures can be included in the training, such as:

- providing a rationale for the adaptation
- teaching the vocabulary related to the adaptation
- giving explicit instructions (e.g., modeling, examples, feedback)
- using visual, oral, and written instructions (e.g., videotapes, diagrams) on correct implementation (Anderson-Inman et al., 1996; Day & Edwards, 1996)

Also, users may require training in computer literacy, keyboarding skills, input devices (e.g., speech-to-text software, touch-sensitive mouse, trackball mouse, touch screen), and output devices (refreshable Braille displays, screen readers). Certainly, the quality of the tutorials to teach individuals how to use devices or to serve as a backup after more formal training has occurred is an important training consideration.

Table 2.1 shows a rating scale that can be used to determine the overall simplicity/complexity of a device. Potential users and professionals can use the rating scale to determine the feasibility of the device for the user, family, and other professionals (e.g., teachers) who might be involved in the implementation of the device. The rating scale is not meant to limit choices but rather to provide a quick assessment of what assistance AT specialists might need to provide to ensure that the device is used properly and not abandoned because of training or maintenance issues.

CONSIDERING THE NEED FOR AT ADAPTATIONS IN THE INDIVIDUALIZED EDUCATION PROGRAM

In the field of education, IDEA 2004 requires that Individualized Education Programs (IEPs) be developed for all preschool through high school students with disabilities (ages 3 to 21). The IEP team must "consider" a student's need for AT and services so that the student can receive a free, appropriate public education (FAPE) in the least restrictive environment (LRE). IEP teams must "consider" AT to help students compensate for their specific disabilities and to meet the demands and expectations of school environments. Furthermore, "consideration of a child's need for assistive technology must occur on a case-by-case basis in connection with the development of a child's Individualized Education Program (IEP)" (Schrag, 1990, p. 1). For example, for students who are blind or visually impaired, instruction should be provided in Braille and the use of Braille unless the IEP team determines, after an assessment of the student's reading and writing needs presently and in the future, that instruction in Braille or the use of Braille is not appropriate (IDEA, 2004).

Table 2.1 Simple to Complex Continuum of AT Features

Adaptation: Speaking Calculator with Large Keys

Overall Mean Rating of Simplicity/Complexity: 1.6

	Simple Few		Some		Complex Many
Technological Components	1	2	3	4	5
	Simple Easy		Somewhat		Complex Difficult
Ease of Use	1	2	3	4	5
	Simple None		Occasionally		Complex Frequently
Maintenance Demands	1	2	3	4	5
	Simple None		Some		Complex Many
Environmental Needs	1	2	3	4	5
	Simple None		Moderate		Complex Extensive
Training	1	2	3	4	5

IEP teams must have in place a process for determining students' needs for AT on an individual basis. IEP teams must consider ways to help students successfully access the demands or expectations of their educational environments, access the general education classroom, and progress in the curriculum. IEP teams often choose from an array of adaptations or modifications that promote students' learning. Instructional adaptations consist of changes to teaching procedures, curriculum, management, materials and technology, and the physical environment to facilitate learning (Bryant et al., 2008). Assistive technology devices and services are certainly viable adaptation options.

Psycho-educational assessments serve as an important step in providing decision makers a wealth of information about an individual's academic achievement and functional performance in cognitive, sensory, motor, language and speech, psychosocial, and self-help domains. Goals for academic skills, language development, social and emotional skills, functional skills, motor development, or work-related skills are identified for the individual. AT must be considered in light of the individual's needs as a possible related service to promote access to the curriculum, facilitate independence, and empower the individual to compensate for challenges.

IEP team members gather assessment data about the student's needs from the psycho-educational assessment process and from the speech/language and sensory-motor evaluations, if they were conducted. Additionally, specialists must conduct technology evaluations to determine the setting demands (i.e., tasks individuals perform in different environments and the requisite abilities needed to perform these tasks) and the needs and strengths of individuals in relation to these demands. AT devices can then be selected based on their features and how the features match the individual's abilities and promote independence.

As a part of the total educational program, the need for AT devices and services for infants and toddlers and secondary-level students must also be considered. Individualized Family Service Plans (IFSPs) for children birth through age 2 and statements of transition service needs and interagency responsibilities for older students can include provisions for AT to meet the student's individual needs. (See Smith, 2000, for a detailed discussion of IEPs, IFSPs, and transition.) For example, a communication device could be identified by the speech/language pathologist as essential for developing language skills and cause–effect responses for a toddler. The communication device then would become a part of the IFSP along with the appropriate support for the family and child to ensure proper use of the device.

For older students, transition service needs and interagency responsibilities, which become a part of the IEP document, are critical for identifying services to promote a smooth transition from secondary to postsecondary settings. Therefore, individuals with disabilities, diagnosticians and psychologists, and service providers (e.g., on-campus service provisions, rehabilitation counselors) are challenged to determine appropriate AT devices and services at the secondary level that students can learn to use, which can transfer easily to the postsecondary setting.

AT can be identified in IEPs as part of the special education program, as a related service, or as a supplementary aid. AT can be designated as an accommodation that allows participation in the general education curriculum; AT can also be designated as a related service when it is deemed necessary to involve other professionals (e.g., AT specialists) to deliver services. For example, when AT is included as part of the special education program, an IEP goal might be that, using word prediction software, Maria will compose papers that include at least five paragraphs in narrative format consisting of a beginning, a middle, and an ending. In this case, the AT allows Maria to participate in a typical general education activity of writing stories that otherwise might be quite difficult for her to achieve. As a related service, training on a communication device may be part of language therapy if the device is intended to assist with interactions and conversations. Finally, if the AT device is used in place of another material, then it could be identified as a supplementary aid (e.g., computer instead of paper and pencil). Table 2.2 provides key ideas for IEP team members to consider when deciding the need for AT devices and services.

AT ADAPTATIONS IN THE REHABILITATION FIELD

In the rehabilitation field, one of the purposes of the Rehabilitation Act Amendments of 1998 is to empower individuals with disabilities to achieve employment, economic self-sufficiency,

Table 2.2 IEP Team Key Ideas to Consider for the Selection of Assistive Technology Devices and Services

1. Identify information about the needs and strengths of the individual and how these relate to AT device options.
2. Identify how the AT device can promote a free, appropriate education.
3. Identify the areas in which an AT device could promote independence, access, and success in the general education classroom.
4. Identify how it will be determined whether the individual is benefiting from using the device.
5. Identify individuals and training that are necessary to ensure that the user of the AT device will be supported in various environments (e.g., school, home, work).

independence, and inclusion and integration into society. Assistive technology devices and services are included under the heading "rehabilitation technology," meaning the systematic application of technologies, engineering methodologies, or scientific principles to address the barriers encountered by individuals with disabilities in areas such as education, rehabilitation, employment, transportation, independent living, and recreation (Rehabilitation Act Amendments of 1998). Individuals are assessed for the need of rehabilitation technology devices and services to enable them to develop the capacity to perform in a work environment. Each state develops a plan that includes strategies to be used to address the needs of individuals identified during the assessment process. States must identify how AT devices and services will be provided to individuals at each stage of the rehabilitation process.

The vocational rehabilitation counselor and individual with a disability must develop an individualized plan for employment. The plan must include a description of the vocational rehabilitation services necessary to help the individual achieve employment, including the use of AT devices and services (Rehabilitation Act Amendments of 1998). Assistive technology devices can facilitate participation in postsecondary and vocational settings and are an integral part of an effective support system used by people with disabilities. Although AT devices are rarely the only support needed, it could be argued that the use of AT devices can assist individuals with disabilities to function more independently (Bryant et al., 1999). Thus, AT has widespread application across environments and fields to empower people with disabilities to lead fulfilling lives. In the next section, we provide information about frameworks that can be used to help decision makers consider an individual's need for AT adaptations and services.

SELECTING AND EVALUATING THE USE OF AT ADAPTATIONS

There are different perspectives about how to select and evaluate the use of AT adaptations. In this section, we present two: the SETT Framework and the Adaptations Framework.

SETT Framework

Professionals can benefit from having a framework for considering, selecting, and evaluating adaptations, including AT. We begin by describing the SETT Framework, which was developed by Joy Zabala. Joy is an assistive technology practitioner, professional developer, and consultant in assistive technology and leadership. As an independent practitioner, she provides services to state departments of education, school districts, consumers of assistive technology, and others across the United States and abroad. She also serves as a consultant or advisory board member to several state and federal projects. She is a founding member of the QIAT Consortium and the developer of the SETT Framework, which is widely acknowledged as an excellent model for assistive technology service delivery. We present Joy's perspectives about the SETT Framework.

SETT is an acronym for Student, Environments, Tasks, and Tools. The SETT Framework provides a structure for collaborative groups to work together and think well about the assistive technology devices and services that are needed to provide a student with disabilities access to educational opportunities. When using the SETT Framework, each person shares individual knowledge in order to build the team's collective knowledge of the student, the environments in which the student is expected to function, and the tasks that the student needs to be able to do to be an active learner in those environments. When the team's knowledge about the student, environments, and tasks has been built and analyzed, they are able to consider what system of assistive technology tools (devices and services) is necessary for the student, in identified environments, to do expected tasks. According to Zabala, the development of the SETT Framework was needs based. When AT first emerged, there was great hope that the "right" tools would help most students with disabilities make major strides in their educational programs and their lives. From the start, a great effort was made to match the needs of the individual to the features of devices, and many seemingly "right" tools were put in place. However, underutilization and abandonment of AT devices were occurring at an unacceptably high rate. Thus, many individuals were not benefiting much from the early promise of AT. It became increasingly clear that tools "worked" better when they (devices and services) were based on matches. The matches would consider not only the individual and the tools, but also the factors related to the environments in which the tools were expected to be used and the tasks that those environments required and/or that were very important to the individual.

As pointed out by Zabala, an important feature of the SETT Framework is that it supports collaborative work by helping IEP team members understand that each person on the team brings critical expert knowledge in some area to the work of the group. When using the SETT Framework, each person shares his or her individual knowledge of the student, the environments, and/or the tasks in order to build the team's collective knowledge. Team members can then use their collective knowledge to consider whether assistive technology tools (devices and services) are required by the student. If they are, team members can develop a system of tools that is student centered, environmentally useful, and task focused. In other words, they can provide tools that can be used by the student to do expected tasks in a way that is compatible with the student's customary environments. By working through the SETT Framework together, IEP teams develop not only a solid basis for tool selection, but also a shared vision of when and how the tools should be used by the student. This helps the team understand the links among IDEA, the IEP, and assistive technology in educational settings. It also helps all members of the team know when, how, and for what purpose assistive technology is integrated into the student's educational program.

Finally, Zabala emphasizes that families play a critical role in all planning of the educational program of students with disabilities, including being a part of assistive technology decision making and implementation. The SETT Framework encourages and honors the role of families because it requires the family's perspective and expertise, particularly in the area of the Student, but also in the Environments and the Tasks.

We now turn our attention to a discussion of the Adaptations Framework, which we developed more than 10 years ago (Bryant & Bryant, 1998).

Adaptations Framework

The Adaptations Framework can be used to help professionals, families, and users decide on the type of adaptations that would be most beneficial to enable an individual to become more independent and achieve success with tasks in any environment (Bryant & Bryant, 1998; Bryant et al., 2008). Decision makers may use the Adaptations Framework to determine that (1) the individual requires an AT adaptation to meet specific needs; (2) the individual requires a different type of AT adaptation than what is presently being used; (3) the individual does not need an AT adaptation to meet his or her needs at this time; or (4) further information is required and additional evaluation is necessary, which may include an AT evaluation. In Chapter 3, we discuss AT evaluation, which can be conducted to select appropriate devices if decision makers require further information about matching devices to individual's needs.

The Adaptations Framework consists of setting-specific demands, person-specific characteristics, AT adaptation options, and evaluation. In this section, we provide descriptions of these components of the framework. Table 2.3 presents questions to help decision makers use the Adaptations Framework.

Table 2.3 Questions to Facilitate Use of the Adaptations Framework

Adaptations Framework	Questions
Setting-Specific Demands:	
	What are the expectations (e.g., punctuality, task completion)?
Tasks	What tasks are associated with being successful in this setting (e.g., reading, writing, answering the telephone, working a cash register)?
Setting-Specific Demands:	
	What prerequisite knowledge is needed?
Person-Specific Characteristics:	What are the person's sensory, motor, language, and cognitive capabilities in relation to the tasks?
Functional Capabilities	
	How do the person's specific abilities match the requisite abilities?
Person-Specific Characteristics:	What are the person's sensory, motor, language, and cognitive limitations in relation to the task?
	What prevents the person from functioning independently?
Functional Limitations	How do the person's disabilities interfere with the requisite abilities?
	What supports are there to meet the person's needs?
AT Adaptations:	What adaptation solutions exist for the person to perform the tasks?
Features	How do the features correspond to the person's capabilities and limitations?
	Do the adaptations require environmental considerations such as electricity, furniture, and location?
	What training does the user require to use the adaptation correctly?
	What training does the service provider require to assist the user in using the adaptation?
	What training do family members require to assist the family member in using the adaptation if necessary?
Evaluation of Effectiveness:	Is the individual making good progress using the AT adaptation?
Monitoring Progress	Is the person using the adaptation properly?
	Is additional training required?
	Is the person capable of keeping pace with peers?
	Is the person comfortable with the adaptation?
	What data should be collected to determine the person's progress?
	Is the person capable of working independently?
	Is the person able to access the setting demands successfully?
	Is the person able to accomplish the tasks of the setting?
	What are the effects of the use of the adaptation?
Setting-Specific Demands:	What is the setting (e.g., classroom, workplace)?
	What are the expectations (e.g., punctuality, task completion)?
Tasks	What tasks are associated with being successful in this setting (e.g., reading, writing, answering the telephone, working a cash register)?

Setting-Specific Demands

People encounter many settings as they go about their daily business. Classrooms, offices, movie theatres, sports venues, restaurants, public facilities, and grocery stores are all examples of different settings or environments. These settings present specific demands that people must be able to address to be successful in those settings. Setting demands include (a) tasks people must do and (b) the requisite abilities or skills people need to perform the tasks successfully (Bryant & Bryant, 1998).

In an activity of daily living setting, for example, in the grocery store (the setting), individuals must be able to select food items (task). To do so, they must be able to read a grocery list or remember what is needed, locate the items in the store, carry them in some fashion, purchase them, and get the items home (requisite abilities).

In an academic setting including K–12 and postsecondary levels, setting demands are particularly difficult for many students with disabilities. Research findings have informed us about the importance of examining the demands of educational settings that students encounter daily (Bryant & Bryant, 1998; Bryant et al., 2008; Deshler, Ellis, & Lenz, 1996). Setting demands include the curriculum that is taught, how information is delivered to and received by students, and how students demonstrate their understanding of the curriculum (Bryant et al., 2008; Rivera & Smith, 1997). For instance, in the high school or postsecondary classroom (setting), the teacher may expect students to come to class on time, listen to instruction, take notes, read text, and write a report (tasks). To perform these tasks, students must be able to tell time; possess the ability to hear; understand the critical features of the lecture for note-taking purposes; be able to decode and comprehend text; and know how to identify, organize, and produce ideas in written form (requisite abilities for the tasks), respectively. Yet we know that for many students with disabilities, these high school setting demands present challenges that must be addressed.

TASKS

People encounter numerous tasks related to settings on a daily basis whether they are functioning at home, at work, or in the classroom; negotiating public transportation or public facilities; engaging in activities of daily living; or taking part in leisure activities. Although there are legal mandates (e.g., ADA, 1990; IDEA, 2004) for accessibility and to prevent discrimination based on disability, individuals with disabilities encounter an array of issues related to the tasks that we all perform every day and for which AT adaptations are often helpful solutions.

In the public school setting, at the secondary level for example, students are expected to comprehend textbook material (Ellis, 1996; Miller, 2002); solve complex mathematical equations; develop a listening, speaking, and reading vocabulary in a foreign language; demonstrate writing proficiency skills; and use note-taking skills (Suritsky & Hughes, 1996). For students with learning disabilities or sensory impairments, these tasks are daunting without adaptations that allow access to these setting-specific demands.

Similarly, tasks related to other settings must be examined. For instance in a movie theater setting, people need to be able to hear the dialogue. In the home environmental setting, in order to be able to live independently, people need to be able to use bathroom facilities and environmental control features, engage in leisure activities (e.g., watching television, listening to the radio, using a computer), and have safety features (e.g., smoke detectors, fire extinguishers, telecommunications) available. In the work setting, in order to do their jobs, people need to use telecommunications, environmental features (e.g., desk, chair, reference materials), restroom facilities, and so forth. Consider an individual who uses a wheelchair for mobility and works on the second floor of an office building (the setting). If the elevator is not operating or if there is an evacuation of the building (no elevator access), what are the options? Thus, each task (e.g., evacuating from a building, getting to one's office) represents a challenge *if* the task clashes with a person's disability-related limitations. Such "functional dissonance" mandates that adaptations be made so that people can accomplish those tasks successfully (Bryant et al., 1999).

REQUISITE ABILITIES

Requisite abilities are skills that must be demonstrated to accomplish the tasks of the setting demands (Bryant & Bryant, 1998). For instance, the task of "reading the textbook" requires the requisite abilities of seeing print, decoding, comprehending text (including vocabulary), reading fluently, and so forth. The task of communicating with a friend, colleague, or customer requires the requisite abilities of thinking about the message, articulating the words to send the message, having a mechanism for sending the message (e.g., cell phone, voice, sign language, computer-visual or verbal), and having a means for receiving feedback about the message. Many people possess the requisite abilities for these tasks; however, some individuals with disabilities lack the skills that are necessary for performing specific tasks unless AT adaptations are implemented.

Person-Specific Characteristics

As a part of the Adaptations Framework, decision makers examine and assess person-specific characteristics, the person's functional capabilities and limitations, as they relate to the setting's tasks and specifically to the requisite abilities. Decision makers should consider AT adaptations (e.g., specialized software, no tech, low tech, high tech; simple to complex) that will enable the individual to perform the task.

FUNCTIONAL CAPABILITIES

Functional capabilities or strengths refer to cognitive (e.g., reading, writing, reasoning, thinking, processing information), sensory (e.g., visual, auditory), language (e.g., listening, speaking), and motor (e.g., fine, gross) capabilities that individuals use to perform tasks and the associate requisite abilities. Determination of an individual's functional capabilities in relation to setting demands is important for selecting appropriate adaptations. For instance, a student who has a reading disability yet has good listening skills (i.e., functional capability) may benefit from electronic textbooks with a comprehension check to access the reading material for class. Similarly, a student's functional capability, such as visual acuity skills, dictates whether preferential seating, a magnification device, and/or Braille materials should be used for accessing and performing the tasks and requisite abilities associated with the setting (e.g., school, home, work).

FUNCTIONAL LIMITATIONS

Functional limitations are disability-related characteristics that could impair an individual's ability to perform the setting demands (tasks). Functional limitations include difficulties with cognitive or academic skills, sensory abilities, language, and motor skills as they relate specifically to the tasks and requisite abilities in the settings. For instance, a person who has a mathematical disability (e.g., dyscalculia) may exhibit difficulty with computational or word problem-solving skills, tasks of the setting, and the associated requisite abilities (e.g., recalling arithmetic facts, computing problems, interpreting the information presented in a word problem). Functional limitations typically are documented in a psycho-educational assessment including an AT evaluation. Decision makers must determine how a person's functional limitations interfere with the ability to perform specific tasks and the associated requisite abilities. Following the identification of the setting-specific demands (tasks and requisite abilities) and the person-specific characteristics (functional capabilities and limitations) as they relate to the setting, decision makers can examine and make recommendations for possible AT adaptations.

Selection of AT Adaptations

There are several considerations for identifying AT adaptation solutions. The features of the AT adaptations must be carefully examined to determine whether a good match is present with the setting-specific demands and the person-specific characteristics. Also, the attitudes and acceptance levels of all parties involved in the use of the AT adaptation are critically important to ensure use rather than abandonment of the AT adaptation. Finally, although limited funding availability is not a deciding factor on the selection of the AT adaptation, funding options and support for families and users is important to discuss.

FEATURES

The features of the AT adaptations (i.e., types of AT, ease of implementation, maintenance demands, environmental factors, and training requirements) must be examined to determine an appropriate match with the setting demands and the person-specific characteristics. When selecting AT adaptations, decision makers must identify AT adaptations that would enhance the individual's success and independence to function across settings. Independence is one of the most promising and crucial aspects of AT (Bowser & Reed, 1995; Rieth, Colburn, & Bryant, 2004).

Thus, the features of the AT adaptation must be matched appropriately to the individual's needs (i.e., functional strengths and limitations) and to the tasks and requisite abilities required in the setting to facilitate independence as much as possible. For example, if the individual needs to use a computer to type a paper or manage inventory or accounting tasks, being able to access the computer (visually, motorically) would be necessary requisite skills. If the individual has limited fine motor control but has typical visual acuity, then a keyboard adaptation might be appropriate. A touch screen is a possibility because it promotes access by providing a larger area for responding; a key guard would help reduce random keystrokes; or voice recognition software would reduce the need for a keyboard.

When dealing with technology-based AT adaptations, reliability and durability are two critical issues to be considered for successful implementation. Devices that fail or perform sporadically and have parts that break easily will quickly be abandoned unless repair is expedient or "loaners" are readily available (Todis, 1996). In a teacher survey, findings suggested that teachers rate as "very important" the time to program, set up, and customize equipment as well as funds for repair, upgrade, and replacement (McGregor & Pachuski, 1996). Thus, the selection of AT adaptations hinges on careful consideration of the setting-specific demands, the person-specific characteristics, and the features of the devices.

ATTITUDES AND ACCEPTANCE

Attitudes and acceptance are often influenced by a person's comfort level with the AT adaptation; most people do not feel comfortable initially with new devices. Thus, decision makers must acknowledge and address the importance of persistence, training, and support to help users and their families or support systems adjust to the AT adaptations.

The selection of adaptations requires the collaborative decision making of professionals, families, and users; the attitudes and levels of acceptance by all parties involved can be influential in the sustained use of the adaptation. Professionals must be involved in the selection process and encouraged to describe their attitudes about the proposed adaptations. Acceptance of the selected adaptations by professionals is critical if the adaptations are to be integrated properly into the environment (e.g., classroom, work) (Lemons, 2000).

The implications of technology for people with disabilities and their families are critical. Including families in selecting AT devices and hearing their viewpoints is crucial (Bryant et al. 1998; Lemons, 2000; Rieth, Bryant, & Woodward, 2001). Several key ideas should be included in the AT decision-making process. Team members must consider family and cultural viewpoints about disability and how services that are intended to be helpful may be interpreted. Richards (1995) discussed family-related guidelines to be considered when making appropriate setting–person–feature matches. Decision makers must consider family experience and comfort level with technology, their acceptance of the AT adaptations, and the resources that are necessary to help families integrate AT adaptations into their homes and their community contacts. Families should be aware of the expected outcomes of AT adaptations; these outcomes should reflect the needs of the users and their families in promoting independence (Parette & Brotherson, 1996). Assistive technology services, such as training and funding options, must be provided to families and/or caregivers as they work with the user. Selection of AT adaptations that are not accepted by family members will contribute to difficulties between home and school and ultimately to the abandonment of the adaptation by the user (Angelo, Jones, & Kokoska, 1995).

Finally, decision makers must consider the user's attitudes and acceptance level of the adaptation (Carney & Dix, 1992; Rieth et al., 2004). The user's opinions about the types of AT adaptation options, attitudes about using AT adaptations, and interest in trying available options must be considered. Decision makers should be sensitive to the user's attitude about whether or not the AT adaptation will promote his or her independence. Moreover, the motivational level of the user is critical when selecting AT adaptations (Carney & Dix, 1992; Raskind & Bryant, 2002). No adaptation will work if the user is against it, because the device simply will not be used.

FUNDING

Different funding sources are available from which assistance can be provided once the AT adaptation is selected. AT adaptations, such as technological devices, have a wide price range. Although cost should not be the determining factor when selecting an adaptation, decision makers certainly can explore simple and reasonable, low-cost AT adaptations as viable options to match the needs of the user. AT adaptations do not always have to be high-end to be effective for an individual; starting out with a low-tech device could work well to help the individual compensate for a limitation. Locating a funding source can be a problem, but funding alternatives and supplemental funding sources, such as Medicare, insurance, and grants, should be explored (Derer et al., 1996). State rehabilitation offices are possible sources of AT devices and assistance in obtaining funding. Also, for public school students, school districts are responsible for providing AT whether it is done through the district or a community agency (Chambers, 1997).

Evaluation of the Effectiveness of AT Adaptations

Although adaptations have the potential to enhance access to setting demands, promote independence and productivity, and circumvent functional limitations, studies show that almost one third of AT devices are abandoned within the first year of use (Phillips, 1991). This trend is disappointing considering the potential benefits of AT adaptations. Abandonment occurs because users may not be achieving independence, training was insufficient, or numerous equipment issues (e.g., maintenance, reliability) interfere with their success (Phillips, 1992).

Professionals, family members, and users can evaluate whether the AT adaptations help users compensate for specific difficulties (e.g., reading and writing, computer use, access to telecommunications) so that they can meet the demands of the settings. Specifically, is the individual able to perform tasks, master goals and objectives stipulated on education plans, access the tasks of various environmental settings, and achieve independence? Compared to not using the adaptation, is the individual progressing at a rate commensurate with his or her peers? Is accessibility no longer an issue? These are just some of the questions that can be considered to determine the progress of users with adaptations including AT.

Evaluation of the AT adaptation needs to be ongoing to determine if the adaptation continues to meet the individual's needs as he or she matures (e.g., a student in the elementary grades will have different needs than a student in a postsecondary setting; a younger person will have much different capacities than a much older person; an older person with spastic cerebral palsy may have much different motoric challenges than a younger person who may be more ambulatory) and as the setting demands change (public school to workplace setting to leisure activities to retirement). As individuals learn more skills and mature, and encounter increasingly complex setting demands, their needs undoubtedly will change. For example, a child with cerebral palsy who receives physical therapy to develop motor skills will probably benefit from different AT adaptations than an adult with cerebral palsy who has developed some motor skills and has adapted to many of his or her environments. Many disability-related technologies (e.g., screen readers) become dated with the evolution of the mainstream technology, which happens quite rapidly. This factor may actually be more linked to a need to upgrade than to the individual's changing skills, demands, and abilities.

However, as the individual continues to age, his or her AT needs will continue to change to reflect the aging process. For school-age children, as their skills increase and as the academic setting demands become more challenging, AT adaptations at the elementary level (e.g., a pencil grip) may need to be changed to something more appropriate (e.g., a word processing program) to better address the setting–person–feature match.

Evaluation is an integral part of the Adaptations Framework. Reevaluation of any component of the process may be necessary to determine a more appropriate adaptation to satisfy setting demands and user needs and to foster success, independence, and accessibility. Therefore, evaluation of the effectiveness of AT adaptations including AT is crucial.

The Adaptations Framework provides a structure for examining the setting demands, examining information about the individual's needs and strengths as they relate to the setting demands, selecting appropriate AT adaptations, and evaluating the effectiveness of the adaptation to promote access and success. Table 2.4 provides an example of the Adaptations Framework in action. In this case, the setting is the bathroom, where tooth brushing has been identified as a task that an individual needs to learn how to do. We have to think about the task, the person, and the AT adaptation solutions, which will help the person complete the task independently and correctly. Only by carefully evaluating each step of the Adaptations Framework can we begin to ensure a good match between the person's needs and the task at hand. Take a moment to review the framework.

Table 2.4 Adaptations Framework in Action

Setting-Specific Demands		*Person-Specific Characteristics*		*Adaptations*
Task	**Requisite Abilities**	**Functional Capabilities**	**Functional Limitations**	**Simple-to-Complex**
Brushing teeth	grasping brush and paste; squeezing paste onto brush; brushing teeth; rinsing mouth	vision; hearing; cognitive ability to complete task	grasping/fine motor; sequencing difficulties	adapted handle; checklist of steps; electronic toothbrush

SUMMARY

Individuals with disabilities are legally entitled to access environments available to everyone. Adaptations including AT are often necessary to promote access to environmental setting demands. Decision makers, including professionals, family members, and users, must consider the need for AT adaptations and are required to do so according to IDEA (2004).

Adaptations are a common component of the delivery of special education services. As decisions are made about the selection of adaptations, decision makers must consider the setting demands, the needs of the individual, and the types of adaptations. Training is crucial to ensure that AT adaptations will be used and maintained rather than abandoned. Training should be made available for all parties involved and be ongoing with follow-up and support. Evaluation of the effectiveness of the adaptations includes environmental factors, use of the adaptation, use of the adaptation over time, and user progress and must be an integral component of the use of any adaptation.

SCENARIO APPLICATIONS

Scenario 2.1

Develop your own Adaptations Framework chart by thinking about a particular setting and the tasks associated with that setting. Now, develop a case study by considering a person with a disability and identifying possible functional capabilities and limitations for this person. Use the questions in Table 2.3 (setting-specific demands and person-specific characteristics) to help you think about possible adaptations. Record your answers on your chart. Identify several AT adaptations through the Internet, catalogues, or a local AT lab that might possibly be appropriate for your case study. Conduct a feature analysis of the adaptations using the information in the features section and the questions presented in Table 2.3. Select an AT adaptation for your case study. Based on what you have learned in the section on selection of AT adaptations, provide a rationale for your choice. Finally, identify the training you think will be necessary for the AT adaptation you chose for your case study. Talk with a partner and brainstorm a training plan. Share your plan with your peers in class. Identify an evaluation plan for your case study. Share your ideas with a partner or in a small group.

For Discussion

1. What do the 2004 Amendments to IDEA and the Rehabilitation Act Amendments of 1998 say about AT consideration?
2. What are the four components of the Adaptations Framework?
3. Define *setting demands* and provide examples of tasks and requisite abilities.
4. What are examples of functional capabilities and limitations?
5. Explain no assistive and assistive technology adaptations, simple to complex adaptations, and features of adaptations.
6. Describe the considerations for selecting AT adaptations.
7. What AT training should be presented to professionals, families, and users?
8. What are the three components of evaluation? Briefly describe each one.

References

Anderson-Inman, L., Knox-Quinn, C., & Horney, M. A. (1996). Computer-based study strategies for students with learning disabilities: Individual differences associated with adoption level. *Journal of Learning Disabilities, 29*(5), 461–484.

Angelo, D. H., Jones, S. D., & Kokoska, S. M. (1995). Family perspective on augmentative and alternative communication: Families of young children. *Augmentative and Alternative Communication, 11*(3), 193–201.

Alliance for Technology Access. (2001). *Computer resources for people with disabilities* (4th ed.). Alameda, CA: Hunter House.

Americans with Disabilities Act of 1990, Pub. L. No. 101-336, § 2, 104 Stat. 328 (1991).

Bowser, G., & Reed, P. (1995). Education TECH points for assistive technology planning. *Journal of Special Education Technology, 12*(4), 325–338.

Bryant, B. R., Seay, P. C., & Bryant, D. P. (1999). Assistive technology and adaptive behavior. In R. Schalock (Ed.), *Adaptive behavior and its measurement: Implications for the field of mental retardation* (pp. 81–98). Washington, DC: AAMR.

Bryant, D. P., & Bryant, B. R. (1998). Using assistive technology adaptations to include students with learning disabilities in cooperative learning activities. *Journal of Learning Disabilities, 31*(1), 41–54.

Bryant, D. P., Smith, D. D., & Bryant, B. R. (2008). *Teaching students with special needs in inclusive classrooms.* Upper Saddle River, NJ: Allyn & Bacon/Pearson.

Carney, J., & Dix, C. (1992). Integrating assistive technology in the classroom and community. In G. Church & S. Glennen (Eds.), *The handbook of assistive technology* (pp. 207–240). San Diego: Singular.

The Center for Applied Special Technology (CAST). (2004). *Universal design for learning.* Center for Applied Special Technology. Retrieved March 20, 2011, from http://www.cast.org/udl/index.cfm?i=7

Chambers, A. C. (1997). *Has technology been considered? A guide for IEP teams.* Reston, VA: Council of Administrators of Special Education and the Technology and Media Division of The Council for Exceptional Children.

Connell, B. R., Jones, M., Mace, R., Mueller, J., Mullick, A., Ostroff, E., et al. (1997). *The principles of universal design.* Retrieved March 19, 2011, from http://www.design.ncsu.edu/cud/about_ud/udprincipleshtmlformat.html

Day, S. L., & Edwards, B. J. (1996). Assistive technology for postsecondary students with learning disabilities. *Journal of Learning Disabilities, 29*(5), 486–492, 503.

Derer, K., Polsgrove, L., & Rieth, H. (1996). A survey of assistive technology applications in schools and recommendations for practice. *Journal of Special Education Technology, 13*(2), 62–80.

Deshler, D., Ellis, E. S., & Lenz, B. K. (1996). *Teaching adolescents with learning disabilities.* Denver, CO: Love.

Ellis, E. S. (1996). Reading instruction. In D. D. Deshler, E. S. Ellis, & B. K. Lenz (Eds.), *Teaching adolescents with learning disabilities* (2nd ed., pp. 61–126). Denver: Love.

The Individuals with Disabilities Education Improvement Act of 2004. Pub. L. No. 108-446: IDEA 2004.

Lemons, C. J. (2000). *Comparison of parent and teacher knowledge and opinions related to augmentative and alternative communication.* Unpublished master's thesis, The University of Texas, Austin.

MacArthur, C. A., & Haynes, J. A. (1995). Student assistant for learning from text (SALT): A hypermedia reading aid. *Journal of Learning Disabilities, 28*(3), 150–159.

McGregor, G., & Pachuski, P. (1996). Assistive technology in schools: Are teachers, ready, able, and supported? *Journal of Special Education Technology, 13*(1), 4–15.

Miller, S. P. (1996). Perspectives on mathematics instruction. In D. D. Deshler, E. S. Ellis, & B. K. Lenz (Eds.), *Teaching adolescents with learning disabilities* (2nd ed., pp. 313–368). Denver: Love.

Miller, S. P. (2002). *Validated practices for teaching students with diverse needs and abilities.* Boston: Allyn & Bacon.

Okolo, C. M., Cavalier, A. R., Ferretti, R. P., & MacArthur, C. A. (2000). Technology, literacy, and disabilities: A review of the research. In R. Gersten, E. P. Schiller, and S. Vaughn (Eds.), *Contemporary special education research* (pp. 179–250). Mahwah, NJ: Erlbaum.

Orkwis, R., & McLane, K. (1998, Fall). A curriculum every student can use: Design principles for student access. *ERIC OSEP Topical Brief*, 1–20.

Parette, H. P., Jr., & Brotherson, M. J. (1996). Family participation in assistive technology assessment for young children with mental retardation and developmental disabilities. *Education and Training in Mental Retardation and Developmental Disabilities, 31*(1), 29–43.

Parette, H. P., Jr., Brotherson, M. J., Hourcade, J. J., & Bradley, R. H. (1996). Family-centered assistive technology assessment. *Intervention in School and Clinic, 32*(2), 104–112.

Parette, H. P., Jr., Brotherson, M. J., & Huer, M. B. (2000). Giving families a voice in augmentative and alternative communication decision making. *Education and Training in Mental Retardation and Developmental Disabilities, 35*(2), 177–190.

Phillips, B. (1991). *Technology abandonment: From the consumer point of view.* Washington, DC: Request Publication.

Phillips, B. (1992). *Perspectives on assistive technology services in vocational rehabilitation: Clients and counselors.* Washington, DC: National Rehabilitation Hospital, Assistive Technology/Rehabilitation Engineering Program.

Raskind, M., & Bryant, B. R. (2002). *Functional evaluation of assistive technology (FEAT).* Austin, TX: Psycho-Educational Services.

Raskind, M., & Shaw, T. (1996, March). An overview: Assistive technology for students with learning disabilities. In *Council for Learning Disabilities Assistive Technology Symposium*, Las Vegas.

Richards, D. (1995). *Assistive technology: Birth to five years.* Cromwell, CT: ConnSense.

Rieth, H. J., Bryant, D. P., & Woodward, J. (2001). Technology applications for persons with disabilities: Benefits, barriers, and solutions. In I. Pervova (Ed.), *People, time, society* (pp. 86–96). St. Petersburg, Russia: St. Petersburg Press.

Rieth, H. J., Colburn, L. K., & Bryant, D. P. (2004). Trends and issues in instructional and assistive technology. In A. M. Sorrells, H. J. Rieth, & P. T. Sindelar (Eds.), *Critical issues in special education* (pp. 205–225). Boston: Allyn & Bacon.

Rivera, D. P., & Smith, D. D. (1997). *Teaching students with learning and behavior problems* (3rd ed.). Boston: Allyn & Bacon.

Schrag, J. (1990). *OSEP Policy Letter.* Washington, DC: U.S. Office of Education.

Smith, D. D. (2000). *Introduction to special education* (4th ed.). Boston: Allyn & Bacon.

Suritsky, S. K., & Hughes, C. A. (1996). Notetaking strategy instruction. In D. D. Deshler, E. S. Ellis, & B. K. Lenz (Eds.), *Teaching adolescents with learning disabilities* (2nd ed., pp. 267–312). Denver: Love.

Todis, B. (1996). Tools for the task? Perspectives on assistive technology in educational settings. *Journal of Special Education Technology, 13*(2), 49–61.

Wehmeyer, M. L. (1999). Assistive technology and students with mental retardation: Utilization and barriers. *Journal of Special Education Technology, 14*(1), 48–58.

3 ASSISTIVE TECHNOLOGY ASSESSMENTS

This chapter was written by Brian R. Bryant and Minyi Shih.

Chapter at a Glance

Objectives

1. Identify the qualities of effective assessments.
2. Determine how tasks, individuals, devices, and contexts work together to influence the nature of AT assessments.
3. Examine the features of an effective AT assessment to ensure that the individual and device combine to provide an effective person–technology match.

MAKING CONNECTIONS

Think about how assessments are used on a regular basis to gather information about people. What types of instruments are administered, and by whom? What information is gleaned by such assessments, and how are their results used? What kinds of information would be important to obtain concerning AT use? What factors would affect AT use, and how might those factors be examined? Who would conduct such assessments? What would be the purpose of such assessments?

In Chapter 2, we introduced the Adaptations Framework. This chapter explores the evaluation process by examining a number of assessment-related issues. We (a) provide an overview of basic issues in assessment that must be considered when any type of evaluation occurs, (b) discuss AT assessments, and (c) discuss specific components that should be addressed during AT assessments.

OVERVIEW OF GENERAL ASSESSMENT ISSUES

Most assessments are conducted to identify strengths and struggles, determine program eligibility, document progress, select interventions, and/or conduct research (Hammill & Bryant, 1998). In reality, AT assessments may be conducted for all these reasons. The purpose of this section is to identify basic assessment concepts that are considered when assessments for these reasons take place. The assessment concepts include reliability, validity, and frame of reference.

Reliability is defined as the consistency with which an assessment instrument (e.g., test, rating scale, observation checklist) measures a particular construct (Hammill, Brown, & Bryant, 1992). During AT assessments, it is important that the evaluation instruments used yield consistent results so that the results obtained today would be the same if the instruments were administered tomorrow or the next day. When unreliable instruments are used, important decisions can be made based on obtained data, only to end with the discovery that the data were wrong and the decisions flawed.

Validity occurs when an instrument measures what it intends to measure (Salvia & Ysseldyke, 2000). When teachers are asked to complete rating scales on a student's reading abilities, the AT evaluation team expects that the results of the scale will be indicative of the student's reading skills. If the rating scale's results indicate that the student is a poor reader but, when asked to read, the student turns out to be an excellent reader, the scale's results are not valid.

Every evaluation has a frame of reference. Norm-referenced tests compare student performance to that of the student's peers (i.e., the test's standardization or normative sample). Criterion-referenced instruments evaluate performance in terms of mastery of specific skills. Nonreferenced tests do neither; instead, they provide information about performance intrinsic to the individual. Examples of nonreferenced measures are reading miscue analyses and error analyses of math problems (Bryant, Smith, & Bryant, 2008).

Three key assessment concepts are of particular relevance to AT assessments. First, the assessments must be ecological. Second, AT assessments should be practical. Finally, the assessments must be ongoing.

Ecological Assessment

Ecological assessment has as its core philosophy the idea that behavior of any type does not occur in a vacuum or in any single location. Thus, ecological assessments consider the person's multiple environments in which behaviors occur. Ecological assessment is particularly applicable to AT assessments because devices are used in a variety of settings and involve a number of significant people (e.g., professionals, peers, family members). As a result, effective assessments consider the various contexts where the device will be used and the people with whom the user will interact.

As an example, consider a seventh-grade student with learning disabilities who is being evaluated for AT adaptations to print access (i.e., reading) problems. In what contexts or settings does the student have to read text? Typical middle school students attend science class in one room, social studies in another, English class in another, and so forth. So the assessment has to consider each classroom environment and each content-area teacher. It is critical for two reasons that each teacher be a part of the assessment process. First, each teacher has important information about the demands of the class and his or her expectations (e.g., how much material is read, how information is presented during class time) and the student's abilities and behaviors that have been demonstrated in the classroom. Second, the teacher's input, as well as that from parents, peers, and other professionals, demonstrates a level of involvement in the assessment process that will more likely lead to device use after the technology is determined. Teachers who feel that they are involved in the assessment process, whose input was considered, and who participated in on-site trial use of the device are more likely to "buy into" the device's use and participate in training activities concerning its use.

There are a variety of ways in which data can be gathered from teachers, including the use of teacher interviews and ratings scales. We provide an example of rating scales that can be used later in this chapter, as part of a case study. Teachers provide information about a variety of tasks that are assigned to students or expectations of student participation and also can identify, from the teacher's perspective and experience, student strengths and struggles in reading and other academic areas. By having each of the student's teachers complete the scale, an ecological perspective can be gained about the student's characteristics and how they match the demands of the academic environment.

Assistive technology team members may wish to create and use their own rating scales. This task is rather easy and can be accomplished by a simple review of various developmental checklists and scope-and-sequence charts. A sample rating scale that looks at spoken language skills is provided in Table 3.1, which was designed after examining language development texts to identify pertinent skills for examination (Wiederholt & Bryant, 1987). If desired, members of the assessment team can meet with teachers and use the rating scales during an interview as a way to gather data from the teacher. Interviews have the advantage over typical rating scale completion (where the scale is completed by the rater alone) in that the interviewer can probe responses to gather additional information. Regardless of the manner in which data are gathered, the key ingredient is that information is being obtained from a number of people in a variety of settings. This is the importance of ecological assessment.

Practical Assessment

With respect to AT assessments, we use the term *practical* in its dictionary sense: "pertaining to or concerned with practice or action" (*Webster's Universal College Dictionary,* 1997, p. 620). Thus, ideas presented under ecological assessment are continued by actually using the device in the settings (e.g., the classroom, the workplace) where the student's actions will take place. Practical assessments allow the user to gain experience using the device in natural environments and receive training on the device simultaneously (recall that providing training in the natural environment was introduced as an AT service in Chapter 1). Practical assessment also allows for training on the device to be conducted with various people (e.g., teachers, co-workers, supervisors) in the user's multiple environments, which is another AT service. After a device has been selected and matched to the user, assessment continues in multiple contexts where the device will be used.

Assistive technology assessment team members may wish to create their own checklists that most appropriately match the contexts of the individual. Or, they can use existing commercially prepared checklists; a copy of one can be found later in this chapter. Either way, gathering data across multiple environments, while training people within those environments, can be time well spent during the AT assessment.

A second feature of practical assessment is seeking information and participation from specialists. Think of AT assessment teams in terms of "cafeteria plans." *Cafeteria plan* is a useful term that describes the availability of a number of options. The insurance industry uses the term to describe plans that have a variety of options (e.g., disability riders, unemployment compensations) that policy holders consider as they purchase the policy, in the same way that one goes through the line at the cafeteria and selects items from among those laid out by servers.

Table 3.1 Checklist of Spoken Language Strengths and Weaknesses

Spoken Language Rating Scale

Rate the individual's spoken language abilities by reading each item on the rating scale and responding to each item using the following descriptors:

1 = Not at all like the student
2 = Not much like the student
3 = Somewhat like the student
4 = Very much like the student

The ability to. . .				
. . .attend to the speaker	1	2	3	4
. . .verbalize complete thoughts	1	2	3	4
. . .name common objects when given a verbal description	1	2	3	4
. . .describe more than one dimension/trait of an object	1	2	3	4
. . .provide concise descriptions of common objects	1	2	3	4
. . .use conventional grammatical word order	1	2	3	4
. . .use prosody (stress, intonation, pitch) to aid meaning	1	2	3	4
. . .use inflectional endings to provide meaning	1	2	3	4
. . .give verbal directions in logical order	1	2	3	4
. . .relate simple personal experiences in proper order	1	2	3	4
. . .adapt language appropriately to different situations	1	2	3	4
. . .pronounce words appropriately for age	1	2	3	4
. . .speak clearly and distinctly	1	2	3	4
. . .participate in conversations appropriately (does not monopolize)	1	2	3	4
. . .identify rhyming words	1	2	3	4
. . .produce rhyming words	1	2	3	4
. . .answer what, where, and who questions (literal comprehension)	1	2	3	4
. . .answer why, how, and what if questions (inferential comprehension)	1	2	3	4
. . .identify multiple meanings of words	1	2	3	4
. . .use compound sentences (uses conjunctions to combine complete thoughts)	1	2	3	4
. . .understand simple prepositions	1	2	3	4
. . .follow simple directions	1	2	3	4
. . .give opposites when requested	1	2	3	4
. . .identify synonyms on request	1	2	3	4
. . .use contractions appropriately	1	2	3	4
. . .talk in sentences of six or more words	1	2	3	4
. . .mark tense appropriately	1	2	3	4
. . .formulate questions to elicit desired response	1	2	3	4

Source: From Wiederholt, J. L. and Bryant, B. R. (1987). *Assessing the reading abilities and instructional needs of students.*

Table 3.2 Members of an AT Assessment Team

• Student/client	• Physical therapist
• Family members	• Physician
• Diagnostician	• Psychologist
• General education teacher	• Special education teacher
• Occupational therapist	• Speech/language Pathologist
• Paraprofessional	• Others as needed

Table 3.2 lists professionals who should be "on call" for membership on the AT assessment team. As is depicted in the table, the user should always be a member of the team. A member of the user's family, if available, should also be a member of the team. An AT specialist, if available, should be a member of every team. If the user is a student, at least one teacher should be a team member. If the student is receiving special education services while also attending classes in general education, then a special educator and a general educator should be team members. We would also suggest that building principals serve on AT assessment teams, if for no other reason than to demonstrate support of the team's actions and provide leadership in AT implementation in the school. Speech/language pathologists should always be key team members when augmentative and alternative communication devices are being considered. Assistive technology considerations involving seating and positioning issues necessitate team inclusion of physical and occupational therapists. When decisions are being made concerning vocational rehabilitation, rehabilitation counselors should be members of the team. We would argue that counselors also should be involved if the user is a student who is transitioning from special education services into rehabilitation services, whether those services will be provided in postsecondary or workplace settings. Other members of the AT team should be selected as needed and as appropriate.

Ongoing Assessment

A major purpose of assessment is to document the presence of a disability and determine placement eligibility. Such assessments usually occur once, and the information is secured in the student's cumulative folder for reference and archival purposes (Rivera & Bryant, 1992). Assistive technology assessments, on the other hand, never end. Assessments continue in one form or another indefinitely, because the use of devices is monitored and evaluated continuously with follow-ups and follow-alongs (Cook & Hussey, 2002) to ensure that the decisions of the assessment team were accurate and that the device is being used effectively and as recommended. In addition, ongoing assessments ensure that AT decisions that were initially helpful do not become obsolete or inappropriate (Dell, Newton, & Petroff, 2008).

Throughout the course of this text, we discuss the benefits of AT in helping a person compensate for functional limitations. For the technology to be effective, it must be matched to the individual; meshed with other devices, services, and individuals; and evaluated constantly to make sure that the technology adaptation is valid; that is, the adaptation is benefiting the individual as hypothesized. Think of AT use as a hypothetical experiment, a testing of a hypothesis, so to speak. In this line of thinking, the AT assessment team hypothesizes that a particular device will benefit the individual in compensating for disability-related or functional limitations (Bryant & Bryant, 1998). The hypothesis is made after a thorough evaluation of the individual and the contexts within which he or she learns, works, and plays. Sometimes the hypothesis proves correct (i.e., the device is helpful), but sometimes the hypothesis proves false (i.e., the device does not result in expected performance gains). The hypothesis must be tested continuously over time until it is proven correct, which is a critical yet too often overlooked evaluation component. For more information about why ongoing assessments are so important, see Personal Perspective 3.1 with Dr. Penny Reed, a noted authority in the field of assistive technology assessment.

PERSONAL PERSPECTIVE 3.1

Penny Reed, Ph.D., is a national consultant in the field of special education specializing in assistive technology services. She was founder and director of the Wisconsin Assistive Technology Initiative, a statewide technical assistance project on assistive technology funded by the Wisconsin Department of Public Instruction from 1993 to 2003. She has been a teacher, consultant, and administrator in the field of special education for over thirty years. Much of her experience involved working with children with physical and multiple disabilities, which led to her interest in assistive technology. Dr. Reed has worked for local school districts, education service agencies, and state education agencies and has taught both graduate and undergraduate courses at the post secondary level. In 1992, Dr. Reed received the National Leadership Award from the Technology and Media Division of the Council for Exceptional Children.

Dr. Reed is co-author of the *Educational Tech Points* (Bowser & Reed, 1995), *Navigating the Process, Educational Tech Points for Parents* (Bowser & Reed, 1997), *Educational Tech Points: A Framework for Assistive Technology Planning* (Bowser & Reed, 1998), *Assistive Technology Pointers for Parents* (Reed & Bowser, 2000), Assessment for Assistive Technology (Reed & Best, 2001) and Supporting Physical and Sensory Capabilities Through Assistive Technology (Best, Bigge, & Reed, 2001) in *Teaching Individuals with Physical, Health, or Multiple Disabilities*, *How Do You Know It? How Can You Show It?* (Reed, Bowser, & Korsten, 2002), *A School Administrator's Desktop Guide to Assistive Technology* (Bowser & Reed, 2004), *Considering the Need for Assistive Technology within the Individualized Educational Program* (Castellani, Dwyer, McPherson, Reed, Rein, & Zabala, 2005), Assistive Technology and the IEP (Reed & Bowser, 2005) in the *Handbook of Special Education Technology Research and Practice*, and Reed, P., Bowser, G., & Kaplan, M. (2008). *The Assistive Technology Trainer's Handbook*, Roseburg, OR: National Assistive Technology in Education Network. She is editor of *Designing Environments for Successful Kids* (2003) and co-editor of *Assessing Students' Need for Assistive Technology: A Resource Manual for School District Teams* (Reed & Lahm, 2004).

Dr. Reed is a member of the Leadership Team for Quality Indicators for Assistive Technology Services (www.qiat.org) and in that role works with others to develop guidelines and materials to help school districts evaluate and improve their assistive technology services. In the past two years, Dr. Reed has co-authored the content for a website on assistive technology for The Center for Technology in Education at Johns Hopkins University (www.matnonline.com). She maintains a website (www.educationtechpoints.org) through which she can be contacted.

1. Why is AT assessment such an important dimension of working with individuals who have disabilities? AT assessment is often the starting point in the process of providing appropriate AT services. It is the first service mentioned in IDEA and must include "a functional evaluation in the child's customary environment." Not every child with a disability must have an AT assessment, but when questions arise about a child's need for AT and the consideration process within the development of the IEP is not able to answer those questions, then an AT assessment or evaluation is required. The manner in which the AT assessment is carried out is

(continued)

critical to successful use of AT in the future. The requirement that the AT evaluation process must include a functional component that takes place in the child's customary environment shows great wisdom. There are hundreds, perhaps thousands of tools that can be considered AT. But if a tool or tools are recommended that do not function well in the classrooms, hallways, cafeteria, gym and other customary environments, then they are not useful and will be abandoned. The AT assessment has to include one or more trials of the proposed AT in the settings where the student needs to use it in order to determine if it is a reasonably good choice. The student's preferences and willingness to use any tool will impact the effectiveness of the AT. Discovering those preferences are critical at the assessment stage so that neither time nor money is wasted on a tool that will not be accepted by the user.

An assessment process that includes the teacher(s) and paraprofessional(s) who will be expected to implement regular use of the AT is also critical to its success. While someone with AT expertise is needed to help plan and guide the AT assessment process, that person cannot be the sole decision maker. Successful AT use only occurs when the AT is used on a daily basis to accomplish meaningful tasks. That means that those individuals who manage those environments and tasks must have a stake in the selection and planned implementation of the AT tools.

2. When the Individualized Education Program (IEP) team "considers" assistive technology, what are some key factors that should be taken into account? Consideration of the need for AT starts with the question, "What is it this student needs to be able to do during the next twelve months that he either cannot do or does with such difficulty that it is not functional?" This "task" focus is the cornerstone of effective AT consideration. IEP teams that start with this focus are better able to work through a process that leads them to think about what strategies or tools, including AT, might help the student overcome barriers and be better able to learn new information, stay engaged in classroom tasks, and demonstrate knowledge. Members of the IEP team are in a position to have observed the student's struggles and successes over the past months and can contribute to the consideration process by sharing those observations. Knowing that a student understands information better when she sees and hears it at the same time can be the critical piece of information that leads the team to consider using a means of visually projecting key points in addition to oral lectures or providing a trial with talking word processing when Christina has a writing assignment.

Another critical factor is that someone on the IEP team must either have a basic understanding of the types of tools that constitute "AT" or they must have access to a resource where they can get that information. That resource may be an online resource such as the Tech Matrix (www.techmatrix.org) or a person whom they can contact with questions. This does not mean that an AT "expert" must be on every IEP committee, but rather that the team members are trained to know their own limitations and seek help from an appropriate resource when needed.

3. How do issues such as age and culture influence the assessment process? Even young students and those who are functioning at a young age have opinions and preferences. Part of the task in completing an AT assessment is to find out what those are. Research shows that self-determination is a critical factor in successful AT use by adults. Self-determination is learned by gradually making more decisions for oneself free of undue pressure or influence. As with other skills, students need opportunities to practice making choices and decisions about their AT use in order to become proficient. They can begin with limited choices and clear parameters as they acquire skills. As students grow and mature they can become increasingly active participants in the AT assessment process and in the development of their IEPs. Willingness to use a specific AT tool is often the deciding factor in whether AT is successfully used or abandoned. Both age and culture work together to impact that willingness. For example, young teens are especially sensitive about using anything that appears different. Their opinion has to play a critical role in AT assessment or even the "best" tool will sit unused.

4. How can families be involved in the assessment process? Families need to be an integral part of the AT assessment process. They are the experts on their child. They typically know more about their child's strengths, interests, and needs than anyone else. Parents should be active members of the AT assessment team helping to plan the process, contribute information, analyze the data, and make the decisions.

5. Why is ongoing assessment so important? Ongoing assessment of the student's performance using AT is a component of the evaluation of effectiveness that is part of successful AT use. Although the AT assessment yields initial data on which to base selection decisions, there has to be an ongoing way of monitoring the AT use and its success or difficulties. Early in the implementation of AT it is important to collect data on whether or not the AT is causing the expected changes in performance. Is the student able to overcome the barriers that the AT was expected to minimize? Can the student accomplish the tasks that led to the selection of AT in the first place? What has changed? Is the student able to act more quickly, more in depth, more clearly, more effectively, more independently, with less support? These are the things that can only be addressed through ongoing assessment and monitoring. In addition, change has become a constant in our lives. The student will learn new skills, move on to a new environment, and encounter new performance demands. Monitoring the effectiveness of the AT use is required in order to address and plan for these changes.

Source: Reprinted with permission from Psycho-Educational Services.

ASSISTIVE TECHNOLOGY ASSESSMENTS

Assistive technology assessments should incorporate a multidimensional assessment model that recognizes the dynamic interplay of various factors across contexts and over time (see Table 3.3) (Raskind & Bryant, 2002). As already implied, selecting AT devices requires careful analysis of the interplay among (a) the user's specific strengths, struggles, special abilities, prior experience/ knowledge, and interests; (b) the specific tasks to be performed (e.g., compensating for a reading, writing, or mobility problem); (c) specific device qualities (e.g., reliability, operational ease, technical support, cost); and (d) the specific contexts of interaction (across settings—

Table 3.3 Examination of Technologies, Individuals, Tasks, and Contexts

TASKS	INDIVIDUAL
The specific tasks/functions to be performed (e.g., reading, writing, remembering) and the requisite skills associated with the tasks	The individual's specific strengths, weaknesses, special abilities, prior experience/ knowledge, and interests
DEVICE	**CONTEXT**
The specific device (e.g., reliability, operational ease, technical support, cost)	The specific contexts of interaction (across settings such as school, home, work; and over time such as over a semester or a lifetime)

Source: From Raskind, R. and Bryant, B. (2002). *Functional evaluation of assistive technology.* Austin, TX: Psycho-Educational Services. Reprinted with permission.

school, home, work; and over time—over a semester or a lifetime). Raskind and Bryant provided a framework for systematically determining the most appropriate and potentially effective device considering the four major components described above and depicted in Table 3.3. Many of the components of the model were described in our adaptations model in Chapter 2. They are reviewed again here with specific reference to AT assessment.

Tasks

As part of living and breathing on planet Earth, people perform a myriad of tasks and functions. These pertain to independent functioning, academics, play, work, and so forth. As we noted in Chapter 2, each task has requisite skills (in actuality, smaller tasks) that lead to the completion of the larger task (Bryant & Bryant, 1998). Part of an ecological assessment is identifying what tasks are to be performed, in what settings or contexts the tasks are performed, and who are significant players (e.g., co-workers, job coaches, teachers) in those settings. Documentation of these tasks provides a contextual mapping of the person's life and activities.

Context

Context is an important consideration when conducting AT assessments (Raskind & Bryant, 2002). The specific contexts of interaction (across school, home, and work settings and over time, whether a semester or a lifetime) are examined as the assessment team examines how an AT device fits into a person's daily routine. For example, if a boy uses a wheelchair, all the various places he goes, along with his mobility needs, are considered. How are his classrooms configured? What does his home look like? What accessibility issues must be considered? Clearly, numerous questions must be asked. If a young girl uses an augmentative communication device, what must be programmed into the device to meet her communication needs? Who are her communication partners? How can the device fit in with her practicing the drums? These questions relate to the contexts within which she lives or travels—that is, where she lives. When these and other questions are considered, the person–technology match comes into a clearer focus.

Individual

The individual who will use the device is central to the assessment (Raskind & Bryant, 2002). The person's specific strengths and functional limitations in a variety of areas (e.g., sensory, affect, cognitive, motor), prior experiences, and interests all must be examined by the assessment team. An examination of the individual's cumulative records will yield considerable information in all of these areas. For example, juniors in high school who have been receiving special education services since third grade have been tested and retested dozens of times over the course of their academic lives, and there is a wealth of anecdotal data that has been collected in their school folders over the years. Before conducting additional assessments, these records should be thoroughly reviewed and data should be extracted. If "holes" appear (e.g., there is a lack of data on sensory and motor skills) and the need for additional data gathering is identified, then additional testing should take place.

Testing can include gathering quantitative and qualitative data. Quantitative data consist of norm-referenced test scores that compare a person's assessment performance to that of a peer group; intelligence test scores are perfect examples. Criterion-referenced tests also yield quantitative data in that they identify areas of mastery; for example, students demonstrate mastery of double-digit addition when they achieve a preset criterion (e.g., 9 of 10 items correct) on a test. Checklists of observed behavior also can yield quantitative data, depending on how the checklist is scored. Qualitative data are not reported as numeric comparisons or in terms of achieved mastery. Rather, they are data that can be accumulated through anecdotal observations, interviews, document review, and rating scales that yield descriptive information. Qualitative information can also be obtained by watching examinees and recording their actions (e.g., body tension, facial strain, grimaces) during testing. Additional information can be gleaned through error analyses of missed test items. For instance, a student's response of 51 for a subtraction item "94 – 45 = ?" may result in the clinical observation that he does not apply regrouping knowledge and instead always subtracts the smaller number from the larger number. All data are helpful in assessment because they provide information that is valuable in identifying strengths and functional limitations. Very often in AT assessments, the strengths and struggles relating to use of a device appear self-evident.

In summary, effective assessments yield quantitative and qualitative information that, together, is useful in making adaptation decisions. Neither source of information is sufficient in and of itself. It should be remembered that the more data that are gathered, the more reliable will be the decisions that are made based on available data.

Device

Assistive technology teams have a wide selection of devices from which to choose (Raskind & Bryant, 2002). That is a good thing, because it allows team members to begin the assessment process with a corpus of potential technologies that can be considered during the assessment process. Unfortunately, not all AT devices are created equal, and it is necessary for the devices themselves to be evaluated. Raskind and Bryant (2002) have created a rating scale that can be used to examine certain types of devices. Assistive technology team members should create their own checklists for each type of device they prescribe (e.g., wheelchairs, augmentative communication devices, input/output devices for information technology). Through personal experiences, literature reviews, or interviews with users, AT assessment team members can complete evaluations on a variety of devices and consider those evaluations when making decisions.

Care should be taken not to become enamored with a specific device before the evaluation takes place. More than one parent or practitioner has come away from a product demonstration workshop with the feeling, "Now, *that* is what my child [student] needs!" Sadly, not all devices that appear spectacular during demonstrations meet expectations when purchased. Each device must be evaluated according to specific criteria. Usually those criteria relate to reliability (i.e., consistency of use), validity (i.e., does the device do what it is intended to do?), technical support (e.g., does the toll-free tech support number have a human being on the other end, and is the local sales representative capable of providing on-the-spot technical assistance?), and cost (what is the cost-benefit ratio?). Regarding cost, we have often heard two sides disagree over a particular device because of the device's price tag. In all cases, the bottom line should be whether the device meets the needs of the user. If two devices are equally reliable, yield valid results, and the vendors offer equal technical support, we would follow the lead of generic prescription drugs and select the less expensive device. But that should be the decision of the assessment team based on the information at hand.

Assistive Technology Consideration

IDEA 1997 for the first time mandated that the IEP team consider whether a child receiving special education requires AT devices and services. The Wisconsin Assistive Technology Initiative (WATI) (2004) noted that "when considering a child's need for assistive technology, there are only four general types of conclusions that can be reached:

> When considering a child's need for assistive technology, there are only four general types of conclusions that can be reached:
>
> 1. The first is that current interventions (what ever they may be) are working and nothing new is needed, including assistive technology. This might be true if the child's progress in the curriculum seems to be commiserating with his abilities.
> 2. The second possibility is that assistive technology is already being used either permanently or as part of a trial to determine applicability, so that we know that it does work. In that case the IEP team should write the specific assistive technology into the IEP to insure that it continues to be available for the child.
> 3. The third possibility is that the IEP team may conclude that new assistive technology should be tried. In that case, the IEP team will need to describe in the IEP the type of assistive technology to be tried, including the features they think may help, such as "having the computer speak the text as the student writes." The IEP team may not know at this point a specific brand or model, and should not attempt to include a product by name, since they do not know if it will perform as expected. Describing the features is the key step for the IEP team in this situation.
> 4. Finally, the last possibility is that the IEP Team will find that they simply do not know enough to make a decision. In this case, they will need to gather more information. That could be a simple process of calling someone for help, or going to get some print, disk, or online resources to help them better "consider what AT might be useful. It could also be an indication that they need to schedule (or refer for) an evaluation or assessment of the child's need for assistive technology." (p. 7–8)

There are several ways for IEP teams to satisfy the consideration provision. The WATI Assistive Technology Considerations Guide (see Figure 3.1) is one example of an excellent evaluation tool that can be used by school districts. Devised in 2004 by the Wisconsin Assistive Technology Initiative, the Guide provides a workable framework for AT considerations.

Another excellent tool for AT consideration is the Assistive Technology Consideration Quick Wheel (see Figure 3.2). The Quick Wheel was developed by the Technology and Media (TAM) Division of the Council for Exceptional Children (CEC), and the Wisconsin Assistive Technology Initiative. On one side of the wheel, this handy tool provides the definitions of AT devices and services, as well as information about low-tech, mid-tech, and high-tech alternatives for composing written material, communication, reading, learning/studying, math, motor aspects of writing, and computer access. On the other side of the wheel there are AT resources (e.g., titles of books and journals) as well as information about low-tech, mid-tech, and high-tech alternatives for activities of daily living, control of the environment, position and seating, vision, hearing, recreation, and mobility.

ASSESSMENT COMPONENTS

Once it has been determined that a student can benefit from AT it is time to actually conduct assessment by looking at a variety of issues. What are the contexts that have to be considered? What are the user's strengths and struggles? What to-date experiences does the person have with technology? What technology should be considered, and is it a quality device? What is the match between the technology and potential user? These questions form the basis for the remainder of this chapter. The Wisconsin Assistive Technology Initiative (WATI, 1998) recommends a nine-step

WATI Assessment Forms

WISCONSIN ASSISTIVE WATI TECHNOLOGY INITIATIVE

WATI Assistive Technology Consideration Guide

Student's Name ______________ School ______________

1. What task is it that we want this student to do, that she is unable to do at a level that reflects his/her skills/abilities (writing, reading, communicating, seeing, hearing)? Document by checking each relevant task below. Please leave blank any tasks that are not relevant to the student's IEP.
2. Is the student currently able to complete tasks with special strategies or accommodations? If yes, describe in Column A for each checked task.
3. Is there available assistive technology (either devices, tools, hardware, of software) that could be used to address this task? (If none are known, review WATI's AT Checklist.) If any assistive technology tools are currently being used (or were tried in the past), describe in Column B.
4. Would the use of assistive technology help the student perform this skill more easily or efficiently, in the least restrictive environment, or perform successfully with less personal assistance? If yes, complete Column C.

Task	A. If currently completes task with special strategies/accommodations, describe.	B. If currently completes task with assistive technology tools, describe.	C. Describe new or additional assistive technology to be tried.
❒ Motor Aspects of Writing			
❒ Computer Access			
❒ Composing Written Material			
❒ Communication			
❒ Reading			
❒ Learning/ Studying			

FIGURE 3.1 WATI Assistive Technology Consideration Guide

Source: Wisconsin Assistive Technology Initiative (2004). *WATI Assistive Technology Consideration Guide.* Wilton, WI: WATI. Reprinted with permission.

WATI Assessment Forms

Task	A. If currently completes task with special strategies/accommodations, describe.	B. If currently completes task with assistive technology tools, describe.	C. Describe new or additional assistive technology to be tried
❒ Math			
❒ Recreation and Leisure			
❒ Activities of Daily Living ADLs			
❒ Mobility			
❒ Environmental Control			
❒ Positioning and Seating			
❒ Vision			
❒ Hearing			

5. Are there assistive technology services (more specific evaluation of need for assistive technology, adapting or modifying the assistive technology, technical assistance on its operation or use, or training of student, staff, or family) that this student needs? If yes, describe what will be provided, the initiation and duration.

____

____

Persons Present:______________________________ Date: __________

FIGURE 3.1 *(Continued)*

approach for conducting AT assessments (see Figure 3.3). In this chapter, we use a case study for Ryan Reider, a 12-year-old seventh grader attending middle school in Saugus, Massachusetts. In the case study, we demonstrate how the assessment process can be accomplished using a sample instrument, the *Functional Evaluation for Assistive Technology* (FEAT, Raskind & Bryant, 2002). The case study implements many of the features associated with WATI's nine-step approach.

Considerations of Various Contexts

As already stated, it is important to look at the various contexts within which the device will be used. To do so, one can identify the various contexts within which the individual works and plays and then examine requisite skills needed to accomplish expected tasks. The evaluator identifies

Assistive Technology Consideration
Quick Wheel
After discussing the student's present level of educational performance and developing the measurable annual goals, if you are concerned that the student may need assistive technology to help meet any of the goals in this area:
MOBILITY
Walker
Grab bars and rails
Manual wheelchair including sports chair
Powered mobility toy
Powered scooter
Powered wheelchair
Adapted vehicle for driving
CONSIDER:
LOW TECH ..... MID TECH ..... HIGH TECH
DON'T FORGET
There are many other tools, this list is just to help you get started.
RECREATION
HEARING
VISION
POSITION AND SEATING
CONTROL OF THE ENVIRONMENT
S OF DAILY LIVING (ADLS)
IDEAs that Work
U.S. Office of Special Education Programs
idea PARTNERSHIPS
Council for Exceptional Children
ASSISTIVE TECHNOLOGY RESOURCES—
Books
Bowser, G. & Reed, P. (1998). Education Tech Points: A Framework for Assistive Technology Planning. Winchester, OR: CATO; P.O. Box 431, Winchester, OR 97495; www.edtechpoints.org
Golden, D. (1998). Assistive Technology in Special Education: Policy and Practice. Council of Administrators of Special Education, Fort Valley State University, 1005 State University Drive, Fort Valley, GA 31030
Reed, P. (Ed.). (2000). Assessing Students' Need for Assistive Technology. Oshkosh, WI:WATI; www.wati.org
Reed, P. & Bowser, G. (2000). Assistive Technology Pointers for Parents. Winchester, OR: CATO; www.edtechpoints.org
Journals/Newsletters
Closing the Gap, Closing the Gap, P.O. Box 68, Henderson, MN 65044; www.closingthegap.com
Journal of Special Education Technology, Free with TAM Membership (a division of CEC); jset.unlv.edu
Special Education Technology Practice, Knowledge by Design, 5907 N. Kent Ave., Whitefish Bay, WI 53217-4615; www.setp.net
Internet Sites
www.closingthegap.com – Searchable database of AT plus articles from their newsletter.
www.fctd.info – Family Center on Technology and Disability. Extensive AT Resource reviews, user-friendly resource library and more.
www.LDonline.com – Section on AT. To get to it, go to LD In Depth and then Technology.
www.tamcec.org – The web site of the Technology and Media Division of CEC.
trace.wisc.edu – Links to adaptive freeware and shareware for computer access.
www.wati.org – Wisconsin Assistive Technology Initiative has WATI assessment forms, updates, lending library, information, best practice tips, and more.
Developed by the Technology and Media Division (TAM) of the Council for Exceptional Children and the Wisconsin Assistive Technology Initiative.
Funding comes from the U.S. Department of Education, Office of Special Education Programs (Cooperative Agreement No. H326A80005)

FIGURE 3.2 The Assistive Technology Consideration Quick Wheel

Source: From Technology and Media Division—Council for Exceptional Children/Wisconsin Assistive Technology Initiative (2004). *Assistive Technology Consideration Quick Wheel.* Arlington, VA: TAM-CEC. Reprinted with permission. Council for Exceptional Children. For more information, visit www.cec.sped.org.

Step 1. Team Members Gather Information
The team members review the students strengths and struggles, environment, and task, and determine whether additional testing is needed to yield complete information.

Step 2. Schedule Meeting
Team members set a time when they can gather to discuss the assessment.

Step 3. Team Completes Problem Identification Portion of the AT Planning Guide at the Meeting
The student's strengths/difficulties are listed, the student's multiple environments are identified, and the tasks he or she is expected to accomplished are determined.

Step 4. Prioritize the List of Tasks for Solution Generation
Tasks are prioritized and potential solutions are generated.

Step 5. Solution Generation
A variety of general solution, such as "needs voice output" may be presented, or specific AT devices may be recommended.

Step 6. Solutions Selected
After discussing the various options that are available, the team members make specific decisions about AT devices needed.

Step 7. Implementation Plan
Team member identify a specific plan of action, which would include equipment trials, personnel responsible for implementing sections of the plan, and follow-up meetings to discuss progress made.

Trial Use:

Step 8. Implement Planned Trials
The plan identified in Step 7 is implemented, and responsible team members record their observations for later analysis and review.

Step 9. Follow up on Planned Date
Team members reconvene and discuss how the plan was implemented. Final decisions are made.

FIGURE 3.3 WATI's Nine Steps of an AT Assessment

Source: From Assistive Technology Assessment Directions/Procedure Guide, pages 16–17. Adapted with permission, Wisconsin Assistive Technology Initiative.

the frequency (i.e., daily, weekly, or monthly/less frequently) with which each task is accomplished in the various settings examined.

One might also wish to anticipate the potential usefulness of an AT device across the settings identified in the previous section. Areas examined in this part of the scale might be the device's compensatory effectiveness, compatibility, social appropriateness, portability, support requirements, and potential appropriateness over time (Raskind & Bryant, 2002). Once the technology is identified and implemented, one would then want to examine the extent to which the technology application has generalized across the settings identified earlier.

After Ryan was referred for an AT evaluation, the AT specialist in the school district interviewed Ryan's teachers, and the Contextual Matching Inventory was filled in to identify the settings demands (i.e., what teacher expectations are) for each of Ryan's classes (see Figure 3.4). The Contextual Matching Inventory has two components. Part A, "Identification of Specific Settings and Demands," is composed of 44 specific tasks (demands). There is space on the form for ratings across six possible settings. The form is completed either by asking the professional to read and

FEAT

Functional Evaluation for Assistive Technology

Contextual Matching Inventory

Name: Ryan Reider

Examiner Name: Dr. Perry

Date: 12-18-01

Part A. Identification of Specific Settings and Demands

Context (Settings):

1. Resource classroom
2. Science classroom
3. Social Studies classroom
4.
5.
6.

Directions: Based on interviews with people in up to six different settings, rate the frequency with which each task is required in each classroom/setting. D = Daily, W = Weekly, M = Monthly, or even less frequently. Write NA if not required.

Task: The individual is expected to . . .	Setting 1	Setting 2	Setting 3	Setting 4	Setting 5	Setting 6
listen to lectures.	D	D	D			
listen to directions/instructions.	D	D	D			
listen to and/or work with peers/coworkers.	D	D	D			
listen to audiotapes/videotapes/CDs.	W	M	D			
listen to announcements.	D	D	D			
speak to teachers/peers/coworkers.	D	D	D			
make class/workplace presentations.	M	M	W			
communicate during class/workplace discussions.	D	D	D			
read textbooks/handouts/reports/letters.	D	D	D			
read from chalkboard/overhead/and so forth.	D	D	D			
read resource materials (e.g., dictionary, encyclopedia, library books).	D	D	D			
read assignment/instruction sheets.	D	D	D			
read test questions.	W	M	W			
read computer text.	W	M	W			
write test answers.	W	M	W			
write papers (reports, term).	M	M	M			
write stories/essays/poems.	W	M	M			
write homework/work assignments.	D	D	D			
copy from chalkboard/text (words/numbers).	D	D	D			
take notes.	D	D	D			
spell words (in isolation and in continuous text).	D	D	D			
compute.	D	W	M			
solve math word problems.	D	M	M			
use math in applied settings/conditions.	D	W	M			
work with manipulatives.	W	W	M			
use a calculator.	W	W	M			
remember recently presented information that has been heard.	D	D	D			

10 9 8 7 6 5 4 3 2 1 06 05 04 03 02

FIGURE 3.4 Contextual Matching Inventory

Source: From M. Raskind and B. Bryant (2002). *Functional evaluation of assistive technology.* Austin, TX: Psycho-Educational Services. Reprinted with permission.

Part A (cont.)	Setting					
	1	2	3	4	5	6
remember recently presented information that has been read.	D	D	D			
remember information learned previously.	D	D	D			
remember sequential information.	D	D	D			
use time-management skills.	D	D	D			
organize work space.	D	D	D			
organize information.	D	D	D			
organize assignments/projects.	D	W	W			
manipulate objects/materials.	D	D	D			
use pencil/pen/marker.	D	D	D			
use keyboard.	W	W	W			
draw/cut/paste/do artwork.	M	W	M			
maintain good posture/positioning.	D	D	D			
attend to task.	D	D	D			
work well with others.	D	D	D			
stay in place.	D	D	D			
cooperate with teachers/peers/coworkers.	D	D	D			
Summary/Remarks	D	D	D			

Part B. Additional Issues Relating to Contextual Matching

Directions: Based on previous experiences and the situations encountered during the evaluation, write the number (1 to 5, 1 being low, 5 being high) that best corresponds to the anticipated use of the technology in the settings identified in Part A. If the noted use is not applicable, write NA.

Potential Use of the Technology	Setting					
	1	2	3	4	5	6
Compensatory effectiveness	5	5	5			
Compatibility with existing technology	3	4	3			
Social appropriateness	3	3	3			
Ease of integration (considering potential conflict such as noise, time, etc.)	5	4	4			
Space availability	5	5	3			
Appropriateness of space (consider physical environment, such as lighting, noise level, etc.)	5	5	4			
Availability of appropriate furniture	5	4	2*			
Availability of supporting equipment	4	4	2			
Availability of required technical support	5	5	5			
Appropriateness of technology for current use	5	5	5			
Appropriateness of technology for use next year	5	5	5			
Appropriateness of technology for use over the next 2 to 5 years	5	5	5			
Appropriateness of technology for use over the next 6 to 10 years	5	5	5			
Ease of portability across contexts/settings	5	4	3			

Summary/Remarks *space is very limited

FIGURE 3.4 *(Continued)*

rate the tasks or via interviews. Part B, "Additional Issues Relating to Contextual Matching," pertains to important generalization issues. Part B is best completed by the professional who is most familiar with AT adaptations and barriers that can impair their successful implementation.

In Ryan's case, three teachers were interviewed. By examining their ratings, it is clear that the teachers' expectations (listen to lectures, read and gain information from textbooks, and write to convey what he has learned to his teachers) are in line with the typical middle school classroom. Because of Ryan's reading disability, it is also apparent that he might have difficulty in his classes because they all involve reading text to gain access to important subject matter.

Considerations of Strengths and Struggles

It is important to determine the individual's strengths and struggles across a variety of academic and cognitive tasks (e.g., listening, memory, organization, physical/motor). A person who knows the individual's behaviors could rate the individual's abilities in the areas of interest. It would be beneficial for more than one rater to complete the scale in order to gain an ecological perspective.

Information from the scale can be used to identify potential areas of difficulty that may be circumvented by AT. Also, the examination can help identify areas of strength on which a device can capitalize to bypass a specific difficulty (Bryant, Seay, & Bryant, 1999; Bryant & Bryant, 1998). This is particularly important when setting demands and requisite abilities are identified for the student and the strengths and struggles must be considered (see Chapter 2).

The FEAT uses the Checklist of Strengths and Limitations (see Figure 3.5) to provide information about the strengths and struggles a person has in the following areas: listening, speaking, reading, writing, mathematics, memory, organization, physical/motor, and behavior. Ryan's teachers were asked to complete the checklist by placing a check mark in the column to designate whether Ryan is weak, average, or strong (when compared to his or her peers) in the behaviors listed.

The checklist is useful for two reasons. First, Ryan's teachers play an important role in the evaluation—they know Ryan and his strengths and struggles. An effective ecological assessment demonstrates to all parties involved in the assessment that they have a valuable role in the assessment process, and their judgments are carefully considered. Second, the AT evaluation team needs as much information about Ryan as it can accumulate, and Ryan's teachers are a valuable source of such information.

An inspection of the completed checklist in Figure 3.5 demonstrates that Ryan has strengths in all areas except reading and writing, which is where his primary functional limitations exist. This information is helpful, because the team has hypothesized that screen reading technology can benefit Ryan, but only if Ryan has listening and thinking strengths. Based on the information provided by the checklist, this is the case. If Ryan had listening problems, he would not benefit from screen reader technology because his listening problems would present another obstacle to overcome.

Considerations of Technology Characteristics

A factor that is too often overlooked in an AT evaluation is the device itself. As we stated, people can become smitten with what a particular device is supposed to do but fail to look at such qualities as the technology's dependability or the vendor's technical support record. It is important to examine the specific device being used in the assessment in such areas as reliability, efficacy of purpose, compatibility, screen presentation, operational ease, and technical support. We agree with Raskind and Bryant, who noted that technology that is not trustworthy is best left in the showroom.

FEAT

Functional Evaluation for Assistive Technology

Checklist of Strengths and Limitations

Name: Ryan Reider

Rater: Ms. Knowles

Date: 12-18-01

Directions: During technology evaluations, specific limitations that may require compensatory intervention must be identified. It is also critical to identify specific strengths that the technology can tap into during compensation. Place a check in the appropriate column (Weak, Average, Strong) that in your opinion best depicts the abilities of the person being rated, when compared to age-mates, in the areas being evaluated.

Listening	**Weak**	**Average**	**Strong**
Differentiates between relevant and irrelevant information		✔	
Hears and understands the spoken word		✔	
Understands basic directions			✔
Pays attention to speaker for an appropriate timespan			✔
Comprehends rapid speech		✔	
Distinguishes differences among sounds/words			✔
Responds appropriately to requests/instructions			✔
Other (specify)			
OVERALL LISTENING SKILLS			✔
Speaking	**Weak**	**Average**	**Strong**
Pronounces words clearly and consistently			✔
Speaks with appropriate vocabulary			✔
Speaks with appropriate grammar			✔
Speaks well in everyday situations			✔
Discusses content that is appropriate to situation			✔
Can adjust language based on communication partner			✔
Speaks well, with appropriate tone, pitch, loudness			✔
Other (specify)			
OVERALL SPEAKING SKILLS			✔
Reading	**Weak**	**Average**	**Strong**
Has requisite visual abilities			✔
Reads words accurately	✔		
Understands meaning of individual words	✔		
Reads with speed/fluency	✔		
Is able to maintain place on page			✔
Understands different sentence structures (e.g., simple, complex)	✔		
Understands the meaning of connected text (i.e., phrases, sentences, paragraphs)	✔		
Other (specify)			
OVERALL READING SKILLS	✔		
Writing	**Weak**	**Average**	**Strong**
Applies capitalization/punctuation rules	✔		
Spells correctly	✔		
Writes neatly with little difficulty			✔
Uses appropriate grammar	✔		
Uses appropriate vocabulary	✔		
Edits/proofs well	✔		
Writes well conceptually	✔		
Applies sense of audience effectively	✔		

10 9 8 7 6 5 4 3 2 1 06 05 04 03 02

Additional copies of this form (#0274) may be purchased from Psycho-Educational Services 5114 Balcones Woods Dr., #307-163, Austin, TX 78759, 512/335-1591

FIGURE 3.5 Strengths and Limitations Scale

Source: From M. Raskind and B. Bryant (2002). *Functional evaluation of assistive technology.* Austin, TX: Psycho-Educational Services. Reprinted with permission.

Writing (cont.)	**Weak**	**Average**	**Strong**
Other (specify) keyboarding skills while writing	✔		
OVERALL WRITING SKILLS	✔		
Mathematics	**Weak**	**Average**	**Strong**
Understands basic number concepts			✔
Calculates basic arithmetic problems			✔
Knows basic math vocabulary			✔
Calculates quickly			✔
Applies math concepts to life situations			✔
Has a sense of reasonable versus unreasonable answers (i.e., can estimate)			✔
Other (specify)			
OVERALL MATHEMATICS SKILLS			✔
Memory	**Weak**	**Average**	**Strong**
Has long-term recall of previously learned information (words/objects/designs/pictures)		✔	
Has short-term recall of recently presented information (words/objects/designs/pictures)		✔	
Follows simple directions in sequence			✔
Follows complex directions in sequence			✔
Other (specify)			
OVERALL MEMORY SKILLS		✔	
Organization	**Weak**	**Average**	**Strong**
Understands cause/effect relationships	✔		
Manages personal and work time		✔	
Manages personal and work space		✔	
Makes plans to accomplish tasks	✔		
Organizes ideas into a cohesive whole		✔	
Can understand abstract concepts		✔	
Other (specify)			
OVERALL ORGANIZATION SKILLS		✔	
Physical/Motor	**Weak**	**Average**	**Strong**
Exhibits physical strength/endurance			✔
Has good posture			✔
Controls objects (grasps/manipulates)		✔	
Moves about freely			✔
Has good positioning/orientation			✔
Other (specify)			
OVERALL PHYSICAL/MOTOR SKILLS			✔
Behavior	**Weak**	**Average**	**Strong**
Stays on task		✔	
Can work with peers		✔	
Takes care of personal/school property		✔	
Cooperates with people of authority			✔
Other (specify)			
OVERALL BEHAVIOR SKILLS		✔	

Summary/Remarks

FIGURE 3.5 *(Continued)*

Once screen readers, along with optical character recognition technology, were determined to provide a possible compensatory strategy to help Ryan work around his reading disability, the AT Specialist used the FEAT's Technology Characteristics Inventory to evaluate device-specific characteristics such as its reliability, dependability, and operational ease. The specialist chose to evaluate a number of devices (including one marketed by the fictitious XL Technologies), before one was selected for the evaluation, which would exclude any inappropriate devices from consideration. A review of Figure 3.6 demonstrates that the device received high ratings in the areas examined and was thus selected to be a part of the evaluation process.

Considerations of Technology Experience

It may be helpful to identify the individual's prior experience with AT devices. An assessment team member has a conversation with the individual being evaluated. Based on the discussion, the examiner rates the individual's expertise in using specific devices. This could be accomplished by identifying various devices that have potential to compensate for difficulties in the areas of spoken language, reading, memory, mobility, organization, and so forth.

So far we have received information from Ryan's teachers and the AT specialist who evaluated the technology, but we have not received information from Ryan himself. As a member of the AT evaluation team, Ryan's participation provides an important contribution to an ecological assessment. The AT specialist interviewed Ryan concerning his experiences with technology using the Checklist of Technology Experiences (see Figure 3.7). Using the checklist, the specialist can identify whether Ryan has used technology in the past and, if so, determine whether the experiences were positive or negative. If Ryan had negative previous experiences with technology, these negative experiences may adversely affect proposed technology interventions. Conversely, if Ryan has experienced success with assistive technology, it is more likely that Ryan will be optimistic that the device can be helpful. In this instance, Ryan has had minimal experience using technology, except for a word processor that he has used with little success.

Considerations of the Person–Technology Match

Every AT assessment should examine the interplay between the individual and the device while performing specific tasks and/or compensating for specific difficulties. The Individual–Technology Evaluation Scale (see Figure 3.8) provides information about the person's interaction with the AT device that is being evaluated. A series of questions are asked relating to compensatory effectiveness, interest, ease of use, comfort, operational ease/proficiency, and behavioral responses (Raskind & Bryant, 2002).

Also as part of the FEAT, Raskind and Bryant (2002) provide a series of device-specific worksheets that are used during the evaluation. In this case, the AT Specialist selected the Optical Character Recognition/Speech Synthesis devices (see Figure 3.9). The specialist and Ryan work in a step-by-step fashion to create a Ryan–technology match. During the evaluation, observations are made within three key areas: Technology Features/Options (e.g., speech rate, font style preferences, background and text color), User's Reactions (e.g., how Ryan responds to the scanning speed and speech quality of the synthesis), and the User's Ability (i.e., whether the user can recognize scanning areas and follow the cursor). At the end of the worksheet, the AT Specialist can record and examine other Ryan–technology match features. As Ryan interacts with and uses the technology, the specialist carefully observes him and makes annotations on the worksheet and on the Individual-Technology Evaluation Worksheet, as shown in Figure 3.9.

The Individual–Technology Evaluation Scale and the device-specific worksheets can be considered the "nuts and bolts" of the AT assessment, because they help the specialist and Ryan

FEAT

Functional Evaluation for Assistive Technology

Technology Characteristics Inventory

Name: Ryan Reider

Examiner Name: Dr. Perry

Technology: Optical Character Recognition

Manufacturer: XL Technologies

Date: 11-8-01

Directions: It is important that an assistive technology (AT) device be evaluated prior to conducting an AT evaluation for a particular individual. Based on prior experience with, or prior knowledge about, the device, circle the number that best corresponds to each characteristic of the technology that is being considered (circle NA if not applicable). Identify the . . .

reliability/dependability of the technology (i.e., does it break down or fail in any way).	NA	Low Reliability 1	2	3	4	High Reliability 5
extent to which the technology accomplishes its purpose.	NA	Very Low 1	2	3	4	Very High 5
extent to which the technology can be used for multiple tasks.	NA	Very Low 1	2	3	4	Very High 5
extent to which the technology can be customized/ individualized.	NA	Very Low 1	2	3	4	Very High 5
extent to which the technology is compatible with supporting technologies.	NA	Very Poor 1	2	3	4	Very Good 5
appropriateness of the auditory output.	NA	Very Poor 1	2	3	4	Very Good 5
appropriateness of the screen presentation or visual display.	NA	Very Poor 1	2	3	4	Very Good 5
social appropriateness of the technology.	NA	Very Low 1	2	3	4	Very Good 5
extent to which the commands and operational procedures are intuitive, straightforward, and logical	NA	Very Low 1	2	3	4	Very High 5
ease of learning to use the technology.	NA	Very Low 1	2	3	4	Very High 5
operational ease of the input device/method	NA	Very Difficult 1	2	3	4	Very Easy 5
level of technical support offered by the manufacturer (e.g., toll-free numbers, clear and concise documentation).	NA	Very Poor 1	2	3	4	Very Good 5
effectiveness of online assistance/service.	NA	Very Low 1	2	3	4	Very High 5
ease of installation.	NA	Very Difficult 1	2	3	4	Very Easy 5
Overall Rating		Very Low 1	2	3	4	Very High 5

Summary/Remarks ______________________________

10 9 8 7 6 5 4 3 2 1 06 05 04 03 02

Additional copies of this form (#0277) may be purchased from Psycho-Educational Services 5114 Balcones Woods Dr., #307-163, Austin, TX 78759, 512/335-1591

FIGURE 3.6 Technology Characteristics Inventory

Source: From M. Raskind and B. Bryant (2002). *Functional evaluation of assistive technology.* Austin, TX: Psycho-Educational Services. Reprinted with permission.

FEAT
Functional Evaluation for Assistive Technology
Checklist of Technology Experiences

Name: *Ryan Reider*

Examiner Name: *Dr. Perry*

Date: *12-18-01*

Directions: Many people have had prior experience with technology. Based on discussions with, or knowledge of, the individual, place a check in the column that best depicts the experience with the devices listed. If a technology is not appropriate for the evaluation, check NA. Space is provided to list additional devices not presented. If the individual has experience with technology, comments about those experiences (e.g., setting, how long the person used the technology, how positive/negative the experience was) can be noted in the Summary/Remarks sections.

Listening-related Abilities: Experienced with . . .	**A lot**	**Some**	**None**	**NA**
assistive listening device				✔
variable speech-control tape recorder/player				✔
conventional tape recorder/player				✔
Other (specify)				
Reading-related Abilities: Experienced with . . .	**A lot**	**Some**	**None**	**NA**
optical character recognition/speech synthesis			✔	
tape recorder/player/Books on Tape			✔	
Books on Disk/CD			✔	
speech synthesis			✔	
Other (specify)				
Writing-related Abilities: Experienced with . . .	**A lot**	**Some**	**None**	**NA**
conventional word processor		✔		
talking word processor			✔	
semantic (mind) map software			✔	
outlining program			✔	
word prediction			✔	
conventional spell checker (integrated)			✔	
conventional spell checker (stand-alone)			✔	
talking spell checker			✔	
alternative keyboard			✔	
speech synthesis/screen review			✔	
abbreviation-expansion (shorthand)			✔	
grammar checker			✔	
speech recognition			✔	
outlining program			✔	
Other (specify)				

Summary/Remarks

Ryan stated that he hates to write so doesn't like to use the word processor, even though he knows how to use it.

10 9 8 7 6 5 4 3 2 1 06 05 04 03 02

Additional copies of this form (#0275) may be purchased from Psycho-Educational Services 5114 Balcones Woods Dr., #307-163. Austin, TX 78759, 512/335-1591

FIGURE 3.7 Checklist of Technology Experiences Completed

Source: From M. Raskind and B. Bryant (2002). *Functional evaluation of assistive technology.* Austin, TX: Psycho-Educational Services. Reprinted with permission.

Math-related Abilities: Experienced with . . .	**A lot**	**Some**	**None**	**NA**
conventional calculator				✔
talking calculator				✔
on-screen (computer-based) calculator				✔
math processing software/electronic worksheets				✔
Other (specify)				
Memory-related Abilities: Experienced with . . .	**A lot**	**Some**	**None**	**NA**
personal data managers (stand-alone)				✔
personal data organization software				✔
tape recorder/player				✔
free-form database				✔
Other (specify)				
Organization-related Abilities: Experienced with . . .	**A lot**	**Some**	**None**	**NA**
personal data managers (stand-alone)				✔
personal data organization software				✔
free-form database				✔
calendar programs				✔
Other (specify)				

Summary/Remarks(*continued*)

FIGURE 3.7 (*Continued*)

FEAT

Functional Evaluation for Assistive Technology

Individual–Technology Evaluation Scale

Name: Ryan Reider

Examiner Name: Dr. Perry

Date: 12-19-01

Technology and Setting: OCR/Resource, Social/Studies, Science Classes

Compensatory Goal/Task: Assit reading

Part A. Individual–Technology Match (Use Individual–Technology Evaluation Worksheets as necessary)

Directions: Circle the number that best corresponds to the level of match for the specified area. If the statement is not appropriate for the evaluation, circle NA. Identify the . . .

effectiveness of the technology in enhancing accuracy/quality.	NA	**Not Effective** 1	2	3	4	**Very Effective** (5)
effectiveness of the technology in enhancing speed/efficiency.	NA	**Not Effective** 1	2	3	4	**Very Effective** (5)
effectiveness of the technology in enhancing ease.	NA	**Not Effective** 1	2	3	4	**Very Effective** (5)
overall effectiveness of the technology in helping the individual compensate for the difficulty.	NA	**Not Effective** 1	2	3	4	**Very Effective** (5)
degree to which the person was interested in using the technology.	NA	**Not Interested** 1	2	3	(4)	**Very Interested** 5
degree to which the individual was proficient in using the technology.	NA	**Not Proficient** 1	2	3	(4)	**Very Proficient** 5
degree to which the individual was comfortable using the technology.	NA	**Not Comfortable** 1	2	3	(4)	**Very Comfortable** 5
degree to which the technology "tapped into" (i.e., utilized) the individual's strengths.	NA	**Very Low** 1	2	3	4	**Very High** (5)
degree to which the technology fostered the individual's special talents.	NA	**Very Low** 1	2	3	(4)	**Very High** 5
degree to which the individual sustained attention using the technology.	NA	**Not Attentive** 1	2	3	(4)	**Very Attentive** 5
extent to which the evaluator needed to support the individual in the use of the technology.	NA	**Much Support Needed** 1	2	3	(4)	**No Support Needed** 5
extent to which the technology can be utilized by the individual across tasks/functions.	NA	**Very Low** 1	2	3	4	**Very High** (5)
individual's ability to learn to use the technology during the evaluation.	NA	**Low Ability** 1	2	3	4	**High Ability** (5)
extent to which the individual was able to resolve difficulties when the technology did not work properly.	NA	**Low Ability** 1	2	3	(4)	**High Ability** 5
individual's reaction when making an error while using the technology.	NA	**Very Negative** 1	2	3	(4)	**Very Positive** 5

10 9 8 7 6 5 4 3 2 1 06 05 04 03 02

FIGURE 3.8 Individual–Technology Evaluation Scale

Source: From M. Raskind and B. Bryant (2002). *Functional evaluation of assistive technology.* Austin, TX: Psycho-Educational Services. Reprinted with permission.

Part A. Individual–Technology Match *(cont.)*

individual's perceived usefulness of the technology.	NA	**Not useful** 1	2	3	4	**Very Useful** (5)
perceived cost/benefit ratio.	NA	**Very Low** 1	2	3	(4)	**Very High** 5
BASED ON INFORMATION ABOVE, OVERALL "MATCH" BETWEEN THE INDIVIDUAL AND THE TECHNOLOGY.	NA	**Very Poor** 1	2	3	(4)	**Very Good** 5

Evidence of performance enhancement (include information used as a basis of comparison—be specific; see *Summary and Recommendations Booklet,* Section IX). Increased reading speed and comprehension

Part B. General Technology Literacy

Directions: Based on the findings of the evaluation, circle the number that best corresponds to the individual's level of ability for each specified area. Identify the individual's . . .

overall computer/technological knowledge/literacy.	NA	**Very Poor** 1	2	(3)	**Very Good** 4
overall ability (i.e., working knowledge) to use computers/technology.	NA	**Very Poor** 1	2	(3)	**Very Good** 4
keyboarding proficiency (if applicable). SPEED	NA	**Very Slow** 1	(2)	3	**Very Fast** 4
ACCURACY	NA	**Very Poor** 1	(2)	3	**Very Good** 4

Part C. Other Considerations

Directions: Based on observations made during the evaluation, respond to each item below with anecdotal remarks.

Posture/Seating: Erect posture demonstrated-no seating difficulties

Body orientation: Tended to turn his body away from the monitor and keyboard

Hand/arm positioning: Appropriate positioning demonstrated

Range of motion: Sufficient movement no problems demonstrated

Visual-height, distance, angle: No apparent difficulties

FIGURE 3.8 *(Continued)*

FEAT

Functional Evaluation for Assistive Technology

Individual–Technology Evaluation Worksheet

Name: Ryan Reider

Examiner Name: Dr. Perry

Date: 12-19-01

Technology and Setting: OCR/Resource, Social Studies, Science classes

Compensatory Goal/Task: compensate for reading difficulties

Optical Character Recognition/Speech Synthesis

Part A. Technology Features/Options

Directions: This worksheet is to be used in conjunction with the Individual – Technology Evaluation Scale to address the specific attributes of Optical Character Recognition/Speech Synthesis. As appropriate, consider the effects of the following items in evaluating the individual–technology match. Check items considered and record comments.

Check		Comments
✔	Speech rate	Difficulty comprehending rates above 180 wpm. Most comfortable between 150-175 wpm
✔	Speech lone/pitch	Prefers low voice Disturbed by high pitch
	Speech volume	
✔	Highlighting words	Highlighting helps focus attention
	Masking	
✔	Font style	Prefers arial
✔	Font size	Prefers 14-16
n/a	Letter spacing	
✔	Line spacing	Double spacing is easier to read
✔	Background color	Prefers light blue background with
✔	Text color	black text
✔	Highlight color	No preference
✔	Graphic vs. "actual" text	Text only view easier to read
Reading/speaking by:		
	Word	
	Sentence	
	Line	
	Paragraph	
✔	Continuous	Prefers continuous reading. Stops speech on own
	Selected text	
	Study tools	

FIGURE 3.9 Individual–Technology Evaluation Worksheet

Source: From M. Raskind and B. Bryant (2002). *Functional evaluation of assistive technology.* Austin, TX: Psycho-Educational Services. Reprinted with permission.

Part A. Technology Features/Options *(cont.)*		
Directions: This worksheet is to be used in conjunction with the Individual – Technology Evaluation Scale to address the specific attributes of Optical Character Recognition/Speech Synthesis. As appropriate, consider the effects of the following items in evaluating the individual–technology match. Check items considered and record comments.		
Check		**Comments**
n/a	**Write/edit scanned text**	
n/a	**Other**	
Part B. User's Reactions		
Directions: This worksheet is to be used in conjunction with the Individual – Technology Evaluation Scale to address the specific attributes of Optical Character Recognition/Speech Synthesis. As appropriate, note the user's reaction to the following items in evaluating the individual–technology match. Check items considered and record comments.		
Check		**Comments**
✓	**Scanning speed**	Tolerates scanning speed
✓	**Scanning errors**	Not bothered by the few errors
✓	**Speech quality**	Not complaints about voice
✓	**Speech accuracy**	No concerns
___	**Other**	
Part C. User's Ability		
Directions: This worksheet is to be used in conjunction with the Individual – Technology Evaluation Scale to address the specific attributes of Optical Character Recognition/Speech Synthesis. As appropriate, note the user's ability in relation to the following items in evaluating the individual–technology match. Check items considered and record comments.		
Check		**Comments**
✓	**Recognizes scanning errors**	identifies about 50s of errors
✓	**Follows cursor**	able to follow cursor

FIGURE 3.9 *(Continued)*

determine if the technology "works" as projected. It should be noted that the specialist conducted Ryan's AT evaluations in his science classroom, during a time when the classroom was unoccupied. Although it is not always possible to conduct the assessment in the student's natural environment, that is the ideal location for the evaluation.

Information Summary

After the evaluation took place, the AT Specialist completed the FEAT's Summary and Recommendations Booklet (see Figure 3.10). Here, the specialist wrote comments concerning each of the FEAT forms. Note that comments in Sections IX, X, and XI are particularly informative. In Section IX, the specialist compared Ryan's performance with the technology to his performance without the technology on the Gray Silent Reading Test (Wiederholt & Blalock, 2000). Ryan's gain in comprehension (in this case, listening comprehension—but comprehension of text material nonetheless) provides supportive evidence for the effectiveness of the technology. Section X includes information about expectations that accompany device use and how support should be provided if the technology fails or if further training is deemed helpful. Finally, Section XI provides information about how follow-up evaluations should occur. Recall that we made the case earlier that AT assessments are ongoing. Simply providing the technology and assuming it will be beneficial is insufficient. Follow-up evaluations are essential to document how the technology is helping Ryan meet the setting demands of the classroom or, if the device is not helpful, what can be done to further assist Ryan.

FEAT **Functional Evaluation for Assistive Technology**	**Summary and Recommendations Booklet**

Section I. Identifying Information

Name: Ryan Reider

Gender: M Age 12 Grade: 7 School/Employer: Saugus Middle School

Evaluation Date: 12-10-01 Referred by Mr. Knowles

Disability/Difficulty: Reading/writing City, State of evaluation: Saugus MA

Evaluation Coordinator: Dr. D. M. Perry

Parent(s)/Guardian(s): Sandra & Kevin Reider

Home address: 12 Sanka Drive

City, State, Zip: Saugus, MA 01906 Telephone: 781-555-1212

Section II. Background Information

Prior Evaluation(s): Psycho-Ed. 1999 Dr Wis Superior Intelligence significant reading & writing deficits

Medical/Psychological Information: No problems noted

School/Educational History: B/C/D/ student but was given considerable support in Elem school

Employment History: N/A

Interests/Hobbies: skateboarding snow boarding baseball soccer

Section III. Assistive Technology Team Members

Name	Position/Affiliation
Ryan Reider	Student
Sandra & Kevin Reider	Parents
D. M. Perry, PhD. OTR	District AT specialist
M. E. Einstein	Science Teacher
I. C. Cartographer	Social Studies Teacher
V. C. Knowles	Resource Teacher
G Patterson	Paraprofessional

Section IV. Purpose of Evaluation/Expected Outcomes

To examine potential technologies that could be used to compensate for Ryan's difficulties and increase his opportunity for success in a variety of setting that require reading and writing proficiency.

10 9 8 7 6 5 4 3 2 1 06 05 04 03 02

FIGURE 3.10 Summary of Ryan's AT Assessment

Source: From M. Raskind and B. Bryant (2002). *Functional evaluation of assistive technology.* Austin, TX: Psycho-Educational Services. Reprinted with permission.

Section V. Summary of Results: Contextual Matching Inventory

Part A demonstrates that the three classes examined (i.e. resource, science, social studies) require considerable reading which exacerbate Ryan's weaknesses.
After conducting the evaluation Part B was completed. For the most part the technology (OCR) should be seamlessly integrated into the classes. Although limited space and resources in the social studies classroom may make used in this setting more difficult the social studies teacher is committed to its use. Attn should be paid to Ryan's reactions to using the technology. If successful the technology should be useful for may years. Speech recognition is likewise useful.

Section VI. Summary of Results: Checklist of Strengths and Limitations

Ryan demonstrated strengths in all area except for reading and writing. In these area most skill areas are deficient. Because Ryan's other areas are strong it would appear that his strengths can be used to help compensate for his limitations in reading and writing.

Section VII. Summary of Results: Checklist of Technology Experiences

Ryan has little experience using technology. The experience he has had was with word processing. He does not like to write so he does not like using the word processor. This may be because of poor keyboarding difficulties.

Section VIII. Summary of Results: Technology Characteristics Inventory

The OCR and speech recognition technologies both achieved relative high ratings, thus their use is encouraged. Of particular interest and value was the determination that technical support by the manufacturer is easy to come by and dependable.

FIGURE 3.10 *(Continued)*

Section IX. Summary of Results: Individual–Technology Evaluation Scale/ Comparisons of the Results of Previous and Current Adaptations

Directions: The first four items from Part A of the Individual–Technology Evaluation Scale deal with the compensatory effectiveness of the assistive technology. To document the effectiveness, check the appropriate boxes to note the presence/absence of previous and current strategies/adaptations and note the outcome/level of performance. Then use the remaining space to make additional comments regarding the "match," technology literacy, and other considerations.

Compensatory goal/task: compensate for reading difficulties

Part A. Individual–Technology Match

Comparison of Previous and Current Adaptations

Previous efforts:

☑ **No strategy/adaptation:**

Outcome/level of performance: GSRT Silent Reading Quotient = 68; TOWE Essay = 71

☐ **Non-AT strategy/adaptation:**

Outcome/level of performance:

☐ **AT strategy/adaptation:**

Outcome/level of performance:

Current efforts:

☑ **No strategy/adaptation:**

Outcome/level of performance:

☐ **Non-AT strategy/adaptation:**

Outcome/level of performance:

☐ **AT strategy/adaptation:** OCR System, Speech Recognition

Outcome/level of performance: Silent Reading Quotient = 105; TOWE = 90

Ryan's use of OCR demonstrated considerable improvement over print reading without adaptations. His silent reading quotient increased from 68 to 105 using OCR. Reading rate also increased by about 50%. Speech recognition technology was also successful. Ryan's writing skills improved considerably as evidenced by his increased standard score (71 to 90) on the essay portion of the TOWE.

Additional Comments:

Used technologies without difficulty. Interested in using technologies evaluated. Ratings with the technologies were 4s and 5s demonstrating positive responses with the devices. The overall rating of 4 for each device provides encouragement for successful implementation.

Part B. General Technology Literacy

Poor keyboarding skills did not deter use.

Part C. Other Considerations

No significant problems were noted in Ryan's posture, although he did tend to approach the monitor in an awkward angle.

FIGURE 3.10 *(Continued)*

Section X. Recommendations for (check one)

___ Listening ___ Speaking ✔ Reading ✔ Writing ___ Mathematics
___ Memory ___ Organization ___ Physical/Motor ___ Behavior

Desired Outcomes(s)/Compensatory Goal(s): increase skills in each area allowing for success in Ryan's classes requiring reading & writing

Technology(ies)/specific product manufacturer(s): XL Technology OCR system. EZ speech recognition

Supporting Technologies/Equipment/Materials Needed: Computer (pentium-high system requirements) furniture space

Source(s) of Acquisition: SPED funds District vendors

Application(s)/Compensatory Task(s): Read texts of various types (e.g. textbooks, worksheets); write papers

Context(s) of Use: Resource science and social studies classes with possible use in other settings (e.g., library, home) if effective.

Physical Environment(s): Resource, science & social studies classrooms.

Positioning: No special adaptations need other than usable computer furniture

Reason(s) for Selection of Technology: Technology has been used successfully with other students. Evaluation showed improvement in Ryan's reading and writing with technology applications.

Instructional/Technical Support:

Method of Contact/Communication: Telephone, FAX, E-mail with manufacturers
Contact Person: XL Technologies, Dave Larsen, EZ Speech Vay Weider
Contact Location: XL Milwaukee, WI; EZ Sacramento, CA
Frequency/Duration of Support: As needed

Training:

Location: Saugus Middle School
Date(s) of Training: 2-15-02 Initial training
Trainer(s): Dr Perry
Training Method(s): Hands on using devices in classroom, interaction between Ryan & his teachers with parent participation

Section XI. Follow-up and Reevaluation Plan

Directions: Provide specific remarks as to how the effectiveness of the technology is to be monitored during use and how the evaluation team will follow up on its recommendations.

Person(s) Involved: Dr Perry will lead AT team

Date of Follow-up: Approximately one month after initial training
Method of Contact: Phone/e-mail/fax

Location of Follow-up: Saugus Middle School
Evaluation Method: Interview and observation All team members to be contacted. Will compare compensatry effectiveness with evaluation results. Focus on classroom integration.

Specific Setting Demand Tasks Targeted for Follow-up (from Part A of the Contextual Matching Inventory): Ease of completing and completion of reading and writing activities.

FIGURE 3.10 *(Continued)*

SUMMARY

Assessment plays an important role when dealing with individuals with disabilities. Ecological assessments account for the varying influences that affect a person's life, whether those influences are in school, at home, or among peers and colleagues. Practical assessments are authentic in that they deal with the reality of a person's situation. That is, practical assessments deal with real-life, daily circumstances a person encounters; thus, they are a natural extension of ecological assessments. Ongoing assessments acknowledge that decisions made during assessments are actually hypotheses that must be examined over time. Assessment team members gather data about a person and make decisions based on those data. If the decisions are made based on reliable and valid practices and instruments, the decisions are *probably* right, but may not be entirely accurate. Ongoing AT assessments follow along with the person using the device to make sure that the decisions were indeed accurate and that the device is fulfilling its purpose to the desired extent. But there are times when the hypothesis is wrong—the device is not doing what it was intended to do, and the individual is not benefiting from the person–technology match as intended. Without ongoing assessments, the hypothesis goes untested, and the potential benefits of AT devices and services may not be fully realized.

In this chapter, we also presented Raskind and Bryant's (2002) model for AT assessments that considers four critical considerations: tasks to be performed, the individual performing the task, the device that will be used to perform the task, and the contexts within which the device will be used. By considering each of these considerations, it is more likely that a valid person–technology match will be made.

Finally, we presented specific components that should be considered during assessments. We asked the following questions:

What are the contexts that have to be considered?

What are the user's strengths and struggles?

What to-date experiences does the person have with technology?

What technology should be considered, and is it a quality device?

What is the match between the technology and potential user?

By discussing these questions, we provided the basis for an ecological, practical, and ongoing assessment that can lead the way for effective AT implementation.

SCENARIO APPLICATIONS

Scenario 3.1

You are the parent of a child who has a learning disability in reading. You are satisfied that your child's teachers have worked with him diligently over the past two years to help remediate his reading weaknesses, but the reading weaknesses remain. What would you say to the IEP committee to ensure that AT is considered for your child? If the committee decides that AT should be considered, use what you have learned concerning ecological, practical, and ongoing assessment to construct a list of questions that you feel should be addressed during your child's AT evaluation. To which professionals should the questions be addressed? Once you have come up with the questions, put yourself in the shoes of the professionals on the team. How would you react to the parent's questions? How would you go about finding answers to the questions?

Scenario 3.2

Think of all of the tasks you do on a typical day, from when you wake up to the time you go back to bed at night. Then list an early morning task, a midmorning task, what you do at lunch, what you do during the afternoon, what you do at suppertime, and what you do in the evening before you retire at night. Then think about the challenges you would face doing these tasks if you were blind or had fine motor problems. Generate a series of questions that must be addressed by the AT assessment team as they seek to find a "you–technology match" to help you perform your daily activities.

Scenario 3.3

You are the Assistive Technology Specialist who is serving as the assessment team leader. You have to conduct an AT evaluation for Ryan, the student discussed in this chapter's case study. Given what you have learned about the assessment process, generate a list of 10 questions that should be considered during an ecological and practical AT assessment. Then identify what ongoing assessments should be conducted to ensure that Ryan's needs are being met by the device or devices that were selected.

For Discussion

1. How would you judge an AT assessment as effective for the user?
2. How do tasks, individuals, devices, and contexts work together to influence the nature of AT assessments?
3. How do professionals and parents judge an effective person–technology match?
4. Compare and contrast considerations for contexts during an AT evaluation?
5. Why is AT evaluation an on going process? Think back to Dr. Reed's Personal Perspective to help you answer this question.

References

Bryant, D. P., & Bryant, B. R. (1998). Using assistive technology adaptations to include students with learning disabilities in cooperative learning activities. *Journal of Learning Disabilities, 31*(1), 41–54.

Bryant, B. R., Seay, P. C., & Bryant, D. P. (1999). Using assistive technology to help people with mental retardation compensate for adaptive behavior deficits. In R. Schalock (Ed.), *Issues in adaptive behavior assessment.* Washington, DC: AAMR.

Bryant, D. P., Smith, D. D., & Bryant, B. R. (2008). *Teaching students with learning and behavior problems in inclusive settings.* Boston: Allyn & Bacon/Pearson.

Cook, A. M., & Hussey, S. M. (2002). *Assistive technologies: principles and practice* (2nd ed.). St. Louis, MO: Mosby.

Dell, A. G., Newton, D. A., & Petroff, J. G. (2008). *Assistive technology in the classroom.* Upper Saddle River, NJ: Merrill/Pearson Education.

Hammill, D. D., Brown, L., & Bryant, B. R. (1992). *A consumer's guide to tests in print* (2nd ed.). Austin, TX: Pro-Ed.

Hammill, D. D., & Bryant, B. R. (1998). *Learning disability diagnostic inventory.* Austin, TX: Pro-Ed.

Raskind, M., & Bryant, B. R. (2002). *Functional evaluation for assistive technology.* Austin, TX: Psycho-Educational Services.

Rivera, D., & Bryant, B. R. (1992). Mathematics instruction for students with special needs. *Intervention in School and Clinic, 28*(2), 71–86.

Salvia, J., & Ysseldyke, J. (2000). *Assessment.* Boston: Houghton-Mifflin.

The Technology and Media (TAM) Division of the Council for Exceptional Children (CEC) & The Wisconsin Assistive Technology Initiative (WATI). (n.d.). *Assistive technology consideration quick wheel.* RESNA, VA: TAM.

Wisconsin Assistive Technology Initiative (2004). *The WATI assessment package.* Retrieved March 20, 2011, from http://dpi.wi.gov/sped/pdf/at-wati-assessment.pdf.

Webster's Universal College Dictionary. (1997). New York: Gramercy Books.

Wiederholt, J. L., & Bryant, B. R. (1987). *Assessing reading abilities and instructional needs of students.* Austin, TX: Pro-Ed.

4 ASSISTIVE TECHNOLOGY DEVICES TO ENHANCE MOBILITY FOR INDIVIDUALS WITH PHYSICAL IMPAIRMENTS

Chapter at a Glance

Objectives

1. Describe how wheelchairs and other wheeled mobility units help individuals develop mobility.
2. Describe the components of a standard wheelchair.
3. Explain seating and positioning issues.

MAKING CONNECTIONS

Think about how you maneuver through the course of a day. Where do you go? How do you get there? What obstacles do you sometimes encounter? How do you overcome those obstacles? What might be different types of mobility impairments? What obstacles might be present for those with mobility impairments? How do they face those challenges? How might those obstacles be overcome with and without mobility adaptations?

The purpose of this chapter is to examine issues related to mobility and to identify how people with mobility impairments function by using a variety of mobility-related AT devices. We begin by (a) introducing mobility adaptations and the devices that help people with physical disabilities compensate for their mobility challenges. We then (b) overview basic seating and positioning design considerations that are particularly relevant to mobility. Information is then presented on specific types of wheelchairs, including manual and power chairs. We conclude the chapter by (c) describing other seating and positioning issues. It is important to note that we do not discuss mobility issues for people who have sensory or cognitive impairments. Mobility issues for individuals with these conditions are discussed in the chapter that deals with independent living.

INTRODUCTION TO MOBILITY ADAPTATIONS

The rationale for AT adaptations is that the skills for accomplishing tasks of various settings may not be present because of disability-related functional limitations; when these limitations are present, adaptations are made. Thus, if people are unable to move about because of a physical or health condition, we must find a way to use their strengths to help them develop mobility. This section of the chapter examines why and how this is done using wheelchairs and other wheeled mobility units.

Reasons for Wheeled Mobility Adaptations

According to the U.S. Census Bureau (2009), about 2.7 million Americans ages 15 and older use wheelchairs on a daily basis, with another 9.1 million people using ambulatory aids such as canes, crutches, or walkers. Most people use wheelchairs because they cannot walk, but many people use them because they have heart problems or other concerns that make walking difficult or impractical. Wilson divided users into three categories: those who have lost function in their lower limbs, those who have unstable posture, and those with general physical problems.

Lower-limb dysfunction can result from many conditions. One of the most common causes of lower-limb problems is spinal-cord injury, which occurs predominately in males ages 16 to 30 (Hardman, Drew, & Egan, 2007). About 10,000 spinal cord injuries occur each year, about half of which are the result of automobile accidents. Traumatic brain injury (TBI) also can cause acquired mobility impairments. According to Karp (1999), about 373,000 Americans sustain TBIs each year, and about one-fourth of those exhibit lifelong functional limitations, including limitations associated with mobility. Other causes of lower-limb problems include arthritis, cerebral palsy, polio and postpolio syndrome, muscular dystrophy, stroke and brain trauma, amputation, amyotrophic lateral sclerosis (ALS, sometimes referred to as Lou Gehrig's disease), Friedreich's ataxia, multiple sclerosis, and myasthenia gravis, to name a few (Karp, 1999; Wilson, 1992).

Brain trauma and cerebral palsy can cause unstable posture severe enough to result in a loss of walking ability, even with the help of walkers or crutches. Spinal cancer can also cause postural instability that necessitates mobility adaptations. In these instances, some functional use of lower limbs exists, but mobility is so impaired that wheelchairs or other units are needed for moving about. At times, people with health impairments will use wheelchairs or some other wheeled mobility device to conserve energy. A colleague told us a story in which a layperson was quite surprised to see an individual in a wheelchair stand and walk, but such an observation is not uncommon.

General physical problems affecting the lower limbs can result from a number of conditions. For example, people break their legs or have surgeries that result in temporary use of a wheelchair. For some, obesity limits their ability to walk; for them, the condition may have concomitant conditions (e.g., shortness of breath, stress) so profound that wheelchair use is mandatory. Older people sometimes fall and sustain leg injuries that require temporary mobility adaptations. Older individuals may experience knee and hip joint problems resulting in arthritis and rheumatism.

Each condition presents its own challenges to the user and those who are responsible for making mobility adaptations. For instance, people with arthritis may benefit from raised seats on their wheelchairs so as to make transfers from the chair to bed or auto easier; larger wheels to make it easier to self-propel; or brake extensions to make it easier to lock the wheels. Also, people with muscular dystrophy have special needs for their mobility devices. If excessive spinal curvature exists, lumbar support will likely be required, as will full-length armrests to support the curvature. Because muscular dystrophy is often diagnosed at a young age, the chair should have seat and armrest growth capabilities so that it can be used as the child grows up (Batavia, 1998). These are but two examples of special considerations that are made depending on the wheelchair user's specific physical attributes.

Types of Wheeled Mobility Units

Before we begin our discussion of wheeled mobility units, we provide a Personal Perspective 4.1 by Michael Haynes to set the stage for this content.

PERSONAL PERSPECTIVE 4.1

Michael Haynes has 20 years of personal and professional experience in dealing with life with a disability. His expertise is in the field of kinesiology, recreational therapy, and adaptive fitness and wheelchair sports. Mike teaches youths and adults with physical disabilities how to recreate and adapt activities to enjoy life to the fullest. He competes in wheelchair sports including basketball, hand cycling, tennis, triathlons, road racing, football, and softball. He also coordinates and enjoys outdoor adventure programs including snow skiing, water skiing, SCUBA diving, and hunting.

How Did You First Get Involved in Wheelchair Athletics?

I had become independent with all my activities of daily living and was back at UT [the University of Texas] studying accounting, but there was still something missing in my life. I had always been active in sports and was looking to fill the void in my life. I met a guy at a Mexican food place and over a couple of margaritas he talked me into coming out to play wheelchair basketball. I met some of the guys on the team and realized that they were real athletes who trained hard and competed at local, national, and international events. When I saw that there was an opportunity to travel, compete, and see the world, I was hooked.

What Recreational Opportunities are Available for People with Physical Disabilities?

Twenty years ago when I became injured, there were just a few sports that had been developed. WWII veterans developed wheelchair basketball when they got back from the war, and the revolution began. Today, the sky is the limit.

There is a sport for everyone. Traditional sports like tennis, softball, and football were adapted just enough to meet our needs. Other sports like quad rugby changed the whole aspect of the game and started to develop to meet the specific needs of various disabilities. The unique thing about wheelchair sports is that there is a place for everyone. There are recreational teams for those who just want to play and there are highly competitive teams that strive to be the world's best at the Paralympics.

(continued)

For the last twenty years, disabled athletes have been pushing the limits of their disabilities by developing assistive technology. This came in the form of adaptive sports equipment and included sit skis for snow skiing, can-ski for water skiing, downhill mountain bikes, and hand cycles. Athletes have climbed mountains, sailed across oceans, and completed Ironman Triathlon distances.

You're an Accomplished Tennis Player. Describe the Levels of Competition that Exist

Open division is a professional division that is sponsored by the International Tennis Federation (ITF). There is an international circuit with tournaments all over the world that pay prize money by the round. Players must be registered with the ITF and all the rules of regular tennis apply. Players must maintain a ranking of at least top 100 in the world to compete in most tournaments. Players represent their respective countries in World Team Cup and Paralympic competitions.

In *recreational divisions,* the player's skill level determines what division he or she competes in. Sometimes skill level is determined by a combination of sports skill and disability function. In other words, no matter how good some players get, their functional ability may limit them from rising to the professional level. All recreational level players compete for national rankings except novice division.

A: players trying to make it to the pro level, but not in the top 100.

B: recreational players who have been playing for years.

C: first- or second-year recreational players or more functionally disabled.

Novice: beginning players, no national ranking in this division.

These are the men's and women's divisions. We also have quadriplegic divisions for people with limited function in all four extremities including Quad Open, Quad A, and Quad B. We have a national circuit with more than 50 tournaments across the nation culminating in the U.S. Open in California at the end of the year.

You Tell a Great Story About Your First White-Water Rafting Experience. Share Your Experience with Our Readers

My buddy Wes Harley and I went north one summer for the Colorado Triple Crown Wheelchair Tennis Circuit, which included tournaments in Boulder and individual and team competitions in Grand Junction. Between tournaments we camped out in the Rocky Mountain National Park.

We were travelling by ourselves so this meant that we were on our own as far as camp setup. You can't imagine what a spectacle two guys in wheelchairs are while putting up a tent. We were such a sight that people set up chairs so that they could watch the whole ordeal unfold. They didn't offer to help us out of the awkward situation, they just wanted to watch.

The following day we decided to be adventurous and go white-water rafting down the Arkansas River out of Buena Vista, Colorado. We drove to the town early in the morning to make sure that we could take a half-day trip through the Brown Canyon. When we arrived at the booming metropolis of Buena Vista we soon realized that the outfitters had probably never even seen a person in a wheelchair, much less taken someone down the river at 3700 cubic feet per second.

These two Texas boys were not about to let anyone tell us we could not do something. So we quickly devised a plan that would ensure our trip. We would lie! We went into Buffalo Joe's River Trips and told them that we had paddled down half the rivers of North America. We told them exactly how to set up our seating system and where we would ride. All that said, we were off to the river in no time.

Once we had gone down a couple of miles on the river, the scraggly river guy who was guiding our vessel down the canyons turned to us and said, "So, I hear you guys have done a lot of rivers across the states. What's your favorite?" We were busted. I turned to Wes and said, "Should we tell him?" We went on to tell him that we had never done white-water rafting before. We just did not want to be told that they would not or could not take us down the river.

Sometimes you just have to act confident and tell people what they want to hear to do what you want in life.

Are There Additional Risks that a Person with a Physical Disability Takes in Athletics? If So, How are Those Risks Minimized?

Yes, people with spinal-cord injuries have more brittle bones and risk fractures because of non-weight-bearing. Skin breakdown is another concern for people with sensation deficits. We minimize these risks by strapping the limbs down to the chair; you stay with the chair if you flip or fall over. We also use high-tech cushions to prevent skin breakdown from the shearing of playing sports in a wheelchair.

What Advances in Wheelchairs Have Benefited Wheelchair Athletes?

The invention of the sports chair in the early 1980s revolutionized wheelchair sports. It allowed wheelchair users to compete to the best of their ability and push the limits of traditional wheelchair sports. New sports were added every year with minimal adaptations to the new rigid frame wheelchair. Today, wheelchairs are so specialized that each sport has its own chair that meets the needs and demands of the individual sport. They come in three, four, five, and six wheels. There is also a big demand for sports equipment like hand cycles, downhill mountain bikes, water skis, snow skis, and the list goes on and on.

Source: Reproduced with permission from Psycho-Educational Services.

There are different mobility units available to consumers to serve a variety of purposes (Lewis, 1993). Here, we discuss the most common: wheelchairs and motorized carts.

Wheelchairs have been used in this country at least as far back as the 1860s during the Civil War, and there is some evidence that their use dates back to the 17th century (Wilson, 1992). A variety of wheelchairs currently exist and are discussed in terms of manual and power wheelchairs.

Manual wheelchairs are propelled by the user. Some users prefer a rigid frame wheelchair because its fewer parts result in a lighter-weight chair that is easier to maneuver. The rigid chair is energy efficient in that it is easier to push, a benefit not lost among long-term users. Folding frame chairs, although heavier and less energy efficient, are still preferred by many users because they are likely to fit into most vehicles (Karp, 1999). Flexible frames also tend to absorb the typical bumps and vibrations that occur in daily use. With both rigid and folding frame chairs, large driving wheels are located at the back, with the smaller caster to the front. Footrests are provided with both models.

In 1983, *Sports 'N Spokes,* a magazine published by the Veterans Administration, began classifying lightweight chairs (i.e., chairs weighing about 30 pounds or less; Wilson, 1992) as belonging to one of four categories: everyday wheelchairs, sport wheelchairs, junior wheelchairs, and racing wheelchairs.

Everyday wheelchairs, as the name implies, refer to lighter chairs that are used for day-to-day activities. These wheelchairs have a rigid frame, and thus they are easier to push.

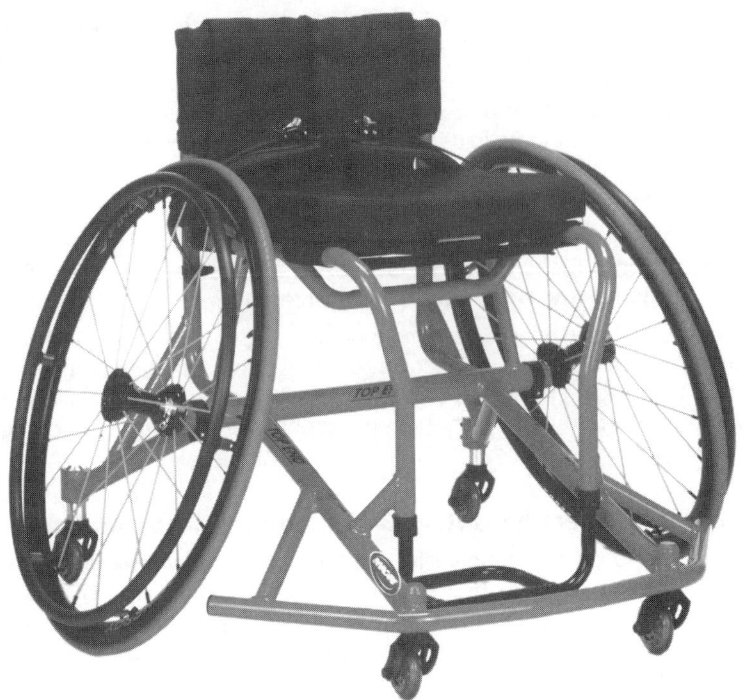

FIGURE 4.1 Top End Paul Schulte Elite BB Titanium Sports Chair
Source: Photo courtesy of Invacare Corporation.

Sport wheelchairs (see Figure 4.1) are specially designed to allow the user to play in such sports as tennis, basketball, hockey, and rugby (Karp, 1999). These chairs have rigid frames that afford greater agility and responsiveness (see Personal Perspective 4.1). Wheel cambers align the top of the wheel inward, expanding the wheelbase outward for stability, thus minimizing the chances of the athlete tipping over during competition. Hockey and rugby players, by the nature of their sports, often collide with one another, so metal guards are included in the chair's base to avoid damage to the chairs and occupants.

The *racing wheelchair* (see Figure 4.2) is a special sports chair designed with speed in mind. Many racing chairs have a single wheel in the front of the chair, and all are made with new alloys that provide stability yet reduce the chair's weight.

FIGURE 4.2 Eliminator OSR Race.
Source: Photo courtesy of Invacare Corporation.

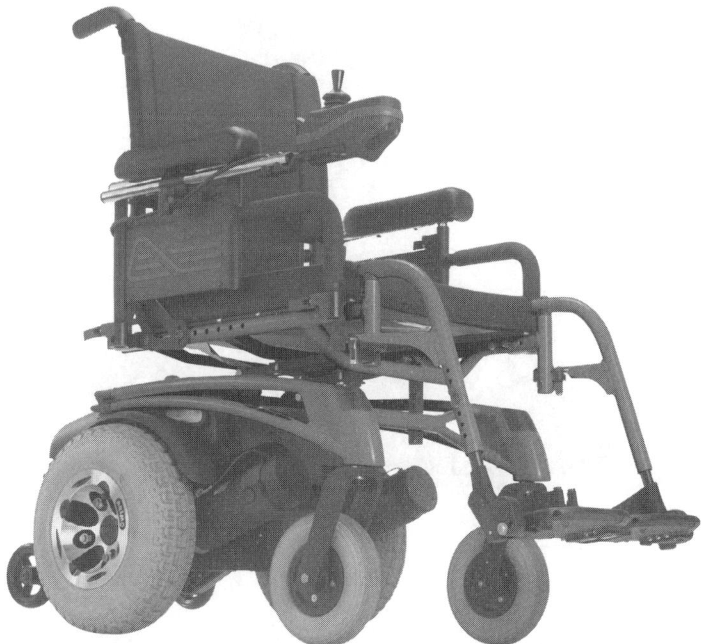

FIGURE 4.3 Quickie P-222SE Power Wheelchair
Source: Photo courtesy of Sunrise Medical.

Powered, or motorized, wheelchairs (see Figure 4.3) are those that have external power supplies (i.e., they are not manually powered by the occupant). Powered chairs satisfy the needs of wheelchair users who have insufficient strength or physical capabilities to manually operate their own chairs and thus would otherwise have to be assisted by others (Angelo, 1997).

Powered chairs come with a variety of options. Users must decide whether to purchase chairs with front-wheel drive (which may provide better traction with changing surfaces, but such chairs may not be sufficiently stable if a tilt system is needed), rear-wheel drive (they may offer a sense of better control, but tipping is a risk—many users equip these chairs with anti-tip devices), or mid-wheel drive (a relatively new option that offers a reduced turning radius and good traction). Not surprisingly, users may not want to select the mid-wheel drive option if they lack good upper body balance (Karp, 1999).

Some professionals prefer manual chairs to powered chairs for their consumers who have sufficient strength to operate a manual chair. But others argue that powered chairs offer users the option of conserving their strength for other activities. Chair use by young children is another issue in the choice between manual and powered chairs. For years, younger children were denied powered chairs for safety reasons. With improved control systems, however, powered chairs are now seen as a viable mobility option for children as young as 2 years of age. The freedom power chairs give children to explore their surroundings makes them an exciting option for older toddlers.

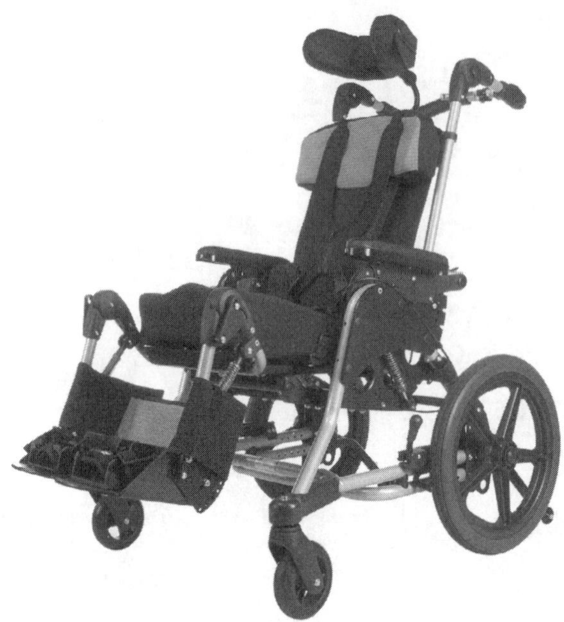

FIGURE 4.4 Kids ROCK Wheelchair.
Source: Photo courtesy of Kids UP, Inc.

As the name suggests, *junior wheelchairs* are designed for children and young teens. Some of the junior wheelchairs are lighter in weight because they are relatively small; they may have rigid or flexible frames. Others, however, are heavier because of the extra equipment they may have for functionality, depending on the child's needs. Figure 4.4 provides an example of a manual junior chair, and Figure 4.5 shows a junior wheelchair that is motorized. One advantage of many of the junior wheelchairs is that they are adjustable and "grow" with the child.

It is important to note that some parents of young children find it difficult to deal with their child's use of a wheelchair. We have heard more than once the story of a mother whose dream is for her child to walk. To her, accepting wheelchair use is an admission of defeat. Only after seeing the child use the chair as a freedom-of-movement tool can she recognize fully its value. Still, it is a difficult adjustment that is an important consideration for wheelchair prescribers and other professional caregivers.

Motorized carts, or scooters as they are also called (see Figure 4.6), tend to be used by people who have better sitting and transfer skills (i.e., moving in and out of the chair) than those who use powered wheelchairs. In addition, because motorized carts use a steering wheel, scooter users must have good use of their upper limbs. Often, scooter users have some ambulatory skills. Motorized carts offer advantages over powered wheelchairs because carts tend to be much lighter and are narrower; thus, they may provide mobility in aisles that otherwise inhibit wheelchair use. In addition, people who have temporary conditions that inhibit mobility may prefer scooters to wheelchairs because they "look" less like a disability vehicle. When compared to manual wheelchairs, scooters and powered chairs have decided disadvantages when they break down (i.e., it is much more difficult to transport broken powered units than manual units) or when they are used in areas that are less accessible (e.g., curb cuts are not available, stairs are not supplemented with ramps).

FIGURE 4.5 TDX Spree with Formula CG
Source: Photo courtesy of Invacare Corporation.

FIGURE 4.6 L-3 Red 3-Wheel Microportable Lynx
Source: Photo courtesy of Invacare Corporation.

Scooter boards are cushioned strips of wood that have small wheels designed to be used on smooth surfaces. The scooter board varies in length, depending on the size of the rider. It may be the same length as the user for full support or may be shorter to allow the rider to exert additional body control. Scooter boards help to develop head and trunk control and upper body and arm strength.

Switch-operated power scooter boards are available for use. When manual boards are used in the prone position, the rider uses his or her arms to reach to the ground and propel the board. Or the board can attach to a rope that can be pulled by someone other than the rider.

When used while lying in the supine position (i.e., with the rider lying on his or her back), the user uses feet for self-propulsion. Finally, scooter boards can be used in the sitting position, with propulsion accomplished using the feet, which frees the hands for grasping.

Several upright mobility units exist for people who prefer to be standing as they move about and who have some use of their legs. These weight-bearing devices allow people to look at others face to face and allow for more vertical movement. *Walkers* have rigid frames that may or may not be folded when not used. Some walkers have postural supports and/or wheels; others do not.

Gait trainers (see Figure 4.7) are used by people, usually children, who may have balance and/or muscle control problems. Users of gait trainers propel the device with their feet. Gait trainers often come with different supports (e.g., chest laterals, leg abductors and prompts,

FIGURE 4.7 KidWalk Gait Mobility System
Source: Photo courtesy of Prime Engineering.

forearm supports), and most are equipped with seats that allow the user to rest when tired or wanting to relax. Adjustments are available to vary the physical supports.

Mobile standers are a third type of upright mobility unit that can be used by people with limited or no use of trunk or leg muscles. Users are supported with pads, and the units are adjustable in height, width, and tilt angles. Users may use their arms to move the unit's wheels. The devices may be equipped with adjusters that reduce weight-bearing capacity, which is important for users who have unstable hips or those who cannot extend their legs fully.

Power assist chairs are recent additions to the wheelchair industry. One such chair, Frank Mobility's e-motion, is composed of a system that incorporates motors, batteries, and software into the chair's wheels (see www.frankmobility.com/e-motion.php). The system is activated as soon as the user pushes on the wheel's rims, and provides power in addition to that provided by the user. When the user lets go of the rim, the system disengages. Such a device creates somewhat of a hybrid between a manual and power chair, giving the user a power boost to assist in mobility. The system does add about 25 pounds to the weight of each wheel, so the extra 50 pounds or so can make the chair more difficult to transport (in and out of a car, for example). However, for the user who requires the extra "push" that the power assist chair can provide, the trade-off is worthwhile. In addition, as technology advances, the weight of the systems might well decrease.

BASIC DESIGN CONSIDERATIONS

Wilson (1992) described the components of a standard wheelchair (see Figure 4.8). Each chair consists of a seat, a seatback, armrests, controls, front riggings, wheels and rear tires, casters, hand rims, and other features. Each is briefly discussed in this section.

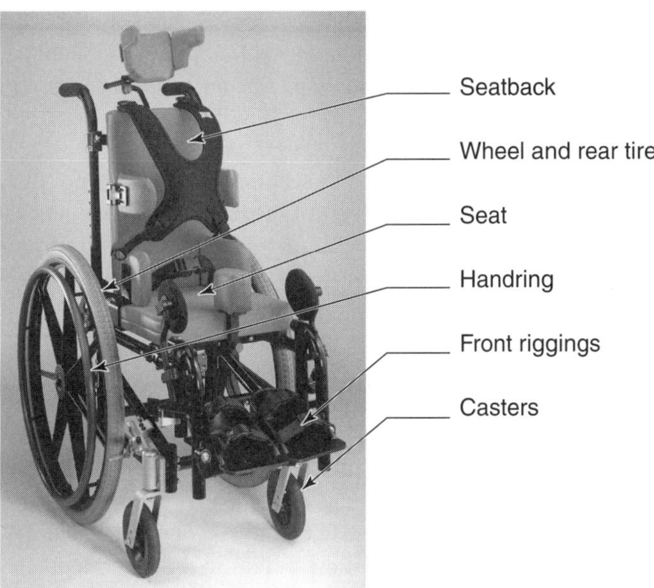

FIGURE 4.8 Components of a Wheelchair
Source: Photo courtesy of Adaptive Engineering Lab, Inc.

Seats

Seat types sent from manufacturers are hammock or sling, both of which are quite flexible. Seats may be solid to provide postural support. In this instance, the seat can be removed so that the chair can be folded, or the solid seat can be specially installed to fold with the chair. When the user's body offers particular challenges, seats are specially fabricated to conform to the user's seating needs. This situation is discussed later in this chapter.

It is generally accepted that seats should be as narrow as possible without making contact that causes pressure sores. Wheelchair seats usually range in size from 10 to 30 inches and are available in 2-inch increments. Although larger seats are available, their size makes the chair more difficult to fold for transport.

Seat depth refers to how long the seat is from front to back. A seat that is too shallow (i.e., short) results in the user's legs extending too far in front of the seat. When this occurs, too much pressure is placed on the body's soft tissues, and pressure sores can develop. In addition, shallow seats inhibit proper foot contact with the footrests. Seats that are too deep inhibit blood flow unless the users slump backward on their chairs or extend their legs outward. Either position is detrimental to comfort, and slumping that results from rotating the pelvis backward can lead to spinal degeneration (Karp, 1999).

Seat height is usually 19½ to 20½ inches, depending on the height of the user. The height of the seat is obviously affected by the size of the cushion. At times the height will be altered to make the user feel more stable. That is, if the seat is tilted slightly to the back, establishing contact between the user's back and the chair back, the user feels more secure than if the posture were forward leaning.

Seatbacks

For years, seatbacks had to be flexible so that they could fold with the chair for storage purposes. Unfortunately, these flexible seatbacks were unable to provide lumbar support, lateral trunk stability, and accommodation to unique positioning needs (Karp, 1999). With the introduction of rigid frame wheelchairs, seatbacks now provide much better support because they pivot downward against the seat rather than closing sideways. New technology also has allowed for the inclusion of back supports on traditional folding chairs.

As with seats, seatbacks should be fitted to accommodate the size of the user. Backs that are too short cause problems when the upper part of the back hangs over and causes discomfort or sores. The height of the device should allow for firm support without restricting motion.

Armrests

Almost all powered wheelchairs have armrests, but manual wheelchairs may or may not have them, depending on the needs and desires of the consumer. There are a number of factors to consider concerning armrests. Karp (1999) offered the following benefits of armrests:

- Armrests can help prevent spinal problems. When you put the weight of your arms on the armrest, you relieve some of the load on your spine.
- Armrests may be important for transfers into and out of the chair.
- Armrests are helpful for shifting your weight in the chair, a crucial habit for the prevention of pressure sores.
- If you have limited upper body balance, your safety may depend on having the added stability armrests provide. (p. 259)

Some people prefer not to include armrests on their chairs because they are simply not needed. Others choose to have flip-up or swing-away armrests installed because they only need armrests some of the time. When not needed, the armrests are pivoted out of the way. Still other wheelchair users choose to have removable armrests that can be easily taken off and put on the chair as needed. Finally, some users choose to have permanent armrests. Some power wheelchair users choose to use sculpted armrests that fit the arms for joystick ease of use. In some instances, straps can be used to keep the arm securely placed in the mould.

Controls

Church and Glennen (1992) discuss a variety of control methods that can be employed by a power chair user. By far the most common control is a hand-controlled joystick, similar to the device used in video games. This application of the joystick allows the user to propel his or her chair in a particular direction. Proportional-drive joysticks allow the user to control the speed and direction of the chair's movement. Microswitch joysticks, on the other hand, offer only on-off alternatives.

Some wheelchair users who require head-stick or chin controls employ remote joysticks. Typically, these types of joysticks offer the same advantages as their proportional-drive counterparts, with the obvious difference being their mode of operation. Less common are controls that are operated by sip and puff or another type of switch. The main point to consider is that power chairs can be propelled by any number of controls, making such chairs a viable alternative for many potential users.

Front Riggings

Front rigging is a generic term that is used when discussing foot and leg rests. Batavia (1998) notes four purposes of riggings:

1. They prevent the users' feet from dragging on the floor as they ride.
2. They support the back of the base of the thigh from pressure sores that result from contact at the front edge of the seat.
3. They allow the knee joint to bend at the preferred angle.
4. They provide the ankle joint with the proper dorsiflexion (i.e., the ankle flexes at the required angle).

Like armrests, footplates can be fixed or detached. Also like armrests, footplates can pivot to allow for easier entry to and exit from the wheelchair or allow for easier access to work tables. In addition, front riggings can be adjusted to allow for straight leg use (i.e., parallel to the ground). Such a configuration allows for comfort for those whose legs are in a cast or who have knee problems (Wilson, 1992).

Wheels and Rear Tires

Wheelchairs usually include two 20- to 26-inch rear spoke or molded wheels that support the tires (standard wheelchair wheels are 24 inches in diameter). Spoke wheels are lighter than molded wheels but require more maintenance. In contrast, molded wheels are more durable. As the size of the wheel increases, maneuverability tends to decrease.

Tires are pneumatic, solid, or airless. Pneumatic tires are air-filled. They can be smooth or treaded, depending on the terrain that is traversed. Smoother areas, such as inside buildings or on

FIGURE 4.9 Colours in Motion Tremor Wheelchair Equipped with "Fatso tire."
Source: Photo courtesy of Colours in Motion.

sidewalks, can be traversed easily with smooth tires. Different tire treads are available for rough or semirough terrains. Pneumatic tires are the most shock-absorbing type of tire; thus, they tend to prolong the life of a chair by reducing shock to its systems. Pneumatic tires also make riding more comfortable.

Solid tires have the advantage of lower maintenance and are firmer than pneumatic tires. Because pneumatic tire blowouts can occur in a work environment that has sharp edges (e.g., broken glass, sharp metal) on the floor, solid tires may be the preferred choice for some locations.

Airless, solid-insert tires offer similar advantages to traditional solid tires. Their shock absorption is superior to standard solid tires but considerably less than pneumatic tires.

Figure 4.9 shows an example of a special tire that can be used to allow wheelchair users access to beaches, the snow, or desert sands. The "Fatso tire" by Colours is one example of how new technology is allowing wheelchair users to participate in recreational opportunities that were once thought impossible. A colleague tells the story of sitting on the beach watching children play in the sand while the children's mother watched in her wheelchair from the boardwalk many yards away. Some time later, while visiting the same beach, he saw the same family playing together making sand castles. The mother's wheelchair had been equipped with "balloon" wheels, similar to those shown in Figure 4.9, which allowed for full family fun at the beach.

Casters

Casters are small front (usually) wheels that allow the wheelchair to be steered. Although casters can be of any size, they range in diameter from 2 to 8 inches, with typical sizes being 5 or 8 inches. Larger casters provide better shock absorption, but smaller casters offer a smaller turning radius and less "fluttering" (i.e., shaking back and forth). The increased maneuverability of smaller wheels should be considered against the inconveniences that are presented by obstacles such as small potholes. Wider, ball-shaped casters improve rolling resistance and allow wheelchairs to be used on sand. Like rear wheel tires, caster tires can be solid or pneumatic or a hybrid of the two.

Hand Rims

Hand rims are usually circular tubes that attach to the driving wheels to allow for control of the chair. Many tubes are made of steel and allow the user to push the chair and keep the hands clean. Some users who have grasping problems find they are helped when knobs or other projections are attached to the tubes. These attachments allow the user to propel the drive wheels using the palms or the meaty portion of the hand.

Other Features

Seat belts, parking locks, anti-tipping devices, and trays are just a few of other helpful tools that can be a part of a rider's wheelchair. These and the many other features available for wheelchair users allow for added safety, comfort, and support. Of particular value are specialized seating and positioning systems, which are described in the next section.

SEATING AND POSITIONING ISSUES

We begin this section by providing a Personal Perspective 4.2 on issues related to seating and positioning.

PERSONAL PERSPECTIVE 4.2

Jamie Judd-Wall has been a leader in the field of assistive technology for over a decade. She is currently in private practice working with individuals with disabilities and their families in Austin, Texas. Jamie has pioneered programs such as "PECS with TECH" and "The 8-Step Process for Assistive Technology Assessment," worked with many companies to develop assistive technology products, authored articles including "Learning and Living with Technology" and published the assessment tools "The Assistive Technology Screener" and "Portfolio Assessment for Students with Severe to Profound Disabilities." Jamie is a frequent presenter at conferences and hosts conferences and training workshops in Austin, Texas.

We have Heard You Talk About the Importance of Positioning when Considering AT. Why is Positioning Such a Critical Factor for Some People with Disabilities?

Positioning is a critical factor for everyone. From the more basic perspective if you aren't positioned properly, you can damage your bones and joints; you may not breathe properly and your circulation may be impeded. From another perspective, when you are uncomfortable or spend your energy maintaining your posture, you can't focus on the task. For people with disabilities, there are many aspects of positioning that play a part in their health and their performance. Many caregivers don't realize the seriousness of the physical damage that can occur as a result of improper positioning. Others don't understand the connection between posture and function.

Some people with disabilities are not able to change their positions and so rely on caregivers and family members. Other individuals, due to aspects of their disability, may not be aware of their position and they don't realize that physical damage has begun to occur, that they are uncomfortable, or that their work is being affected until after the physical damage has occurred or decline in performance has begun.

(continued)

What can Teachers Look for to Ensure that a Student is Positioned Correctly in Classroom Environments?

Teachers should be sure that certain critical supports are in place for every student.

1. **Hip Placement**—Are the student's hips securely placed in the chair so that the upper body has a good base of support? Is body situated so that the person's weight is going to the buttocks? Think of a slouching teenager—that person's weight isn't going to their buttocks—but they can move and reposition themselves where many of our students cannot. Are they using a properly placed seatbelt? The seatbelt should fit into the hip at an angle and provide support down and back maintaining hip placement.
2. **Foot Placement**—Is foot support available? We don't all keep our feet on the ground all the time but chairs that are too tall to allow for solid foot support encourage poor positioning. Imagine sitting on a tall stool with your feet dangling. No matter how long you sit on the stool, you can't put your feet on anything. You may find that your feet or legs fall asleep, your lower back hurts, and your head moves forward into an unnatural position. Now try something simple, like reciting the alphabet. How was that? Imagine that you have been given a more difficult task while in this position. What is the quality of work you are likely to produce? Neat and careful or careless and laden with errors?
3. **Back Support**—Is there good back support? Again, we don't lean back all the time, but when the student leans into the chair back, is it in the right location to help support his or her spine in a "working" posture? There is a strong connection between hip placement and back support. If a person's hips aren't properly situated in their chair, especially a wheelchair, then it is more likely that they aren't well supported by the back of the chair. Gaps between the lower spine and chair should be minimal, especially in students using wheelchairs.
4. **Benefits of Good Positioning**—Good positioning helps you focus on the task, it supports organs, muscles, and joints for proper functioning, and it extends peak performance. Poor positioning at a minimum is uncomfortable and at its worst results in deformities that can require painful and costly surgeries or other procedures.

Describe Muscle Tone as it Relates to Positioning

Muscle tone is a more important positioning factor when it is abnormal, too high, or too low. Low muscle tone means that someone's muscles are too "soft" to assist the person in maintaining proper positioning, like the child who can't hold up his or her head. Low tone is a factor in respiratory and circulatory problems. Children with low tone tend to drop their head and as a result they have difficulty taking full breaths. High muscle tone means that the muscles are too "rigid or stiff" to assist in maintaining proper positioning, like the child who can't bend to sit down. High tone is a major factor in the development of contractures, bone and joint deformities. Very stiff muscles put pressure on joints that, over time, can result in less movement or no movement in joints. Our hope in using positioning devices is that we can bring the person's tone closer to normal so that he or she can have better health; normal skeletal development as well as more control over movements and perform tasks more independently and with less effort.

How Do Reflexes Affect Positioning?

Reflexes take control of your body away from you, like when you hear a loud noise unexpectedly you startle—you may jump, shiver, or yell. You have had a physical reaction that is out of your control. People who have very strong reflexes move their body in certain ways that are out of their control. A person may have their head turned to one side and their arm extended, they may startle repeatedly at seemingly minor sounds or their shoulders may turn one way and their hips the opposite way—without the ability to straighten out. Imagine trying to read a book or look at the teacher's lesson presentation when your head is turned to the left and your arm is reaching out to the right. How can you build friendships when you jump and cry at the slightest noise? When your body is out of your control, you can't do the things that you want to do. Some people are able to learn to overcome reflex patterns. They develop a "cognitive over-ride." Others require the use of positioning aids to provide them with enough support to have freedom of movement. Daily activities many take for granted, like scratching our nose or holding hands with a loved one, are often unattainable for a person with strong reflex patterns.

What are Some of the Devices that are Used to Aid in Positioning?

There is a wide range of items to help in maintaining a proper position. Some are simple home-made items such as a box put under a chair as a footrest or rolled-up towel placed in a strategic location behind a person's head; at other times it is a custom-made wheelchair insert, one that is made specifically to match the curves in a person's spine so that they can sit without pain or discomfort. Designing proper seating and positioning systems for people with severe physical challenges is a specialty service provided by highly trained therapists.

Positioning supports have become part of the bigger picture of assistive technology as environmental controls and communication devices have been blended with wheelchairs or bed controls. Years ago a person using a wheelchair needed an assistant to push them. Then, power mobility became popular and people with disabilities had independent mobility. Today a person with a physical disability can use the environmental controls built into their wheelchair to unlock, open and close doors to their house, turn on and off lights, and even dial the phone and order pizza!

You Do a Lot with Switches. Describe the Importance of Positioning with Regard to Switch Use. [See Chapters 6 and 8 for More Information About Switches.]

Using a switch is a part of the chain of events set in place by positioning. Switches are part of the positioning scenario when we are working with a person whose disability very severely impacts their controlled movement. In many cases, due to the effects of a disability such as cerebral palsy, a person can control the movement of a finger or a foot ... and that's it!

A switch is part of a larger system of technologies that empower the individual. Switch use can be basic—activate the switch and the music goes on—or it can be a complex set of binary choices that control hundreds of functions. Activating the switch accepts the choice given and not activating the switch rejects the choice and another/different choice is offered. For example, you want to spell the word CAT; the letters of the alphabet are put in front of you one at a time. You point your finger when you see the letter you want. So first you see A (don't do anything, just wait), then you see B (again do nothing), then you see C (point your finger now), the C is typed onto your computer and the process begins again, first you see A (this time you point your finger) the A is typed into your computer, finally you need the T- you have to wait a while because T is letter 20 but when it is offered again you point your finger. You are using a finger switch to spell.

Switches can be used in a writing process as I described above, in environmental controls (instead of offering letters of the alphabet, the options are LIGHTS, FAN, TV, RADIO and you point your finger to turn the desired appliance), or augmentative communication devices (in this application the person is offered phrases or sentences that they want to say to a friend, care giver or even pizza toppings, point your finger for pepperoni, mushrooms or extra cheese). In complex systems, all these functions are combined into one electronic mega-system that the individual controls by accepting or rejecting items in the binary series. With imagination and patience, a switch can open incredible doors for a person with a severe physical challenge. Personally, I find switch use to be one of the most exciting and professionally challenging aspects of assistive technology. The difference in a person's life with a switch and without a switch can be staggering.

(continued)

Switches can be accessed virtually by any body part, finger, shoulder, and foot; even tongue and eyes. Clearly, keeping the switch within reach is critical to this process.

Positioning Plays a Critical Role in Food Digestion. Can You Describe How the Two are Related?

There are many things that affect digestion; positioning is one of them. Think of yourself after a big holiday meal—you want to get up and stretch, stand up, walk a little bit; that gives your body space to let your organs work properly. Imagine how uncomfortable it would be if you had to remain in your chair at the dining table for hours without being able to make those simple movements. That is the relationship between positioning and digestion. Movement encourages digestive processes; sitting all the time inhibits it. For some people who are in their wheelchairs for long periods of time, extended sitting, lack of stretching, and lack of weight-bearing positions inhibit their digestive process. These folks have serious difficulties with elimination. An example is found in folks with low tone who don't keep their head up and torso expanded; they aren't giving their intestines enough room to perform peristaltic movement. Just as bones develop contractures, the digestive system can develop blockages. Standing lets gravity help your body process food; weight bearing sends certain signals to your internal organs about what they need to do. Moving, especially weight bearing standing and stretching type movements helps your body move food through your system.

Here's your Chance to Tell our Readers the One Thing you Think is Most Important for Them to Know About Positioning. What Would that be?

First, I would say that positioning issues are important for everyone, not just the person with visible physical challenges. Students without visible physical challenges, such as those with learning disabilities, may be inappropriate and inattentive because they don't have enough positioning support to focus and work. I would encourage teachers and parents to look at positioning issues as part of an overall program for *every* student with a disability. Many students with unacceptable behaviors need a footrest not a time out!

Secondly, if you are working with a person with obvious physical challenges, such as a person with cerebral palsy, imagine yourself in their position—especially without the ability to change postures at any time. If you are finding your limbs getting tingly, your neck or back are feeling stress—imagine having to sit or stand that way while performing academic tasks or using complex communication equipment. Now, you are thinking like a positioning specialist!

Source: Reprinted with permission from Psycho-Educational Services.

People who use wheelchairs come in a variety of shapes and sizes. To help wheelchair users best fit into the chair, seating and positioning specialists work to create the best seating system for the rider. The Wisconsin Assistive Technology Initiative (WATI) provides an excellent document that relates to assessing the seating and position needs with regards to mobility. A segment of that document is provided in Figure 4.10, which asks a series of questions designed to aid in solving seating- and positioning-related challenges.

Anyone who has had to sit or lie in one position for an extended period of time knows how uncomfortable the experience can be. (See Personal Perspective 4.2 for a general discussion of positioning issues.) Seating systems include several wheelchair components such as seat cushions, seat inserts, back inserts, lateral trunk supports, hip guides, pommels, anterior trunk supports, and head supports (Batavia, 1998). Positioning describes the process of supporting a person's posture at a particular point in time using these seating system components. Thus,

WATI Assistive Technology Decision Making Guide

Area of Concern: Seating, Positioning and Mobility

PROBLEM IDENTIFICATION

Student's Abilities/Difficulties	Environmental Considerations	Tasks
What are the student's abilities and difficulties related to seating, positioning and mobility? • Does the student have strengths in any areas that would facilitate their seating and mobility? • Does the student have issues in • Physical-Muscles-strength or weakness; Coordination or other physical issues? • Stability-trunk, extremities; standing, seated or other position? • Endurance-fatigues easily? • What is the student currently using for: • Seating? Positioning? Mobility? Transfers?	What environmental considerations impact seating and positioning? • Where is the student expected to move about? • Do different locations require the same or different types of seating or mobility? • Does the child have an environmental preference? • Does the child require physical assistance in some areas, but not others (restroom, classroom, bus, etc.)?	What task(s) do you want the student to do once they are *seated*? • Use hands? • Use device or learning tool? Stay on task? • What task(s) do you want the student to do once they are *moving*? • Get to and from class? • Move around in the classroom? • Participate in daily activities? • What does the child need to be provided with to be as independent as possible in regards to: seating, positioning, mobility? • Does the child need assistance with transfers, changing positions, accessing mobility or other devices?

Sensory Considerations	Narrowing the Focus
Hypersensitivity or hyposensitivity to stimuli such as visual clutter, different lighting; classroom and background noise; tactile stimulation-surfaces: awareness of physical space / personal space; other individual specific sensitivities	i.e., Specific task identified for solution generation

Solution Generation Tools & Strategies	Solution Selection Tools & Strategies	Implementation Plan
Brainstorming Only No Decision	Discuss & Select Idea from Solution Generation	AT Trials/Services Needed: Date/Length/Person Responsible
		Follow-Up Plan
		Who & When— Set specific date now.

Important: It is intended that you use this as a guide. Each topic should be written in large print where everyone can see them, i.e., on a flip chart or board. Information should then be transferred to paper for distribution, file, and future reference.

FIGURE 4.10 WATI Assistive Technology Decision Making Guide for Seating, Positioning, and Mobility
Source: Reprinted with permission of the Wisconsin Assistive Technology Initiative.

positioning is an important mobility consideration because people who use wheelchairs stay in their chairs for much of the day. It is important to place people in positions from which they can comfortably participate in their daily activities. By paying careful attention to a person's positioning needs, factors can be reduced that may lead to muscle tightness, abnormal postures, and/or restricted movement associated with bone malformation, discomfort, and reduced functional abilities. Proper positioning does more than help a person achieve functionality; however, it is an absolute necessity for the person's physical welfare throughout the lifespan. Comfortable positioning is important for people to be able to pay attention, move their heads so that they can see and hear what is happening in their vicinity, shift their weight or change positions for comfort's sake, breathe easily, and manipulate objects or operate switches. Also, proper positioning in youth may set the stage for the maintenance of abilities later in life.

Positioning not only provides comfort, but it also can reduce further malformations. For instance, for a child with a developing scoliosis (i.e., a lateral curvature of the spine), positioning systems can help control the scoliosis and reduce continual degeneration. In Table 4.1, Batavia (1998) provides a number of positioning questions to consider for wheelchair users and caregivers.

In recent years, technological advances have been made that help improve positioning for wheelchair users. Technologies such as Doppler ultrasound, the Ankle Brachial Index (ABI),

Table 4.1 Questions to Consider for Wheelchair Positioning

YES	NO	NA	CONSIDERATION
____	____	____	1. Are postural supports properly installed on the frame?
____	____	____	2. Is the seat depth acceptable?
____	____	____	3. Is the seat width acceptable?
____	____	____	4. Is the back height acceptable based on the user's activity level?
____	____	____	5. Is the foot height level acceptable?
____	____	____	6. In the frontal plane, in the pelvic level, are the shoulders and eyes horizontal, and is the nose vertical?
____	____	____	7. In the sagittal plane, is the pelvis in a neutral tilt and the shoulders and head balanced?
____	____	____	8. Are the rear wheels positioned properly with respect to the user's arms?
____	____	____	9. Are straps and seatbelts positioned properly?
____	____	____	10. Does the chest harness provide proper clearance around the neck?
____	____	____	11. Is the pommel positioned distally, between the knees, rather than proximally, into the groin?
____	____	____	12. Do lateral trunk supports allow for acceptable clearance of the auxiliary region so that there is no pressure to the brachial praxis?
____	____	____	13. Is there sufficient space between the lapboard and the abdomen to allow for clothing comfort and respiration?
____	____	____	14. Is the frame stable when the user is in the wheelchair?

Source: Adapted with permission from Batavia, M. (1998). *The wheelchair evaluation: A practical guide*. Boston: Butterworth-Heinemann.

pressure mapping systems, pulse oximetry, and video fluoroscopy can help therapists and clinicians gain valuable information that can used to make positioning decisions. For example, data from these and other assessments can help manufacturers customize seats and seatbacks for wheelchair users.

To conclude, positioning ensures comfort and function (i.e., promotes maximum use of the body that helps a person to be ready to perform activities) while promoting access to a variety of environments and allowing for a positive self-image. When used in conjunction with each other, positioning and mobility allow people freedom to move about comfortably in their multiple environments.

OTHER SEATING AND POSITIONING ISSUES

As the chapter title suggests, we have focused on mobility concerns for people with physical challenges. But there are other seating issues that merit attention. For example, most occupational therapists will express due appreciation for the modern advances in seating cushions. New technologies are being advanced almost daily to help reduce "pressure sores," sometimes better known as *bed sores*, that often occur with the use of wheelchairs. But many would also state that low-tech options such as pillows, cushions, and wedges are also invaluable in solving day-to-day positioning challenges.

Also of interest are various seating systems that are used in daily activities. The *Rifton Toddler Chair* is one example. These chairs encourage normal sitting posture and are often found in day care centers that cater to young children with special needs. *Corner chairs* help children and adolescents maintain leg extension and helps to reduce what is known as extensor thrust, which occurs when a flexed leg in involuntarily extended when the bottom of the person's foot is stimulated. Padding on the chairs provides for extended comfort. *Side lyers* are just what the name implies, a cushioning system that allows a person to lie down on his or her side while being provided with cushioned supports. The system provides needed postural control for accomplishing daily living tasks such as playing, watching television, or simply relaxing in a typical position. *Bolsters* are foam-filled upholstered tubes that are frequently used by therapists to improve people's gross motor movements, balance, strength, and muscle tone to help with various seating and lying positions. Finally, *sit and stand chairs* are commonly found in the homes of many elderly people, but they are extremely helpful for people with physical disabilities as well. The chairs are comfortable recliner-type seats that, with the press of a switch, elevate the person into a near-standing position. The front sections of the chair fold down as the back of the chair elevates, allowing the feet to be positioned firmly on the floor as weight transfers from the seat to the feet and legs.

SUMMARY

In this chapter, we provided an overview of mobility issues for people with physical disabilities and mobility needs. We first introduced mobility adaptations by discussing various physical impairments and their attributes. We also presented a number of devices that are available to people with mobility needs. Manual and electronic wheelchairs were presented, along with a variety of other wheeled mobility units that are available (e.g., scooter boards, sport wheelchairs). We then presented information on the various design features (e.g., wheelchair backs, wheels) available for wheelchair users. Finally, we discussed briefly a number of positioning issues for people who use wheelchairs. These issues are especially important to allow the wheelchair user to move about with comfort and efficiency.

SCENARIO APPLICATIONS

Scenario 4.1

For several years, marathon, 10K, and 5K racing have been popular athletic events for people who use wheelchairs. Find a wheelchair racer and interview the athlete. How did he or she become interested in the sport? How long has the person been racing? What are the person's most interesting, most exciting experiences? What kind of support group is available to wheelchair athletes? Does the person compete in other sports? These are but a few of the questions that you can ask to gain information about this growing sport. Find out how one might go about gaining additional information about wheelchair racing. What Internet sites are available? (Some are listed in the appendix.) Is there wheelchair racing support groups or clubs in the city in which you live? Take some time to learn about wheelchair athletics and what it means to its participants.

Scenario 4.2

It is difficult for some parents of young children to accept the fact that their children will have to use a wheelchair. Yes, their children have had difficulties moving about, but there has always been hope that the therapy being received will result in their children's being able to walk. This is not the case in this instance. Consider the thoughts going through these parents' minds. How will they reconcile their expectations with the reality that their child will be using a wheelchair, perhaps for his or her entire life? It might be helpful to interview a parent who went through this experience to find out what thoughts occurred as this situation was encountered. Or perhaps you can find a disability support group online and conduct an interview with a parent. How have the person's thoughts changed, or not changed, over time? Did anyone support the parent as the child was being fitted for his or her chair? What might that parent say to another parent encountering the same situation?

Scenario 4.3

Go to a medical supply store that sells wheelchairs. Inquire about the cost of features listed in this section. How much do they cost? How are the features fitted for the user? Is there a person at the store who is qualified to fit the features to the individual? If not, what services are available for fitting customized features? Also, does the store help the user with identifying funding sources?

Scenario 4.4

Contact an occupational therapist who specializes in wheelchair positioning. Ask questions about the job. What got him or her interested in this line of work? With what ages does the therapist prefer to work and why? What specialized training has the person received and from where? How does he or she keep abreast of the latest developments? What equipment has been recently made available on the market? How has wheelchair positioning changed in the years the therapist has worked in this area? What would be the person's advice to anyone considering this line of work? Think of some more questions on your own to get a good feel for what a wheelchair-positioning expert does. In addition, ask if you might be able to watch the person as he or she works with a wheelchair user on positioning issues.

For Discussion

1. What various wheelchairs are available to people with mobility needs? How would one go about selecting the best wheelchair? What design features should be considered? How can these various wheelchair options help individuals with mobility challenges?
2. What are the components of a standard wheelchair?
3. What are the issues related to seating and positioning? Think back to Jamie Judd-Wall's Personal Perspective 4.2 to help you answer this question.
4. With whom would you consult when purchasing a wheelchair? What questions might you ask? How would you determine whether the answers to your questions were accurate? Where might you go to obtain more information about wheelchairs?
5. You are an athlete with a physical disability who is interested in wheelchair racing. What concerns might you have about taking up the sport? Where would you find information on wheelchair racing? What exercise regimen would you have to adhere to? What specialized equipment would you want to acquire?
6. Wheelchair positioning is a specialized area. Why might someone be inclined to be an occupational therapist and specialize in wheelchair positioning? How would you go about your training to become an occupational therapist? What might be the pluses and minuses of the profession as it applies to wheelchair positioning? Where might you work?
7. If you were to conduct an interview with Michael Haynes, what questions would you ask him, and what responses do you think he might provide based on his Personal Perspective?

References

Angelo, J. (1997). *Assistive technology for rehabilitation therapists.* Philadelphia: E. A. Davis.

Batavia, M. (1998). *The wheelchair evaluation: A practical guide.* Boston: Butterworth Heinemann.

Church, G., & Glennen, S. (1992). *The handbook of assistive technology.* San Diego, CA: Singular.

Hardman, M. L., Drew, C. J., & Egan, M. W. (2007). *Human exceptionality: School, community, and family* (9th ed.). Boston: Allyn & Bacon.

Karp, G. (1999). *Life on wheels: For the active wheelchair user.* Cambridge, MA: O'Reilly.

Lewis, R. B. (1993). *Special education technology.* Pacific Grove, CA: Brooks/Cole.

U.S. Census Bureau. (2009). *Statistical abstract of the United States.* Washington, DC: Author.

Wilson, A. B. (1992). *Wheelchairs: A prescription guide.* New York: Demos.

5 ASSISTIVE TECHNOLOGY DEVICES TO ENHANCE SPEECH COMMUNICATION

This chapter was written by Brian R. Bryant and Guliz Kraft.

Chapter at a Glance

Objectives

1. Identify the components of language and their role in language development.
2. Determine the purpose of alternative and augmentative communication, specifically with regard to unaided and aided communication.
3. Examine the components of an augmentative and alternative communication system and how they combine to provide individuals with severe speech problems the opportunities to communicate on a daily basis across environments.

MAKING CONNECTIONS

Think about how often you communicate throughout the day. How do you communicate? With whom do you speak? What are the topics of conversation? Are the conversations formal or informal? What are the purposes for your communications? What skills do you have to possess to communicate effectively? What if you did not possess those skills? How might you communicate otherwise?

From the time you woke up this morning, you probably have communicated with dozens of people, depending on the time of day it is when you are reading this. The purpose and form of each communicative act probably differed in some way. But, more or less, your day has been made easier because of your ability to communicate ideas to someone.

The purpose of this chapter is to examine the communicative act, particularly for those who have disability-related communication problems that require the use of AT. We do so by (a) introducing the nature of augmentative and alternative communication systems, (b) describing various techniques for aided communication systems, (c) providing an overview of nonelectronic and electronic devices, and (d) explaining speech generation devices (SGDs) and evidence-based practices. We begin by providing Personal Perspective 5.1, by Dr. Mark O'Reilly and Bonnie O'Reilly, on individuals with autism, who can benefit greatly from the use of augmentative and alternative communication (AAC) devices. The O'Reilly's describe some common AAC devices that seem to be most effective when working with the range of students with autism (and other individuals with speech and communication needs) to help them better communicate their needs and participate in a variety of environments.

PERSONAL PERSPECTIVE 5.1

Mark O'Reilly is a Professor of Special Education at The University of Texas at Austin. He has over 20 years experience working with individuals with autism and other developmental disabilities. He has held several professional roles in both the United States and Eire including Psychologist, Educator, and Lecturer.

Bonnie O'Reilly is currently a Special Education teacher within the Austin Independent School District. She has worked in a variety of roles with individuals with autism and developmental disabilities for the past 20 years in Eire and the United States.

1. What are the unique characteristics of individuals with autism for which AAC technology is a necessity to promote communication and independence? Communication difficulty is one of the primary characteristics of individuals with autism. In fact, approximately 50% of this group never learns to speak. There are a variety of communication deficits with those who do speak. Interventions to increase appropriate communication are therefore the primary target for early intervention with children with autism. Without intervention many of these individuals remain at a prelinguistic level of communication. By prelinguistic communication we mean that individuals use actions such as pointing to a desired object or leading an individual to a desired object or activity. Hence, as many of these people do not speak or possess severe deficits in speech/communication AAC is a very viable strategy. Further, autism embraces a wide range of abilities and strengths. For example, 70% of individuals with autism have intellectual disabilities while the other 30% fall within the normal range of intellectual ability. AAC devices and strategies can be used to meet the communication needs of a broad range of differing abilities. For example, an individual with severe autism and severe intellectual disabilities may be taught to exchange a picture of a cup to access a drink at lunch time. On the other hand, an individual who is higher functioning but non-verbal can create sentences using a speech output device to expand a conversation or tell a joke with a friend or family member. Many individuals with autism, contrary to popular belief, are very motivated to communicate and to interact socially. Their idiosyncratic communication skills are usually only understood by those who know them best, thus limiting their interactions with persons outside of their immediate circle of support. AAC provides them with modes of communication that can be understood by a general audience.

2. How can AAC technology be used to ensure that individuals with autism can communicate in different environments? There are a numbers of important considerations when thinking about generalizability of AAC technology. First, the device or strategy must be capable of being physically used in multiple environments. Some augmentative communication devices can be quite cumbersome and may be difficult to use in some environments (e.g., at the grocery store, on the bus). This being said, with new technology, such as PDAs [personal digital assistants], voice output devices may be very portable and unobtrusive. So the awkwardness of many of the voice output technologies may soon be a problem of the past. Second, it is important

(continued)

that the technology (Picture Exchange Communication System [PECS] or voice output) should be understandable to a novel audience across the settings that you want the person to use the communication device. This is a problem encountered with strategies such as signing, which is not understood by the majority of the population. PECS need to include pictures that are easily read by unfamiliar people. Voice output devices must also be audible and understandable. Third, generalization of the use of communication strategies does not typically happen automatically. So, generalization needs to be programmed across settings and people as part of the curriculum. This entails developing an initial set of generalization goals (e.g., Where will the person use the device? Who will they possibly encounter? What will be the communication need in these multiple environments?). The curriculum should then be structured accordingly with instructional opportunities across these salient environments. A core agenda should be to insure that the user is motivated to use the device to communicate in all environments, so make sure that you target communication opportunities that are important to the person. Finally, train the person to use the device across multiple environments. Do not solely focus on teaching within the classroom, as the person will not automatically generalize. The person must be actively taught in all criterion environments. Also use extrinsic reinforcers during acquisition until the person learns the intrinsic value of communication in these multiple environments.

3. What are examples of low tech and high tech AAC devices that are commonly seen in educational environments? Below are some examples of low tech and high tech AAC that can be used with individuals with autism. There are many variations/combinations of the strategies described below. This field is developing rapidly with new technologies emerging continuously.

Communication boards or books are very common, low tech, and are made by using Mayer-Johnson symbols or pictures. Teachers and family members choose these pictures or symbols. Persons can use the books to request items or activities that are commonly encountered. These are inexpensive, replaceable, and can be very easy to construct and use.

Another low-tech communication strategy is the picture exchange communication system (PECS). Using this system, the person is taught to exchange pictures with a communication partner. This strategy is based on behavioral principles and can be very effective to teach simple communication exchanges and sometimes complicated interchanges for persons with autism.

Simple switch technology, such as *Big Mac*, which is typically a single switch, when pressed emits a recorded message. A teacher/family member to fit a person's communication needs in particular contexts records the message. Individuals who are low functioning usually use these devices.

A *Go Talk* is a device that allows for several pre-recorded messages (from about 4 messages to 20 or above) that are associated with pictures. The person can make simple one-word requests or can construct complex sentences by pressing on these pictures. These are lightweight devices and a single device can be adapted to multiple settings to meet the communication needs of the person.

A *Dynavox* is a portable computer with synthesized speech. These can be programmed to make simple requests or to allow the person to engage in complex communication exchanges. These are excellent devices for higher functioning persons (e.g., those who may have autism but who are intellectually high functioning) as they can allow the person with autism to create their own communication repertoire. They are also used to make simple requests or comments with individuals with more severe levels of disability. It is important for support staff and family to be trained in the use of this device as it involves the use of computer software. Recent developments in hardware technologies (handheld computers) make *Dynavox* technologies highly portable.

4. What support is necessary for families and users to facilitate the use of AAC? Several points can be made with regard to support for families and users. First, it is critical that professionals are adequately trained to address the communication needs of the person and their family. A team of professionals including the family and person with autism should be involved in selecting the AAC strategy and communication goals. In terms of professionals the team could involve special and general education teachers, rehabilitation professionals (for older individuals with autism), assistive technology specialists, speech therapist, occupational therapist. Second, it is very important for those who have an ongoing or daily level of interaction with the person with autism to have input with regard to the selection of communication strategies and types of AAC to be used. Otherwise the goodness of fit between the AAC technology and the person's everyday environment may not match. If consensus is not achieved among all of the stakeholders, then the result will be a technology that is not used, underused, or used improperly. Third, stakeholders in all of the critical daily environments must be trained to work with the person consistently to maximize the full potential of the technology. This involves not only learning how to use the technology, but also learning how to create new communication opportunities for the person with autism on an ongoing basis. Fourth, it is critical that professionals follow up with the family and person with autism on an ongoing basis to ensure that the technology is being adequately used and to determine whether retraining or alternative goals or strategies are necessary. Finally, some of this technology is financially burdensome so it is important to ensure that families have adequate resources to purchase and maintain such technology.

Source: Reproduced with permission from Psycho-Educational Services.

INTRODUCTION TO AUGMENTATIVE AND ALTERNATIVE COMMUNICATION SYSTEMS

Augmentative and alternative communication "includes all forms of communication (other than oral speech) that are used to express thoughts, needs, wants, and ideas" (ASHA, 2011). An AAC system refers to an individual's complete functional communication system that includes a communicative technique, a symbol set or system, and communication/interaction behavior. Each of these AAC components is discussed later.

There are no specific guidelines for the use of AAC systems. Rather, they are generally considered when speech is inadequate for a person to communicate effectively, especially when receptive language exceeds expressive skills.

The use of AAC systems does not mean that a person will not develop speech, or that the system will be the only means to communicate. The word *augmentative* indicates that the system is meant to add to existing abilities. In many instances, speech may be a person's primary means of communication, and the AAC system supplements vocalizations when a particular communication partner does not understand speech. For others, AAC systems may be the primary means of communication. In either case, it is important to begin the use of AAC as early as possible.

When first asked to consider AAC devices, some people express concern that AAC system use will interfere with speech development. On the contrary: The use of AAC systems may enhance speech and language development by relieving the pressure and frustration that comes with ineffective communications and social interactions with others. This question has been addressed for many years, and the prevailing opinion is that the use of AAC systems does not inhibit speech development (Freedom Center, 1996).

The selection, development, and implementation of AAC systems should result from recommendations by a team of professionals and those who interact with the user. A speech-language pathologist with a background in AAC use will usually assume a leadership role in AAC system evaluation team meetings (Angelo, 1997). Because it is important that AAC systems and strategies be used across the user's environments, all people who interact with the user as communication partners should learn how to use the system to communicate effectively with the user. To the extent possible, key communication partners should be members of the evaluation and implementation team and, at the very least, should be trained with the system to become effective communication partners. Of course, the user should always be a team member, and no decisions should be made without his or her advice and consent. Without such consent, there is no guarantee that the device will be used.

One result of a lack of training in the use of AAC systems is the limitation of interactions that might occur. Some AAC users respond rather than initiate dialogue, especially if the user has been taught symbol vocabulary by eliciting responses to nonmeaningful or contrived questions. In all instances, training should occur in naturalistic settings during meaningful conversations that reflect authentic communicative experiences. Initiating and responding to conversational speech should be a focus of instruction because these are important pragmatic skills for language users.

The person interacting with an AAC system user needs to learn new communication skills. Effective skills include communication partners who are appropriately positioned, pause to allow responses, ask easily understood open-ended questions, confirm statements made by the AAC user, and provide elaborations when needed.

Musselwhite and St. Louis (1988) noted that there are three functions of an AAC system:

> **1.** An alternative communication system, substituting to some extent for a vocal mode. This may be a temporary use for a client who is learning to use vocal communication. The goal here is to transmit information though nonvocal means.
> **2.** A supplement to vocal communication for the client who has difficulty with formulation or intelligibility, but who has some usable speech. The term "augmentative" is often used to describe this function.
> **3.** A facilitator of communication, with emphasis on speech intelligibility, output and organization of language, and/or general communication skills. (p. 105)

Lloyd, Fuller, and Arvidson (1997) discuss AAC systems as being divided into two broad categories: aided and unaided. Each category is discussed here.

Unaided Communication

Unaided communication refers to a communication system that does not involve the use of external equipment or devices (Shane & Sauer, 1986); rather, unaided communicators use their body parts, usually their arms and hands, to "speak" (Musselwhite & St. Louis, 1988). Because this text deals with AT, and unaided communication systems by their nature are not assistive technologies, we will not devote a lot of space to discussing unaided systems. Yet no discussion of AAC would be complete without at least a brief overview of such systems. Here we present three types of unaided communication systems: sign languages, educational sign systems, and gestural language codes.

SIGN LANGUAGES

Almost everyone is familiar with sign language systems that are used by people who are deaf. The same systems have been used effectively with some people who have severe communication problems that have nothing to do with deafness (Alvares & Sternberg, 1994).

The most common sign language system in the United States and Canada is American Sign Language (ASL), or Ameslan as it is sometimes called. It has been speculated that Thomas Gallaudet and Laurent Clerc, who adapted the Old French signing system for their use in American educational settings, brought ASL to the North American continent. Others (Woodward, 1978) argue that ASL is a hybrid language that combined French signing with other signing systems that were in use for years in America prior to Gallaudet and Clerc's efforts. Either way, the deaf community has adopted ASL as its unofficial language, and it has also been used effectively with others who have severe communication challenges. It is important to note that ASL has its own syntax that is different from that of English. For instance, Musselwhite and St. Louis noted that the English sentence "'They have already eaten their dinner' would be signed in ASL as 'THEY FINISH EAT NIGHT' or 'FINISH EAT NIGHT THEY'" (p. 121). This is not to say that ASL is an ungrammatical language. On the contrary, ASL is a grammatically different language that possesses its own rules of grammar.

EDUCATIONAL SIGN SYSTEMS

According to Musselwhite and St. Louis (1988), educational sign systems were developed to create a better grammatical correspondence between sign language and regular English. The most common system is Signing Exact English, which was developed as a result of a 1969 meeting among parents, teachers, and deaf adults to help students learn the syntax and vocabulary they will encounter as they read. The sign system is composed of about 4,000 signs that include about 70 common English prefixes, suffixes, and inflectional endings.

GESTURAL LANGUAGE CODES

Although finger spelling is often associated with sign language, it is really its own gestural code. The most common finger spelling system is called the American Manual Alphabet (see Figure 5.1). Obviously, a person who uses finger spelling must have good motor control of one hand, must be able to spell, and must have good visual skills to recognize what is being spelled.

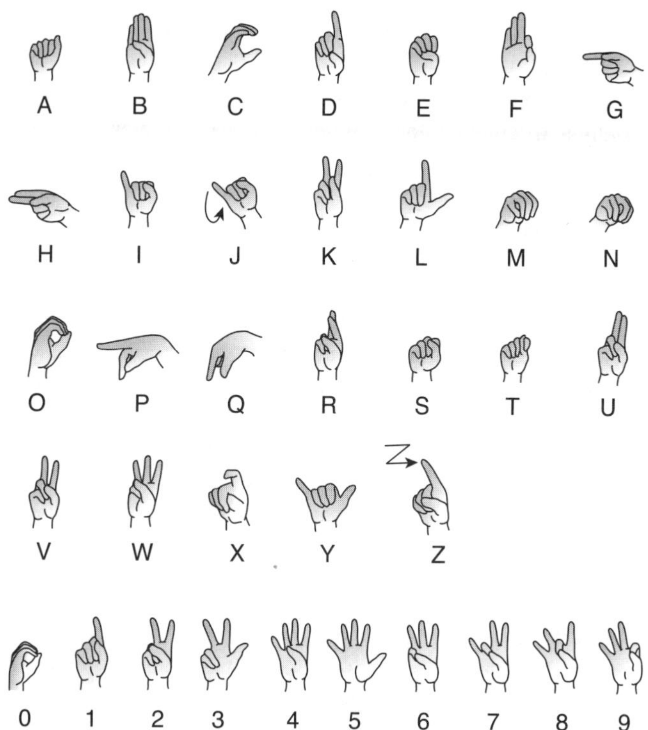

FIGURE 5.1 American Manual Alphabet

A second popular gestural code is cued speech. Cued speech involves hand shapes, hand placements, and nonmanual signals to produce a visible code to help supplement speech reading, sometimes called *lip reading*. Thus, cued speech could be considered a visible partner of speaking. Because cues are used in conjunction with speech reading, cues differentiate phonemes that look similar on the lips. Utterances are cued by dividing what is to be said into consonant-vowel pairs. These pairs are formed by combining the consonant's hand shape with the hand's vowel. Because all cues accompany speech, a cued speech reader sees a multidimensional visual cue (i.e., hand shape, placement, and mouth configuration) for each unique sound of the utterance.

Aided Communication

In contrast to unaided communication systems, aided systems use equipment and/or devices to provide people with the ability to communicate (Brett & Provenzo, 1995). In this section, we provide a brief introduction to symbol systems that form the basis of aided systems, nonelectronic systems, and electronic systems.

Symbols play a similar role as spoken words by representing ideas and concepts. For example, when you hear the word *play*, you think of playing a game and create a mental image to represent the concept. When this mental image is displayed as a picture, the idea of "playing" can be conveyed from one person to another. Some AAC systems, such as the DynaVox/Tango and the Picture Exchange Communication System (PECS), use pictures to help people with significant delays in speech development, such as those with autism. Others, such as Mayer-Johnson's Board Maker Plus!, are software packages that use pictures, voice, sound, and animations as learning tools. According to the Freedom Center (1996), symbols can vary in (a) level of abstraction, (b) style, and (c) size.

LEVELS OF ABSTRACTION

Abstractions in this case occur on a continuum from simple to complex. Simple abstractions are first, and presentations continue through complex stimuli. Life-sized models or miniatures represent the simplest abstraction. Photos (e.g., soup can labels, magazine pictures) also can be used to represent objects. Next on the continuum are exacting colored drawings that contain considerable detail.

Line drawings, next on the continuum, are more detailed than conventional "stick figures." Multiple-meaning icons (i.e., pictures that lend different meanings in different contexts) are considerably more abstract. For example, a picture of the sun can represent "hot," "circular," "yellow," "happy," or whatever concept is selected as being reasonable. Printed words, either single words or phrases, also can be used without pictures to represent concepts and ideas. Spelling, for those who can spell functionally, allows for the highest level of flexibility because it can convey just about any message desired by the communicator.

For the most part, abstract symbols are the most flexible because they provide an unlimited variety of sequences that can be used to generate thousands of messages. Spelling is also versatile because it allows communicators to access all words in their writing vocabularies.

STYLE

Pictures can vary in detail, outline, color, and/or background color. The features of pictures are important because they "belong" to the MC system user. Their selection should be made based on functional use, personal preferences, and the capability of the communicator to deal with the abstraction continuum discussed in the previous section. To reiterate, because the MC system belongs to the user, that user should be integrally involved in decisions about the style of the pictures that are part of the system. Continuous evaluations are made to determine the effectiveness of the user's style choices.

SIZE

In general, larger pictures are easier to use than smaller pictures in terms of vision, cognition, and motor ability. Larger pictures are easier to see, recognize, and point to. The size, spacing, and positioning of pictures is specifically determined for each user's needs. For many young children, full-page-size pictures are preferred when they first use communication boards; some children adapt quickly to smaller (i.e., 1-inch or 2-inch) drawings.

Although it is convenient to fit more small pictures on a page or display, it is critical that the size of the pictures accommodate the user's visual and motor needs. With younger children, it is usually advisable to use pictures no smaller than 2 inches in size. As children grow, or with adult users, size becomes less of a concern and is overshadowed by the need to provide more communication options that come with having more pictures on the board.

SELECTION TECHNIQUES FOR AIDED COMMUNICATION SYSTEMS

The selection technique is chosen according to the user's motor strengths and needs. For example, people who can point will likely use direct selection, whereas a person who has severe motor limitations may prefer scanning with some kind of switch (Shane & Sauer, 1986). Each technique is described briefly here.

Direct Selection

Direct selection systems require some form of directional movement as a means of pointing. The user directly selects the desired item (e.g., object, picture, word) by one of three typical selection techniques: finger pointing, head pointing, or eye gaze pointing. Electronic direct selection devices usually use a keyboard or membrane board that allows the individual to make selections by pressing the pictured item on the display. An example of such a system is provided in Figure 5.2. Here, direct selection is represented in a homemade eye-gaze display. The student

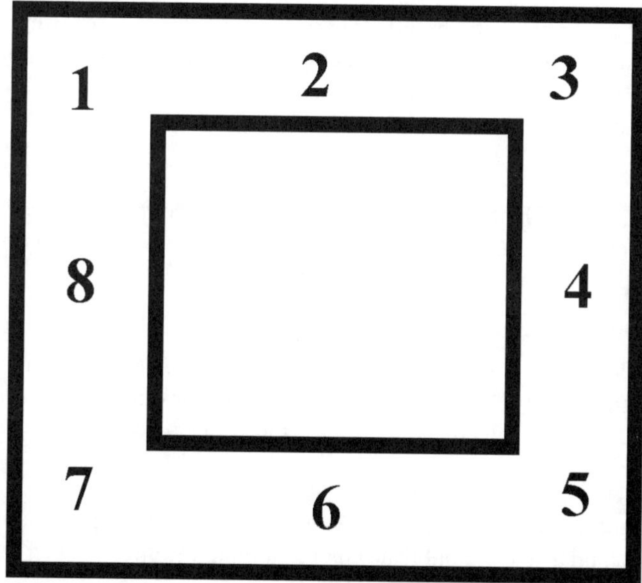

FIGURE 5.2 Simple Eye-Gaze Display to Exemplify Direct Selection

user responds to an addition problem (e.g., "How much is 2 + 2?") by gazing at his or her response. The communication partner, in this case a teacher, follows the student's gaze to identify what number was selected as an answer.

Direct selection systems are preferable to scanning systems for some immature users because they are relatively efficient and easy to learn (Freedom Center, 1996). If the user struggles with pointing, it is best to reduce the amount of physical effort during communication by limiting the selection on the display to only a few larger items.

Scanning

With scanning systems, the user selects his or her choice when the scanner gets to the desired icon in a row or column. With nonelectronic systems, the communication partner points to items individually until the user responds with a facial, motor, or vocal response (Heward, 2000). The pictures or other abstractions are displayed on small communication boards or books, and the communication partner scans through the choices by pointing with finger, stylus, or penlight. One option that is growing in popularity involves attaching Velcro strips to the back of pictures and attaching them to a vest, apron, or pages of a felt book. The use of the strips allows for a portability and alterations that can be made with little effort.

Electronic scanning systems contain items that are displayed on the face of the device. Individual lights or highlights scan the choices and the user activates a switch to select the desired item. The users develop rhythm and timing skills to activate the switch at the precise moment the desired item is highlighted. One of the more sophisticated devices is the Vanguard, which is pictured in Figure 5.3. The Vanguard can be operated with the keyboard, infrared head-pointer, or switch-activated scan.

Auditory scanning is used if the user's visual skills are insufficient to use visual displays. The names of the items are spoken one at a time to the user, who responds when the desired item is heard. Typically, categories are spoken first, followed by items within the identified category. For example, the communication partner could select the following categories: food, sports, and work. The communication partner states a category (e.g., food), and the user makes his or her selection by nodding or blinking. Next, the partner names the items within the specified category (e.g., meat, vegetable), and the process continues until the user communicates his or her intent. Such a scanning technique can occur in row-column, linear, or rotary configurations.

ROW-COLUMN

Items arranged in a grid are highlighted row by row, and the user responds when the desired row is indicated. The items within that row are then offered item by item (column) from left to right. The user again responds when the desired item is indicated.

LINEAR

Linear devices indicate items one by one. In a grid display, the device would individually highlight each item on the top row, then move to the items on the next row one by one. The user waits until the desired item is highlighted and then selects his or her choice.

ROTARY

A rotary device looks somewhat like a clock, with items appearing on the outer edge of the device. A pointer (similar to a second hand) moves around the circle. When the pointer reaches the desired item, the user makes his or her selection.

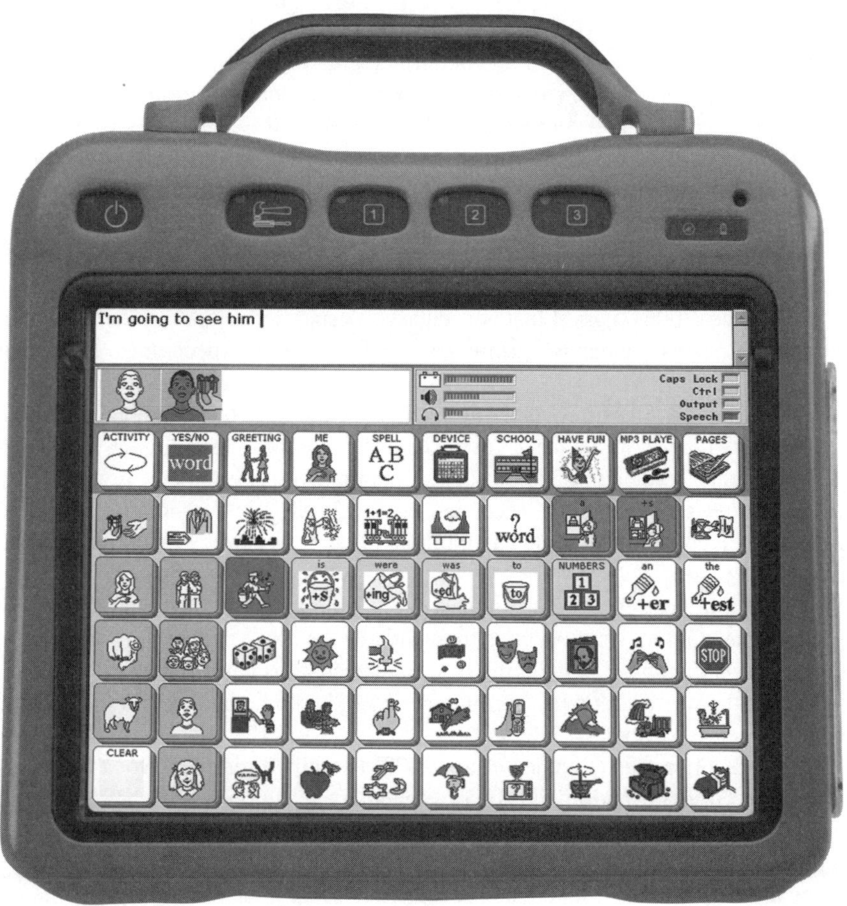

FIGURE 5.3 Vanguard Electronic Scanning System
Source: Courtesy of Prentke Romich Company, Wooster, OH.

OVERVIEW OF NONELECTRONIC SYSTEMS AND ELECTRONIC DEVICES

AAC devices come in a variety of shapes and forms. One of the easiest ways to differentiate and discuss devices is by categorizing them as nonelectronic systems and electronic devices. Each category is described in this section.

Nonelectronic Systems

Nonelectronic systems are often the first systems used with individuals who have severe speech problems because they are flexible and relatively inexpensive. As would be expected, nonelectronic systems use picture displays that are customized for the user's needs and desires. Here, we briefly introduce communication boards, mini-boards, communication books, and eye gaze displays. Before discussing the various types of devices, however, it is important to mention how vocabulary is selected for use on the different displays.

The selection and organization of vocabulary are highly critical for the effectiveness of AAC devices, because they will define the level of communication access for people with complex communication needs (Banajee, Dicarlo, & Stricklin, 2003; Dark & Balandin, 2005; Fem, Ahlsen, & Bjorck-Akesson, 2005). The term *social validity* is often associated with the process conducted by professionals to assess the extent to which a specific vocabulary is useful and appropriate (Karlan & Lloyd, 1983, cited in Dark & Balandin, 2005). To ensure that an AAC device provides quality communication and is socially valid, the vocabulary selection should include (a) a comprehensive vocabulary that is responsive to the specific needs of the user, (b) features that permit an efficient access to messages, (c) content suitable to age, gender, culture, and group membership, and (c) words, phrases, and sentences that are contextually appropriate and relevant.

Liu and Sloane (2006) suggest that vocabulary selected for an AAC system should include a core vocabulary, possess semantic "primitives," and meet user expectations. Each element is described here.

Core vocabulary involves frequently utilized vocabularies in a spoken language and determines the usability of the AAC device. Core vocabularies are the ones commonly used in a given age and developmental level across various (e.g., important verbs, pronouns, prepositions, auxiliaries, and practices environments) (Banajee et al., 2003; Liu & Sloane, 2006). Marvin, Beukelman, and Bilyeu (1994) provide a helpful list of core vocabulary that are commonly used with young children (see Table 5.1).

Semantic primitives refer to the smallest indivisible meaningful units (e.g., basic ideas, concepts, or notions) that may not occur as frequently as the core vocabulary. Some examples of these are *big*, *if*, *would*, *happen*, *think*. Finally, user expectations have to do with the words to be included. That is, the words that a person uniquely uses should be included in the vocabulary as well as common-sense vocabulary.

Banajee and colleagues (Banajee et al., 2003) examined toddlers' vocabulary selection process and categorized a tripartite division of vocabulary selection approaches: developmental, environmental, and functional. According to these researchers, the developmental approach is based on the language acquisition process and involves selecting vocabulary by using developmental language inventories. It takes into account such factors as knowledge of the different word forms (nouns, verbs) and the number of words that children typically use at a certain age or developmental level. The environmental approach takes into consideration the prerequisite vocabulary demanded for communicating in a certain environment or situation. The environment- or situation-specific vocabulary can also be called fringe vocabulary (e.g., *marker*, *paper*, *cookie*, *drink*). Finally, the functional communication approach focuses on the pragmatic aspect of the language and drives AAC vocabularies based on expressed communicational function such as requesting, greeting, and protesting. These vocabularies are highly critical for the development of joint attention for young children (Banajee et al., 2003).

For toddlers, using both core and fringe vocabulary is highly critical; however, studies show that toddlers show more preference of use to core vocabulary than to the fringe examples (Beukelman, Jones, & Rowan, 1989, cited in Banajee et al., 2003). For example, observing 50 typically developing toddlers in a day care center, Banajee and colleagues showed that core vocabulary words for this group included demonstratives (*that*), verbs (*want*), pronouns (*my*), prepositions (*on*), and articles (*the*). Nouns were not represented in the utilized vocabularies. Words with semantic functions included agents (*I*), objects (*you*), pointing objects (*that*) and actions (*go*), possessions (*my*), affirmation (*yes*), negation (*no*), location (*in*), interrogation (*what*), quantity (*some*), and termination (*finished*). Vocabularies describing pragmatic functions included the ones used of taking attention (*you*), maintaining joint attention (*this*), indicating recurrence (*more*), and interaction termination (*finished*).

Table 5.1 Core Vocabulary

Appendix A: Frequently Occurring Home and School Structure Words

about	can	her	must	sometimes	we
after	can't	here	my	somewhere	we'll
again	could	him	myself	than	we're
all	couldn't	his	never	that	well
almost	did	how	no	that's	were
already	didn't	I	not	the	what
also	do	I'll	of	their	what's
an	does	I'm	off	them	when
and	doesn't	if	only	then	where
another	doing	in	or	there	which
any	don't	inside	other	there's	while
are	down	is	our	these	who
aren't	else	isn't	ours	they	why
around	everybody	it	out	they'll	with
as	everything	it's	ready	they're	won't
at	for	let	really	this	would
away	from	let's	same	those	yes
be	had	many	she	to	yet
before	has	may	she's	together	you
being	have	maybe	some	too	you'll
both	haven't	me	somebody	very	you're
but	he	most	someone	was	your
by	he's	much	something	wasn't	yours

N = 138.

Source: Reprinted by permission. Informa Healthcare USA.

Selecting vocabulary for specific activities is accomplished by examining each activity and writing out the words and phrases that might be needed. A display for going fishing, for example, might include "bait the hook," "cast for me, please," and "I have a nibble." The challenge is to select words and phrases that the user will be able to apply to situations as they arise.

NONELECTRONIC COMMUNICATION BOARDS

Communication boards are traditional augmentative communication systems that are convenient enough to be placed on wheelchair lap trays. Communication boards contain a single display of vocabulary words and phrases. The size, number, and position of pictures depend on the user's motor and visual skills and the size of his or her vocabulary. Because the board serves as the user's primary means of communication, it contains as many words and phrases as can fit onto the device. Figure 5.4 depicts a conversation taking place between communication partners using a nonelectronic communication board.

FIGURE 5.4 Nonelectric Communication Board
Source: Courtesy of Mayer-Johnson, Inc.

NONELECTRONIC MINI-BOARDS

Mini-boards have become popular displays of vocabulary words and phrases that fit specific settings or activities. For example, a recreation mini-board will contain pictures that relate to play activities. Mini-boards are used most effectively when vocabulary displays for all activities are prepared ahead of time for different activities and allow the user to select the most appropriate vocabulary for his or her daily activities.

COMMUNICATION BOOKS

Books are excellent vehicles to help provide access to a large vocabulary compilation. Communication categories (e.g., play, work, daily living) or activities (e.g., dining, dating, working) can be found as book chapters that are accessed dynamically as the communication situation warrants. In reality, a communication book is a collection of mini-boards that occurs as chapters and pages within the text. A sample communication book is depicted in Figure 5.5.

EYE GAZE DISPLAYS

Eye gaze displays usually are composed of clear material such as Plexiglas. Pictures of objects are placed along the border of the display so that the communication partner can follow the user's gaze to an item on the display (see Figure 5.6). Eye gaze displays can be made to serve as mini-boards for use in daily activities. When used in this manner, the communication partner identifies the needed display and positions it properly for the user's benefit.

Electronic Devices

Electronic devices are obviously going to be more expensive than nonelectronic devices and involve unique considerations in their selection (Alvares & Sternberg, 1994). In this section, we

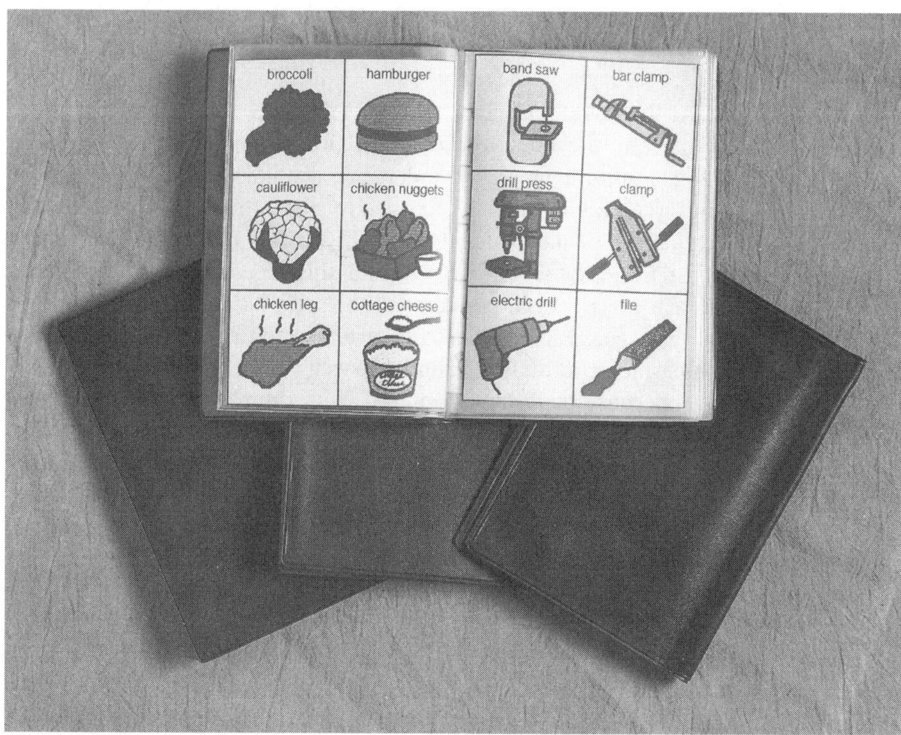

FIGURE 5.5 Communication Book
Source: Courtesy of Mayer-Johnson, Inc.

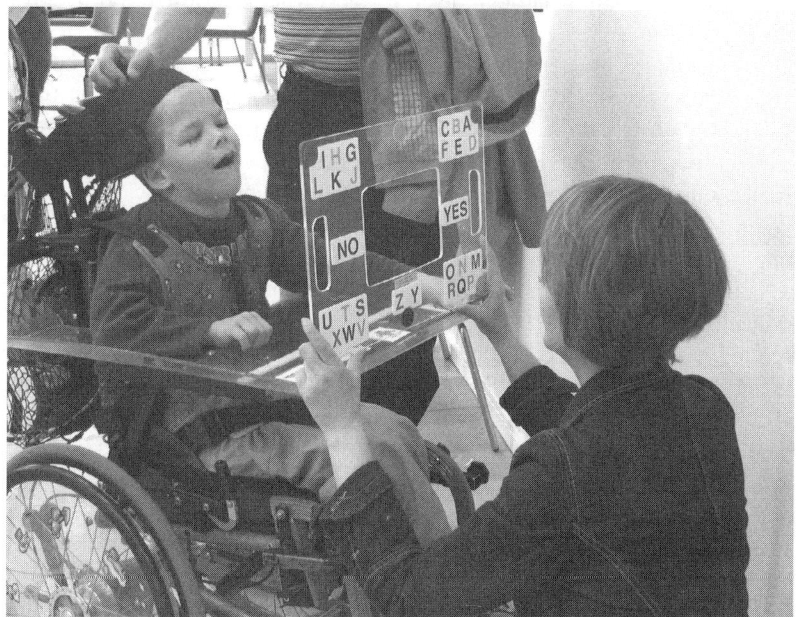

FIGURE 5.6 Depiction of Communication Occurring via the Use of an Eye Gaze Display
Source: Courtesy of COGAIN, www.cogain.org.

provide information concerning (a) advantages and disadvantages of electronic systems, (b) the types of electronic devices that are available, and (c) key features of electronic systems.

ADVANTAGES AND DISADVANTAGES OF ELECTRONIC SYSTEMS

There are several advantages to the selection of electronic communication devices. For the most part, these advantages involve increased independence and options of speech output. Although very young children may not be able to operate an electronic device without assistance, adults are usually capable of independent use. When children are able to communicate successfully without assistance, they learn self-control and independence. Electronic devices can allow independence that nonelectronic systems cannot provide by independent operation of a scanning device with a switch. Nonelectronic systems require considerable assistance from the communication partner. Until fairly recently, speech output has been available only to older children and adults, because there have been too few examples of such technology for young children (Freedom Center, 1996). Now, however, most experts promote the use of speech output devices for young children to mirror speech and language development. Banajee, Dicarlo, and Stricklin (2003) suggest that the use of AAC devices with toddlers between the ages of 24 and 36 months will increase based on three factors: (a) full implementation of Part C of the IDEA 1997, which emphasized AT access for children birth to 3 years; (b) advances in accessible technology; and (c) research that supports the use of AAC devices during early intervention.

When a young child speaks for the first time, parents respond quickly to reinforce language use. The child learns quickly to communicate verbally and experiences the power and success that speech provides. Speech output devices can provide similar experiences. Consider, for example, the child who activates the message "I love you, Daddy." Such a statement will likely result in an immediate response from the child's father, particularly if he had not heard such a statement before the acquisition of the device. Thus, electronic systems have positive attributes that make their use extremely beneficial, even for very young children. Yet disadvantages are also present. These disadvantages involve cost, maintenance, and portability.

Electronic communication systems range in price from about $300 to $7,000. Numerous excellent systems cost about $1,000, but these prices are beyond the means of many families. Although funding is available to help defray expenses, many times funding streams are difficult to identify and access, particularly for families with little experience in dealing with the paperwork and routines that are involved with accessing external funds.

All communication systems, especially electronic systems, require periodic maintenance. Battery charging and vocabulary programming are but two of the more common maintenance procedures that must be worked into a daily or weekly routine. The responsibility for maintenance must be clearly delegated.

The added weight and size of electronic communication systems can add difficulty to making the equipment readily accessible to the user. Because active people change positions and locations frequently, it can be difficult for a system to follow them from place to place. Thus, portability is another legitimate concern. In most cases, the advantages of electronic communication devices outweigh the disadvantages. But such decisions must be made on a case-by-case basis.

TYPES OF ELECTRONIC DEVICES

It is helpful to distinguish the various devices by the kind of input technique they provide. We have already briefly discussed direct selection and scanning. In this section, we reintroduce these features with specific reference to electronic AAC systems. We then introduce three additional features: type of voice, voice quality, and amount of vocabulary.

Direct selection. Membrane keyboards allow devices to be customized for each child's needs with respect to the number, size, and spacing of pictures or other items. An overlay may have a single item or dozens of items. Some membranes require more activation pressure than others, and young children may sometimes find it difficult to apply enough pressure to activate the board.

Some devices offer optical pointing. A small pointing device is positioned on the user's head, and the communicator points to items on the device by moving the head from side to side or up and down.

Some systems are operated by nonscanning switches. For example, a switch can activate a portable tape player with a continuous-loop tape. With this approach, the message is recorded and played repeatedly. Because the tape is a continuous loop, it repeats the message as long as the user continues to activate the switch. Some speech output devices allow the user to speak a single message each time a switch is depressed. These devices use numerous switches, each one responsible for playing a particular message. This is a type of direct selection, because the user selects the switch used for each message.

Scanning. Several MC systems are operated by a single switch, using step, inverse, or automatic scanning techniques. As we discussed earlier, users begin with simple scanning techniques and progress to more complex techniques as their abilities allow.

Type of voice. The two major categories of voices used in electronic systems are synthesized speech and digitized speech (Church & Glennen, 1992). Synthesized speech is produced electronically and is programmed by some form of text-to-speech procedure. Digitized speech is essentially recorded human speech and is recorded using a microphone, usually one built into the device.

Quality of voice. Voice quality varies a great deal, ranging from robotic sounds to voices that are relatively smooth, flexible, and easy to understand. Digitized speech is influenced by the quality of the recording and playback. Early devices used robotic sounds that did not approximate the human voice. Now a variety of male and female voices are available, and the user can select the voice that he or she associates with.

Amount of vocabulary. The number of words that can be used on a device varies according to the device's memory. Many devices provide a large range of memory options, whereas others provide very few. It is better to have too much memory than too little, because people tend to stretch memory as their own vocabulary and skills develop.

SPEECH GENERATION DEVICES AND EVIDENCE-BASED PRACTICES

We have spent this chapter introducing AAC and SGDs and discussing the potential benefits of AAC devices for people with severe speech challenges. We even went so far as to suggest that the term *nonverbal*, as it relates to an individual with profound speech difficulties, may no longer be appropriate—that all people have "speech" in some form and that AAC devices can help people communicate in ways never thought possible just a generation ago.

There remains, however, the discussion of efficacy—just how useful are AAC devices, in particular SGDs, for making beneficial change? On the surface, one would think the answer to this would be self-evident. But given the high stakes involved with AAC use (e.g., the ability to communicate combined with the sometimes significant expense of SGDs), efficacy is a legitimate topic to be discussed. Schlosser and Raghavendra (2003) proposed the following definition of evidence-based practice as it pertains to AAC: "Evidence-based practice is defined as the integration of best and current research evidence with clinical/educational expertise and relevant stakeholder perspectives to facilitate decisions for assessment and intervention that are deemed effective and efficient for a given direct stakeholder" (p. 223).

Golinker (2006) offered a formula for gathering information in order to make evidence-based decisions: BCRE + C/E E + RSP= >> O, where *BCRE* is Best and Current Research Evidence, *C/E E* is Clinical/Educational Expertise, *RSP* is Relevant Stakeholder Perspectives, and *>> O* is Better Approaches to Assessment and Treatment and Better Results (Outcomes). *Best and current research evidence* refers to the research literature that demonstrates that SGDs are valid for the purposes for which they are intended—in most instances, to communicate with others in various contexts at a level and to a degree not occurring without the device. A growing body of data is being collected in this regard, in large part the result of the formation of organizations as the ISAAC and journals such as the *AAC Alternative and Augmentative Communication*.

As shown in Table 5.2, speech/language pathologists (SLPs) have rules generated by the American Speech-Language-Hearing Association (ASHA) that should be followed when dealing with AAC and SGD users. Golinker argues that, by adhering to the prescribed rules, SLPs can use their clinical/educational expertise to help answer questions raised by their clients that may not be covered by research studies. The Rules of Commitment are guidelines for all to consider when working with people who require specialized speech services. These rules can also be of value as guidelines to individuals who are seeking professionals to provide AAC services.

Relevant stakeholder perspectives involves the primary and secondary communication partners who will interact with the AAC user. Golinker suggests that a Social Network (Blackstone & Hunt Berg, 2002) be compiled to demonstrate that the SGD will play an active role across the user's communication contexts (e.g., with family members, neighbors, or co-workers). Such documentation will help make the case for the need of the SGD.

To conclude, efficacy for AAC use involves more than simply compiling a database of existing research. Efficacy also involves the input of a qualified professional and communication networks (i.e., compilation of communication partners). With these three components in place, the likelihood for obtaining funding for the SGDs is likely to improve dramatically (Golinker, 2006).

Table 5.2 AAC Rules of Commitment

Compliance with the following rules will distinguish those who hold in the highest regard the interests of the individual who relies on AAC.

Rule 1: Be committed to the most effective communication system for the individual being served.

The AAC assessment may be the single most important event in the life of a person who relies on AAC. Where that person goes in life will be influenced by communication effectiveness.

Rule 2: Be committed to following your professional code of ethics.

All members of the team must not only agree, but also be motivated to provide the system and services that result in the highest level of personal achievement. In addition, the team must be working toward helping the child develop communicative competence that results in a

Table 5.2 *(Continued)*

spontaneous, interactive exchange of information, feelings, and thoughts. Parents should be asking team members how their educational plan and recommendations are going to help their child communicate effectively.

Rule 3: Be committed to involving the consumer and family in the service delivery process.

Children and parents have rights to assistive technology under the Individuals with Disabilities Education Act (IDEA). Family involvement in the Individualized Education Plan (IEP) process should be motivated by what is best for the child. Parents may need to remind team members that the reason for all these procedures is because of their child. A Consumer-Centered Service Delivery model places the team members and processes in proper perspective. The consumer and family are the focal point, and parents may even decide to request outside supports. Each person on the team has a contributing role in achieving the identified outcomes. Outcomes are influenced by the environment. Defining the roles and responsibilities of the individual team members in this model can have a positive influence on Rule 4.

Rule 4: Be committed to achieving the maximum outcomes for the individual.

Stakeholders are those with an interest in the outcomes of the process. Stakeholders in the AAC service delivery process include the service delivery team and others, including administrators, funding agencies, and so on. Parents need to realize that because of different roles and responsibilities, some stakeholders are vested in achieving different outcomes. Clinicians and therapists tend to be more concerned with outcomes related to clinical results and functional status, whereas administrators and funding agencies will be more concerned with best use of staff time and cost effectiveness for service delivery. Consumers and family members have concerns connected to quality of life and satisfaction issues. Acknowledging differing interests can help teams reach a better understanding of contrasting positions and swifter resolutions to any disagreements.

Rule 5: Be committed to advocating for language.

If the team agrees on the central goal of AAC as being the highest possible personal achievement, then language becomes the focus of assessment and intervention. Unfortunately, many AAC strategies and programs focus on modifying behaviors, such as providing for classroom vocabulary, rather than real communication. The technology is used to promote responses to environmental cues and the child is limited to activating scripted messages. Little language learning is possible when no provisions are made to explore and create self-generated utterances. Parents need to ask questions about the ability of the language representation method and technology to facilitate language acquisition and growth and not just foster routine behaviors and compliance to tasks. A sure sign of a behavior focus to therapy is the prevalence of nouns, colors, and other words that would be considered extended vocabulary. The mastery of basic core vocabulary words should precede the introduction of vocabulary specific to daily activities and academic subjects.

Rule 6: Understand the merits of ALL language representation methods.

The three commonly used language representation methods are single-meaning pictures, spelling, and semantic compaction. The outcome an individual who relies on AAC is able to achieve depends heavily on the language representation method(s) being used. Ease of use at first encounter may not be most effective in the long run.

Single-meaning pictures involve the use of graphic or line drawn symbols to represent single word vocabulary or messages (phrases, sentences, and paragraphs). Reading skills are

(continued)

Table 5.2 *(Continued)*

generally not required for using this method. However, recognition of symbols (especially abstract concepts) is facilitated by the presence of words associated with the symbols. These words, however, are useless and possibly distracting for anyone who cannot read. By the very nature of the system, a large vocabulary also requires a large symbol set. Consequently, having quick access to any symbol can become an issue for augmented communicators needing more than just a very limited number of words or messages.

Spelling, sometimes referred to as traditional orthography, involves the use of the alphabet. Generally, spelling and reading skills are required. Although the symbol set is small, spelling letter by letter is a slow and inefficient AAC strategy. Acceleration techniques such as abbreviation systems and word prediction are commonly used with spelling to reduce the number of keystrokes. However, disadvantages in increasing the memory and reading demands for these acceleration techniques can outweigh any advantages. Research has shown that word prediction is no faster than spelling.

Semantic compaction or "Minspeak" involves the use of a relatively small set of multi-meaning icons that do not require spelling and reading skills. The specific meaning of each icon is a function of the context in which it is used. Minspeak is perhaps the most commonly used AAC language representation method, because of its ability to handle both vocabulary and rules of grammar and support the notion of a core and extended vocabulary.

Rule 7: Support the language representation method(s) for core and extended vocabulary access that best serve the interest of the individual.

Vocabulary selection and organization has been one of the most widely researched topics in AAC. Access to a vocabulary based on the notion of core and extended categories is more important than vocabulary frequency lists to support vocabulary selection. The vast majority (approximately 85 percent) of what we say in daily situations consists of a few hundred core words. Most of these core words are determiners, verbs, adjectives, prepositions, indefinite pronouns, and the like. They are not familiar nouns typically associated with given activities or situations. Rather, situation-specific nouns would be considered extended, or fringe, vocabulary.

Rule 8: Advocate for the AAC system that supports the chosen language representation method(s).

Most individuals reaching the goal of AAC are using multiple language representation methods with the AAC system. Observation of their achievement indicates the use of semantic compaction for core vocabulary access and spelling for extended vocabulary words. Single-meaning pictures appear to have limited use for when the individual only requires access to a small core vocabulary set or for access to extended vocabulary when the individual cannot spell.

Rule 9: Be committed to using language activity monitoring to support clinical intervention.

The most useful and beneficial information on which to base decisions regarding educational and clinical AAC services are analyzed performance data (language samples taken from natural settings). This is done by using automated language activity monitoring, a procedure that is relatively new to the field of AAC. Tools to facilitate the collection and analysis of language samples for individuals who use AAC devices are just now being developed. Use of language activity monitoring will provide team members with detailed information from spontaneous language samples to measure changes in communicative performance. An objective, realistic record of how the child is using technology in different settings will soon be possible. Easy comparisons between vocabulary use, amount of communication, and methods used can be made over time and across activities.

Rule 10: If unable to adhere to any of these guidelines, be truthful about it to the individual, family, and advocates.

If parents are in doubt regarding the commitment of a team member, they must feel empowered to question the continued participation of that member on the team. Not every professional will have the same level of commitment, motivation, and willingness to learn new technologies and strategies. Rule 10 provides an opportunity for any team member to express discomfort with what is being expected of him or her. It also provides for disclosure of being "between a rock and a hard place" relative to making recommendations that may be contrary to administrative directives, such as "Don't write that into the IEP, or the school will have to buy it."

Source: Reprinted with permission from AAC Institute (http://www.aacinstitute.org).

SUMMARY

This chapter provided a very brief introduction to AAC systems. AAC systems were defined, and aided and unaided communication was discussed. Unaided communication systems discussed included sign languages, educational sign systems, and gestural language codes. We then introduced the two common selection techniques used with aided communication systems: direct selection and scanning. We concluded the chapter by discussing the differences between nonelectronic and electronic systems.

Because of the importance of communication, the value of AAC systems for those who need them cannot be overstated. Nor can the need for trained and dedicated professionals to work in and support the field of AAC.

SCENARIOS APPLICATIONS

Scenario 5.1

Think about the role of communication partners. What traits do you find pleasing and annoying in your communication partners? What attributes make for effective communication partners? How might these traits inhibit effective communication when conversing with individuals who have severe speech problems? How might these problems be overcome?

Scenario 5.2

Think about the factors that should be considered when selecting the various features (e.g., levels of abstraction, size) of AAC symbol systems. Then conduct an Internet search using the keywords "augmentative communication." Look for discussions about the factors. Which considerations did you identify that are found in the Internet discussions? Which ones did you come up with that were not mentioned? How could you validate your considerations?

Scenario 5.3

Create your own communication book. Consider first the person who would use the book. Then select a communication context that would likely be encountered by that person. Script a conversation that would take place between communication partners in the identified context.

Then look through magazines to find pictures that could be used to represent vocabulary and phrases that would be used during the conversation. Cut out the pictures and paste them onto a communication book. Then share your work with others and attempt to carry on a conversation using your book. What situations do you presume will be encountered as a result of the conversation? When the conversation is completed, were your presumptions correct or incorrect? What situations did you encounter that were unexpected?

For Discussion

1. What are the components of language, and what is their role in language development?
2. What are the purposes of unaided and aided AAC devices?
3. How do the components of AAC systems relate to individuals with severe speech problems to provide them opportunities to communicate daily across environments?
4. How might you go about identifying strengths and weaknesses across language components? Of what value would your findings be when considering whether AAC systems would be beneficial?
5. How might you approach parents of a young child and discuss the need for an AAC system and the benefits such systems offer? If the parent questioned whether AAC systems might actually stunt language growth, how might you respond?
6. Many people with severe speech problems also have motor difficulties. How might these motor problems interfere with the use of AAC systems, and how can those systems be adapted to foster effective communication?
7. Imagine that it is the year 2100. Describe the perfect AAC system and how it would be incorporated into the life of a person with severe motor, cognitive, and speech problems.
8. Select several devices described in the O'Reilly's Personal Perspective in terms of individuals who might benefit most from them for communication—think person–feature match.

References

Alvares, R., & Sternberg, L. (1994). Communication and language development. In L. Sternberg (Ed.), *Individuals with profound disabilities* (3rd ed., pp. 193–229). Austin, TX: Pro-Ed.

Angelo, J. (1997). *Assistive technology for rehabilitation therapists.* Philadelphia: E. A. Davis.

ASHA. (2011). Augmentative and alternative communication (AAC). Retrieved March 23, 2011, from http://www.asha.org/public/speech/disorders/AAC.htm

Banajee, M., Dicarlo, C., & Stricklin, B. (2003). Core vocabulary determination for toddlers. *Augmentative and Alternative Communication, 21*, 67–73.

Beukelman, D., Jones, R., & Rowan, M. (1989). Frequency of word usage by nondisabled peers in integrated preschool classrooms. *Augmentative and Alternative Communications, 5*, 243–248.

Blackstone, S. W., & Hunt Berg, M. (2002). *Social networks: An assessment and intervention planning inventory for individuals with complex communication needs and their communication partners (SN).* Monterey, CA: Augmentative Communication.

Brett, A., & Provenzo, Jr., E. F. (1995). *Adaptive technology for special human needs.* Albany: State University of New York Press.

Church, G., & Glennen, S. (1992). *The handbook of assistive technology.* San Diego: Singular.

Dark, L., & Balandin, S. (2007). Prediction and selection of vocabulary for two leisure activities. *Augmentative and Alternative Communication, 23*, 288–299.

Ferm, U., Ahlsén, E. & Björck-Åkesson, E. (2005). Conversational topics between a child with complex communication needs and her caregiver at mealtime. *Augmentative and Alternative Communication, 21* (1), 19–40.

Freedom Center. (1996). *Training program in assistive technology.* Unpublished manuscript.

Golinker, L. (2006). *Evidence based practice: Implications for SGD funding*. Paper presented at the ASHA Annual Convention, Miami Beach, FL. Retrieved March 23, 2011, from http://docs.google.com/viewer?a=v&q=cache:VHjNBOOM6pAJ:www.eshow2000.com/asha/2006/handouts/855_1263Golinker_Lewis_057007_111206055142.ppt+Golinker,+L.+(2006).+Evidence+based+practice:+Implications+for+SGD+funding&hl=en&gl=us&pid=bl&srcid=ADGEESjb8ewdf9J8xh5QxJCncTVasmJd5oFP_dTCMbNsNfn66GGv3zfrCDfydVrvKJlSZLk1-b2Til4tcSr3U6Qy7VtVOzsNWVrQRMkjYjAQqAYmRBrt5utDJMotf0zV0d7Pja5uQEJ5&sig=AHIEtbRztkfgPLQDh5nAKKhofovJMNhOlQ&pli=1

Heward, W. L. (2000). *Exceptional children* (6th ed.). Upper Saddle River, NJ: Merrill/Pearson Education.

Karlan, G. R., & Lloyd, L. L. (1983). Considerations in the planning of intervention: Selecting a lexicon. *Journal of the Association for Persons with Severe Handicaps, 8*, 13–25.

Liu, C., & Sloane, Z. (2006). Developing a core vocabulary for a Mandarin Chinese AAC system using word frequency data. *International Journal of Computer Processing of Oriental Languages, 4,* 285–300.

Lloyd, L. L., Fuller, D. R., & Arvidson, H. H. (1997). *Augmentative and alternative communication: A handbook of principles and practices.* Boston: Allyn & Bacon.

Marvin, C. A., Beukelman, D. R., & Bilyeu, D. (1994). Vocabulary-use patterns in preschool children: Effects of context and time sampling. *Augmentative and Alternative Communication, 10*(4), 224–236.

Musselwhite, C. R., & St. Louis, K. W. (1988). *Communication programming for persons with severe handicaps.* Austin, TX: Pro-Ed.

Schlosser, R., & Raghavendra, P. (2003). *The efficacy of augmentative and alternative communication: Toward evidence based practice.* San Diego, CA: Academic Press.

Shane, H. C., & Sauer, M. (1986). *Augmentative and alternative communication.* Austin, TX: Pro-Ed.

Woodward, J. (1978). Historical bases of American Sign Language. In P. Siple (Ed.), *Understanding language through sign language research* (pp. 333–347). New York: Academic Press.

6 ASSISTIVE TECHNOLOGY DEVICES TO ENHANCE ACCESS TO INFORMATION

Chapter at a Glance

Objectives

1. Describe switches and scanning and provide examples of when they can be used.
2. Describe the features of input and output devices and explain considerations for selecting the devices to meet individual needs.
3. Explain the telecommunication issues encountered by individuals with disabilities and the possible solutions for these issues.
4. Describe assistive technology adaptations to promote access to information presented orally and in print.

MAKING CONNECTIONS

Think about the technology tools you access on a regular basis, such as computers, fax machines, voice mail, Internet, electronic media, calculators, cell phones, DVDs, DVR-TiVo®, and so forth. These tools provide you with a variety of information on a daily basis, enrich your life, keep you informed, help you communicate, promote independence, and provide information for decision-making purposes. Now, identify ways in which your life would be changed if access to these devices were not possible.

In this information, electronic, media-driven age, having access to information is critical and empowering. In this chapter, we discuss ways to promote access to information for people with different disabilities. We discuss information access by (a) providing an introduction to information access, (b) discussing switches and scanning as vehicles to enhance access, (c) describing ways to foster computer access, (d) describing some of the latest devices in the telecommunication field, and (e) describing ways to promote access to oral (listening) and written (print) information.

INTRODUCTION TO INFORMATION ACCESS

We live in a technological society where the ability to access information in multiple formats, such as print, computers, and the Internet, is critical to becoming and remaining an informed citizen. Beginning in the early years, children need to learn how to use the devices that provide access to our information-rich society. This knowledge of devices needs to be reinforced by educators and families as children and youth mature. As adults, individuals with disabilities must continue to be able to access the devices that promote independence, keep them informed, and enable them to contribute to and participate in society. There are many ways individuals can access information, including computers, telecommunication, listening, and print material. Each of these has unique features and requires individuals to possess specific requisite abilities to be able to access them. The purpose of this chapter is to present information about how individuals can access information that is conveyed through computers, telecommunications, orally, and in print. We begin by presenting Sam's Personal Perspective 6.1 to provide the reader information about how and why a postsecondary student depends on technology.

PERSONAL PERSPECTIVE 6.1

My name is Sam and I'm 19 years old. I went to Eastland High School and I'm currently attending the University of New Mexico. I enjoy watching movies and playing video games as well as going out with friends. I have just finished my freshman year. It was really good as far as the classes went. I didn't know if I would make friends but I did and technology helped me to do that. I have Asperger's which is a form of Autism. I don't like to point that out but since you are writing about people with disabilities, you need to know that about me. I have always done well in school but I have often had trouble making and keeping friends. I have some ways of making sure that I stay on track with my friends so that I don't seem too different. Still, I know that I come across as shy and sometimes it takes me a couple of seconds to say what I think. Most people think that maybe I don't know what I am talking about but I am usually just making sure of my answer before I say something.

Tell the Readers About the Device(s) You Use

I'm pretty well versed in technology, I use e-mail to communicate with my teachers and I mostly use Microsoft Word to type all my papers. I really like courses were the teachers use WebCT and regularly post their notes, announcements, and study guides online. I don't have to use any kind of real intense assistive technology because I speak well and I communicate in writing without any problems. I am lucky that I got started using technology back in elementary school or maybe even before that because I liked the games. Using the technology seems really natural to me but it also helps me be like one of the crowd. When I use technology to communicate, then nobody, including my professors sees me as different. I like that a lot. I use IM (instant messaging) more than I do the phone because I can get down in writing what I want to say faster than I can say it. Also, everybody does it!

Another technology that I use is the *ITouch*. I have my favorite songs loaded on there and it helps me to block out noise in the library, dorm, or student center. Sometimes, I use it as a calming device, sometimes just for fun, and other times to get me going. It depends on the music, of course. But I do think that it helps me to block out sensory stuff that irritates me.

One other new thing that I have is a *Kindle*. I buy my textbooks in an electronic version and load them on this device. I can carry it anywhere so that I can study or read when I feel like it. Not all my textbooks came this way but it has been great to have it. I have really benefitted from the

(*continued*)

opportunity to seek out places to study without having to drag tons of textbooks. It gives me freedom to select an environment that helps me be my best.

Why Do You Use These Devices?

I use many of these technologies because they help me communicate better with my teachers. E-mailing them helps me better understand what the teacher expects on certain assignments and WebCT helps me know what to expect on any tests coming up. WebCT notes and announcements help me when I miss class to catch up with the material.

The *ITouch* lets me regulate my environment a little more. I can have my ear buds in and people are not upset when I just smile and wave. I can choose when to interact and when to keep to myself. Also, the music helps me to adjust my environment to my needs. Sometimes I can handle certain things in the environment and other days, those things bother me. It gives me a feeling of control.

Kindle is the same sort of thing. When I first went to college, I wasn't sure where I would be able to study. I had been used to a routine with pretty constant surroundings in high school. My family knew what bothered me and they avoided most of those things. At school I had to figure it all out again. Having the *Kindle* allowed me to move through a lot of different spots and figure out where I could actually study. I could have done it without it but the portability of the *Kindle* kind of encouraged me to experiment more.

How Do You Feel About This?

I feel that this technology is great for teaching material and helping students. It lets me be in charge without the world really knowing that I have a disability. Also, because I can control certain things, my disability has less of an impact on me. Also, technology helped me to connect to friends that I probably wouldn't have made face-to-face. We felt a certain comfort level electronically before we had to connect in person.

If You Had a Chance to Tell Teachers About Assistive Technology You Have Used, What Would You Tell Them?

I'd tell teachers, if you have time definitely put your course material and class announcements on WebCT. It really helps students learn better and keep up with classes. I would also tell them that the sooner kids start using a variety of technologies the better. I don't think of them as assistive technology. They are just a part of my everyday life and I'm really good at using them to my benefit. Using a lot of different and readily available technology has been great for helping me to be successful in college.

Source: Reproduced with permission from Psycho-Educational Services.

SWITCHES AND SCANNING

Switches are used to input a signal into a computer, a battery-operated toy, a communication board, an electronic aid to daily living (EADL; see Chapter 8), and so forth. Switches can generate simple responses when an individual pushes the switch to get an action, or more complex responses when multiple switches are used. Some devices, such an electronic communication boards or software, offer many choices from which users can select their response. For example, a communication board may have several food options for the user to select from when indicating that he or she is hungry. Switches are often found in early childhood programs to help students with physical and cognitive challenges to engage in play activities in early childhood programs, at home, and in day care settings. Because the use of switches can promote developmental learning such as cause and effect, social activities such as play, and communication, it is critical that younger children have multiple opportunities to use switches as needed in their learning, social, and home environments.

Scanning is a procedure that draws attention to each item that the user can choose to select (Lewis, 1993). A switch can be pushed to activate the scanning procedure and pushed again when the food item of choice is highlighted. When a switch is used to carry out scanning this is considered to be an *indirect selection method,* meaning that there are several steps involved in inputting a signal and that the individual has to do more than just push a key on a computer (*direct selection method*), for example, to input a signal. Switches and scanning offer individuals with disabilities the ability to manipulate their environment independently and to make choices.

Switches

Questions for decision makers to consider when assessing and choosing switches are included in Table 6.1. Once a switch is selected, users may need time learning how to use the device. Switch instruction should include identifying the switch, activating the switch, and deactivating the switch (Lewis, 1993). For instance, SwitchIt!® Suite (IntelliTools, Inc.) provides four developmental programs to teach the use of switches and to match the user's cognitive and developmental level. Students learn cause-effect, turn taking, concept building, and scanning. Software that helps teachers examine and evaluate how well their students respond to the level of complexity in tasks, the amount of delay in switch activation, and the speed of scanning facilitates more accurate instructional decisional making in selecting appropriate devices to enhance access (see www.synapseadaptive.com/intellitools/newswitchsw.html for illustrations of the SwitchIt! Suite). Characteristics and types of switches are two important topics to think about when selecting switches. To view pictures and product descriptions of multiple types of switches, see www.abledata.com products.

CHARACTERISTICS OF SWITCH DEVICES

Many characteristics must be considered when selecting switches, such as the design of the switch, how a person uses the switch, and how a person receives feedback about the switch's activity. The design of the switch includes its size, the number of activation sites, wireless capability, and the size

Table 6.1 Questions for Decision Makers to Consider When Selecting Switches

Switches
• What devices does the user need to access with a single switch or switch array?
• What are the cognitive, motoric, and sensory abilities of the user?
• What are the best design features for the user?
• What is the best way for the user to activate and deactivate the switch?
• What effort and fatigue factors are involved in using the switches?
• What is an appropriate type of feedback (visual, auditory) for the user?
• Can the user operate a switch and scanning setup?

FIGURE 6.1 Jelly Bean Switch
Source: Courtesy of AbleNet, Inc.

of the sites. For example, a large switch, such as the Jelly Bean® switch (see Figure 6.1), has a 2½-inch activation site to be pushed. This design is particularly effective for users who have limited range of motion and who need a device with a large surface for interaction purposes.

A joystick, on the other hand, has a switch array (activation choices include up, down, left, right) with multiple activation sites. This design requires that the user grasp and manipulate the joystick to activate different sites that have distinctive movements. The user needs to have enough range of motion to activate the different choices and an ability to grasp the joystick and maintain control (Cook & Hussey, 2002).

Switches can be designed for operation in several ways including momentary, latched, and timed activation. *Momentary* operation means that the switch is activated for as long as the user presses the switch. *Latched* operation means that the user presses the switch to turn it on and presses it again to turn it off. Finally, *timed* operation means that the switch can be programmed (using a timer) to stay on for a set period of time and will turn itself off when the time runs out.

There are several ways switches can be used including activation, deactivation, and effort. Switches can be activated using movement, respiration, and phonation (Cook & Hussey, 2002). *Movement* activation can occur with the head, arms, legs, and eyes and can occur mechanically or electrically. Mechanical activation of switches, which uses force, is the most common type of switch activation; these are sometimes called "push switches." Electric activation of switches is based on electrical signals in the body, such as electrodes near the eyes that measure eye movements (Cook & Hussey, 2002). Electromagnetic (light or radio waves) and proximity (heat-sensitive) activation of switches does not require direct body contact. A head-mounted light pointer and remote control are examples of electromagnetic switches. *Respiration* involves breathing where individuals use the breathing actions of inhaling and exhaling to activate the switch. Individuals who do not have fine- and gross-motor control, such as those with quadriplegia, may find this option appropriate for their needs and abilities. *Phonation* activation involves the use of the voice or sound. Voice recognition is a good example of phonation activation (see the Input section of this chapter).

Just as switches need to be activated, users must also be able to release or deactivate them. Like mechanical activation, deactivation also involves the use of force. Therefore, an individual's ability to use force to activate and deactivate switches must be examined. Finally, the amount of effort needed to activate and deactivate switches is a critical component of switch use. Whether it is the use of the head, arm, leg, or hand; the use of inhalation and exhalation; or the use of articulation and loudness, the amount of effort must be considered. Also, the link between effort and fatigue must be considered. If a switch requires a great deal of effort and tires the user quickly, then the usefulness of the switch across time, environments, and tasks is questionable.

In order to know that the activation and deactivation of the switch was successful, the user must receive some type of feedback. For example, an auditory click or response (voice output) tells the user that the switch was depressed successfully. Visually, an action, as with cause-effect software or turning a lamp on or off, provides feedback that the signal was received.

TYPES OF SWITCHES

There are many types of switches available to match the needs of users. Cook and Hussey (2002) identified six types of single-switch options: the paddle switch, which can be activated by body movement; the wobble (provides auditory feedback) and leaf switches, which can be activated by body movement in two directions; level switches, which are much like wobble switches but move in only one direction; pneumatic switches, which involve sips and puffs; and pillow switches, which respond when pushed. Switches can be used singly, or several can be plugged into a switch interface. For example, Macintosh Switch Interface (Don Johnston—see www.donjohnston.com) and DJ PC Switch Interface (Don Johnston) offer multiple switch access for computer use. Switches and the devices to which they will be attached should be examined to determine the type of adapter that will be necessary to link the switch to the device. Cordless switches eliminate the need for adapters but usually have to be directed toward the control panel.

Scanning

Questions for decision makers to consider when assessing and choosing scanning options are included in Table 6.2 (Church & Glennen, 1992). Individuals should receive training if the scanning procedure selected. For examples of switch scanning, see www.synapseadaptive.com/augcom/gus/switch.htm. This site offers an explanation of how a switch is hooked up to a computer and how the scanning feature works. Scanning formats and scanning techniques must be considered when selecting a scanning procedure.

SCANNING FORMATS

Scanning formats generally involve a visual display presented in some sequential manner. The user activates a switch when the scanning procedure highlights his or her choice; thus, multiple

Table 6.2 Questions for Decision Makers to Consider When Examining Scanning Options

Scanning
• Does the user possess the cognitive, sensory, and motor abilities to access scanning formats and techniques?
• What tasks will require scanning?
• What format is best suited for the user?
• What technique is best suited for the user?
• What type of switch will be used with the scanning procedure?

options for a task can be provided from which the user chooses. For instance, a child views four types of toys, each in its own box on a computer screen. The scanning procedure moves from left to right, sequentially highlighting each box as it goes along. The child pushes the switch when the box containing the preferred toy is highlighted. In another example, a student might be working on sound/symbol identification. Several pictures of objects with the same beginning sound and one object with a different sound are displayed in a linear format. The student's task is to activate the switch when the object with the different beginning sound is highlighted.

There are several types of scanning formats; selection of the type should match the user's needs and abilities and the amount of items and information that needs to be addressed. *Linear scanning* involves the vertical or horizontal arrangement of arrays with items to be scanned. The scanning procedure moves left to right or top to bottom, scanning items one at a time, and the user activates the item of choice when it is highlighted. *Rotary scanning* involves the presentation of the items in a circle where again items are scanned one at a time.

To increase the number of items that can be scanned, and thus the information that the user can access, *group-item scanning* can be used. Several items are presented in a group; the groups are scanned sequentially. The user selects the group with the item. The scanning continues of the items in the group until the user selects the specific item. For example, there are three groups: food, school, and recreation. The user selects food. Under food, specific food choices are available, such as French fries or milk. The user selects the specific desired food. In *row-column scanning*, each row is illuminated. The row with the item is selected; each column in the row is illuminated until the user selects the desired item (Cook & Hussey, 2002). For instance, three rows are presented containing letters of the alphabet. The row in which the desired letter is located is selected, then the column in which the letter is located is selected.

SCANNING TECHNIQUES

There are three types of scanning techniques: automatic scanning, step scanning, and inverse scanning. Each type's features must be considered carefully to match the needs of the user. *Automatic scanning* involves scanning items continuously at an established rate, which can be increased or decreased, until the user activates the switch on the desired item. This technique requires the ability to track and attend and requires a certain level of cognitive ability (Cook & Hussey, 2002). *Step scanning* requires the user to activate the switch through each item. The user controls the rate of scanning, and switch activation to select the item or a timing device is triggered to accept the choice. The user must be able to exert sufficient effort to use this technique and not be highly susceptible to a fatigue factor. *Inverse scanning* requires the user to hold down the switch and release it when the item of choice is illuminated. The user must be able to activate the switch for a period of time and have the motor control to release it at the time the item needs to be selected.

COMPUTER ACCESS

Conventional computer access involves using the hard drive, a standard keyboard, and a mouse or touch pad to input information, and a monitor or screen for information output. For individuals with different types of disabilities—such as physical, cognitive, sensory, and communicative—standard input and/or output devices may require modification to promote access and independence. There are many types of computer adaptations that can be identified, depending on the individual needs of users and their purposes for using computers. With the current versions of operating systems for the PC (e.g., Windows® 7, Windows Vista) and for the Mac (e.g., Mac OS X, Mac OS X Snow Leopard; see www.apple.com/accessibility), Web browsers (e.g., Internet Explorer 8, Safari, Firefox), and word processing software (e.g., Office 2007), great strides have been achieved in providing free accessible features across platforms. For example, Microsoft® has a designated site that focuses on accessible input and output features. The Web site, at www.microsoft.com/enable, comes equipped with tutorials and demos to help users better understand how to program their computers to meet their specific needs. Features include magnification and screen readers (e.g., VoiceOver for Mac OS X Snow Leopard) reference tools (e.g., talking dictionary, spell checking, word prediction), touch screen capabilities (On-Screen Keyboard Windows 7), and speech recognition. The reader is referred to the Microsoft Web site to view examples of free, accessible technology.

Input Devices

STANDARD KEYBOARDS

The keyboard that comes with a computer is often called the standard keyboard. When considering adaptations for keyboards to best suit the needs of the user, sometimes starting with standard keyboard adaptations may make sense because they are a simple solution to a possible access issue. Access utilities software can help to facilitate the use of standard keyboards. Access utility software provides visual or auditory cues, and simplifies keyboard operation for individuals who need to increase or decrease keystrokes, who cannot depress more than one key simultaneously, or who may unintentionally strike keys.

Changing the keyboard layout is another adaptation that can be used to facilitate access. The standard keyboard consists of a format, called QWERTY, that was designed many years ago when typewriters were common. The layout of the manual typewriter, and subsequent keyboard, was intended to reduce the jamming of keys that were used frequently. Another keyboard layout, Dvorak, has gained acceptance because the most frequently used keys are on the home row. This layout supposedly limits fatigue for users. Also, there are Dvorak layouts for people who type with only one hand. Finally, alphabetically arranged keys are another type of keyboard layout, which makes sense for individuals who use communication boards with a similar layout. Questions to consider for assessing the needs of the user and determining a good match with the features of standard keyboards are listed in Table 6.3 (Alliance for Technology Access, 2001; Cook & Hussey, 2002).

Table 6.3 Questions for Decision Makers to Consider for Access to Keyboards

Standard Keyboards and Keyboard Additions

- What size keyboard would be most beneficial to meet the needs of the user?
- What size keys would be most beneficial to meet the needs of the user?
- How much pressure will be required to depress the keys?
- How much space between keys would be most beneficial to meet the needs of the user?
- What adaptations are needed to use two keys simultaneously (e.g., shift and key for capital)?
- Will the user need visual or tactile cues?
- Is moisture in the keyboard area a potential problem?
- Can the user reach and target the keys?
- Can keys be released quickly enough to avoid "key repeat" (repetition of depressed key character: kkkkkkkkkkkk)?

KEYBOARD ADDITIONS

For individuals who can use standard keyboards but need adaptations, key guards and moisture guards are available to augment the keyboard. For example, users who have difficulty with fine motor skills and thus have difficulty selecting keys accurately may benefit from the use of a key guard. Key guards provide more separation between keys for easier input and limit the accidental pressing of keys. Moisture guards are another type of keyboard addition, which can protect the keyboard from spillage and other types of moisture. Finally, using labels to color-code specific keys or to provide a tactile cue can help individuals who might benefit from visual or tactile input (Alliance for Technology Access, 2001). Key guards can be purchased from a variety of vendors including Don Johnston, Inc., IntelliTools, and TASH International Inc. Global Computer Supplies carries moisture guards. Questions to consider for determining possible keyboard additions are listed in Table 6.3 (Alliance for Technology Access, 2001; Cook & Hussey, 2002).

JOYSTICKS, TRACKBALLS, DWELL CLICK, TOUCH SCREENS, AND INTERFACE DEVICES

There are a variety of alternative keyboard input devices, including joysticks, trackballs, touch screens, and interface devices. These devices include features that may be beneficial for individuals who have difficulty controlling fine motor movements voluntarily or who lack upper body control. As with any device, selection should be based on a careful evaluation that examines setting demands, person-specific characteristics, and features of devices.

Joysticks are a popular input device for game machines, such as Nintendo, and are found on wheelchairs to promote mobility; thus, they are readily available. Some joysticks can be plugged into the mouse port, and others require special software for the computer to accept them. Joysticks have stationary bases, which make them different from a standard mouse. Individuals who might benefit from using joysticks should be evaluated to determine if they possess the cognitive ability to control multidirectional movement, can benefit from a stationary device, and have the strength that is needed to operate some joysticks.

Trackballs, which replace the mouse and work with keyboards, are alternatives to the conventional mouse and consist of a stationary platform with a movable ball. Some trackballs include the ability to drag and click-lock to minimize hand movements and a chording ability to access keyboard features easily.

For hands-free computer access, the dwell click option is yet another type of device that can be used for input purposes. Through specialized software, individuals can enable dwell clicking that allows access to a standard keyboard or mouse. For individuals who use a head pointer or blinking as their means for accessing the keyboard, the dwell click option is one possible alterative for them. There are different types of software depending on the user's strengths and limitations. For examples of software, the reader is referred to www.naturalpoint.com and www.eyetechds.com.

A touch screen (see Figure 6.2) is a device that is placed on the computer monitor and permits direct selection by merely touching the screen. The touch screen is appropriate for individuals who require a simple input device. Depending on the touch screen, it can be used with switch software or on-screen keyboards (Alliance for Technology Access, 2001).

Interface devices provide the use of switches, alternate keyboards, and other input devices, such as joysticks and speech synthesizers, to access the keyboard and keyboard functions (Alliance for Technology Access, 2001). Interface devices can make communication boards accessible by a switch or alternate keyboard, connect a switch to a computer with scanning options, and permit multiple input devices to be connected, such as several switches, that can activate keyboard functions. The reader is referred to www.abledata.com to view pictures of different types of input devices.

FIGURE 6.2 Touch Screen
Source: Courtesy of KEYTEC, INC., www.magictouch.com.

POINTING DEVICES

Pointing devices, which can be used for direct selection access, are an option for individuals who need an alternative to the mouse and keyboard to input information into the computer because of limited or lack of functional movement of their arms and hands.

An example of a pointer is shown in Figure 6.3, TrackerPro, which takes the place of a mouse for people with little or no hand movement. When combined with a small dot that is attached to a person's forehead, glasses, or the rim of a hat, users are able to access their computer in the same way a conventional mouse provides access.

Pointing devices also can be used to access switches, which can activate a variety of devices including computers, toys, and environmental control units. Pointing devices, including mouth sticks, handpointers, infrared pointing systems, eye gaze systems, and head pointers, have different access options including wires, remote control, and switch control. Both mouth sticks and head pointers require head and neck movements; oral-motor control is an additional requirement to use a mouth stick effectively (Cook & Hussey, 2002). The slant and position of the keyboard must be considered so that the user can reach the keyboard comfortably. Also, games that initially provide large target surfaces that are easier to access can be used to teach the individual how to use the pointing device (Angelo, 1997).

Electronic eye gaze systems can be used by people with physical disabilities to access computers. The user looks at control keys that are displayed on a computer for speech synthesis, typing, and operating computer software. When connected to an environmental control system, eye gaze devices can be used to turn on and off lights, use a telephone, and so forth.

ALTERNATE KEYBOARDS

For users who cannot access a standard keyboard even with access utilities software and keyboard additions, an alternate keyboard might be an appropriate option. Alternate keyboards

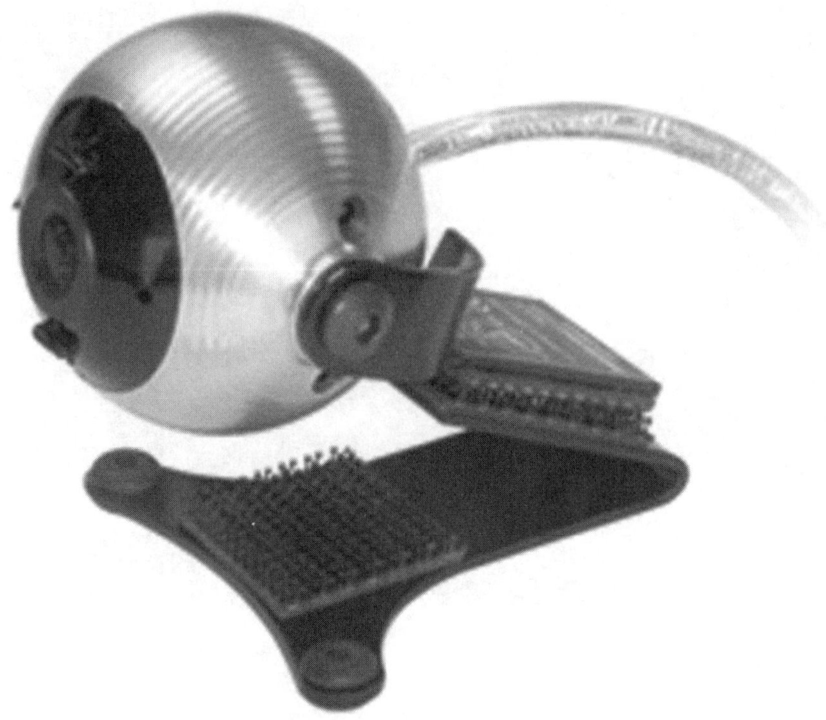

FIGURE 6.3 TrackerPro
Source: Courtesy of Madentec Limited.

consist of keys or switches that replace or add to the traditional keyboard. Keyboards are reduced or enlarged to address access issues by individuals with motor problems, physical disabilities, and so forth (Church & Glennen, 1992). Alternate keyboards include mini-keyboards, on-screen keyboards, and programmable keyboards. Mini-keyboards are characterized by a small surface that requires less range of motion and touch to access the keys. Users may find this type of keyboard less tiring and may be able to benefit from a smaller access area. Individuals who use head pointers, for example, might be able to benefit from these features. TASH International Inc. makes a WinMini keyboard that plugs directly into a PC. This alternate keyboard includes functions for both the mouse and keyboard including adjustments for response rate, key repeat rate, mouse tracking speed, and auditory feedback. The keyboard layout comes in two versions: frequency-of-use and QWERTY. Notably, USB has become the standard connection method for connecting peripherals to different computer platforms. This feature makes compatibility of devices across platforms much more available and "user friendly."

On-screen keyboards provide access for individuals who need to bypass the physical demands of conventional computer input, such as the standard keyboard. Input device options, such as a trackball, touch screen, or mouse, can be used depending on the individual's needs to select words or letters directly on the screen. Some alternate keyboards have scanning options (Alliance for Technology Access, 2001). The on-screen keyboards offer a variety of options depending on the cognitive level of the user and the skills being taught.

Programmable keyboards are enlarged keyboards with wide-spaced keys that connect to the computer and allow easier access for individuals with limited motor control. Programmable keyboards can be used across environments, such as different classrooms, and some can be mounted to laptop computers as well. IntelliKeys® (IntelliTools) comes with six standard overlays that are ready to use with any word processing program or software that has keyboard input. Standard overlays consist of large, well-spaced keys in bright colors so that students can locate letters and numbers easily. Settings can be customized with a special set-up overlay to control the response or repeat rate for students who press unwanted keys or keep their finger on a key too long. Also, IntelliKeys is a flexible switch interface that works with a wide variety of switch software. IntelliTools offers an Access Pac that includes products for teachers to create and individualize curriculum including IntelliKeys, Overlay Maker®, IntelliPics®, and an auditory feedback component, IntelliTalk II®. The reader is referred to www.intellitools.com to view pictures and descriptions of IntelliTools.

VOICE RECOGNITION

For individuals who have physical disabilities and have difficulty accessing the keyboard, voice or speech recognition systems are a good alternate input device. Also, voice recognition may be helpful for some individuals with learning disabilities whose oral language exceeds their written language abilities (King & Rental, 1981). Voice recognition can be used to navigate wheelchairs and operate environmental control units.

Voice recognition systems allow the user to operate the computer by speaking to it. There are two basic systems. The *speaker-dependent system* means that the individual trains the system to recognize his or her voice. The more the voice recognition system is used, the better able it is to understand what the user is saying. The main problem with this system is that sometimes the system does not recognize the speaker's voice because the speaker may have different intonation or pitch, or background noise may interfere with reception. However, this technology is rapidly improving and is beneficial for people who depend on speech recognition as their mode of input. The *speaker-independent system* recognizes a variety of speech patterns from different people without training. Unfortunately, sometimes the vocabulary set that is a part of the software is relatively limited (Cook & Hussey, 2002). Voice recognition systems operate with personal computers and include speech recognition hardware (internal board), software, headphones, and a microphone. The individual dictates into the microphone, and the speech is converted into text on the computer screen.

Continuous voice recognition systems (e.g., Dragon NaturallySpeaking® 10.1) allow the user to dictate without pausing between words. For example, Dragon NaturallySpeaking provides support for letter writing, e-mail work, and Internet browsing. Errors can be corrected by voice or keyboard commands. Questions to consider for assessing the needs of the user and determining a good match with the features of voice recognition systems are listed in Table 6.4 (Cook & Hussey, 2002).

Table 6.4 Questions for Decision Makers to Consider for Voice Recognition Systems

Voice Recognition
• Is the individual capable of articulating speech with consistent vocalization?
• Is there an adequate range of vocabulary in the system?
• Will the voice recognition system be affected by background noise?

Output Devices

SCREEN MAGNIFICATION

Screen magnification refers to enlarged character display on the monitor and includes hardware and software options (Church & Glennen, 1992). For individuals with low vision, screen magnification sometimes can be a simple adaptation to promote access to print displayed on the monitor. Regarding hardware options, monitors come in different sizes. Using a large screen monitor (17 inches, for example) is one way to create a larger visual display for easier print access.

Probably the simplest adaptation is to enlarge the print displayed on the screen through the word processing software program: type size (18 point). Large point size may be able to provide sufficient magnification for some individuals depending on their acuity. Specially designed software also can be purchased that offers magnification solutions for individuals with visual impairment such as macular degeneration and glaucoma. For instance, ZoomText 9.1 (Ai Squared) software (Windows platform) includes an integrated magnifier that has 36× magnification, color filtering for contrast, cursor enhancement to locate the cursor quickly, zooming in and out, and a screen reader. There are speech settings for adjusting voice, rate, and pitch. It offers the capability to read documents, including Web pages and e-mail. See www.aisquared.com for a demo of how this software works.

MAGic™ 6.2 (Henter-Joyce, Inc.) screen magnification software contains color support (up to 32-bit) and an extensive array of list boxes for Microsoft Office. These list boxes help the individual call up lists of frames, links, document reformatting, hyperlinks, and more. MAGic 6.2 screen magnification software is designed to be used with the JAWS® (Job Access with Speech; Blazie) screen reading software for Windows (JAW) screen reader software (see later discussion).

SPEECH SYNTHESIS/SCREEN READING

Screen reading software makes possible electronic spoken language output that involves a synthetic or computerized voice output system (i.e., speech synthesizer). This voice output system can consist of an internal board, which includes a chip or circuit board inserted into the computer or external hardware device, which is a portable external device that connects to the computer and comes with a speaker. Most computers today come with speakers to amplify sound. Thus, speech synthesis is helpful for individuals who are blind or who have low vision, who have a mild hearing loss, or who have difficulties with written language, both reading and writing, and can benefit from auditory feedback.

Many software programs now include both visual and auditory feedback. For example, word prediction programs (see Chapter 7, writing section) may include speech output, which reads back a letter, word, line, sentence, paragraph, or "screen" at a time. For some students, hearing what they wrote may help them catch errors in grammar, spelling, and punctuation that might otherwise go undetected. Also, the user can be alerted to problems regarding the coherence and semantic integrity of the document (Bryant, Bryant, & Rieth, 2002).

There are three techniques for producing speech on computers. First, text-to-speech synthesis involves converting letters and letter combinations to speech sounds. The speech sounds rather robotic. Second, digitized speech involves a person recording words into the system, thus producing human-sounding speech (Church & Glennen, 1992). Finally, linear predictive coding (LPC) is also digitized speech but requires a lot more memory than the text-to-speech technique (Lewis, 1993). When selecting speech synthesis as a solution to promote access, decision makers and users should consider audio output and intelligibility. Audio output is affected by the quality of speakers and amplifiers. Although technology continues to improve so that larger equipment does not always mean better sound quality, it is still true that speakers and amplifiers have a certain size and weight that may affect portability and cost. Intelligibility is another consideration. Speech synthesis features a variety of voices, both male and female, and techniques for producing speech (e.g., digitized speech). Individuals must consider not only the quality of audio output but also the intelligibility of speech. If an individual relies on speech synthesis for expressive language (e.g., communication boards) or for a work environment, then the quality of speech may be particularly important. In most cases the speed, pitch, and tone of voice can be set to accommodate individual preferences. The voice quality of speech synthesizers varies considerably from more "human" to more "mechanical" sounding. In some instances, more mechanical-sounding voices may actually be more intelligible to experienced users; they also allow for faster rates of production.

NaturalSoft's Natural Reader is another popular text-to-speech product. This software converts written text in Microsoft Word, PDF files, and e-mails into spoken words or audio files such as MP3 or WAV for iPods and CD players. Voices include Paul (male—American English), Rosa (female—American Spanish), Louise (female—Canadian French), and Reiner (male—German), among others.

There are a variety of screen reading programs on the market. For instance, JAWS (Job Access with Speech; Blazie) is a speech synthesis program for the Windows operating system, Internet Explorer, and Adobe® Acrobat® Reader. JAWS consists of an integrated voice synthesizer and the computer's sound card to output the content using speakers or refreshable Braille displays. JAWS works with e-mail, word processing programs, spreadsheets, and Web browsers. Finally, eReader (Center for Applied Special Technology; CAST) is screen reading software for both the Macintosh and Windows platforms that provides voice output for content from any electronic source (e.g., Web page, word processing). eReader consists of spoken output, visual highlighting, and document navigation. eReader promotes access to electronic text and supports literacy development. Whether they are work- or school-related, tasks that require access to text on screen can be readily accessible for individuals with disabilities to enable people of all ages to interact with current electronic technology.

TELECOMMUNICATION

Telephones

Access to telephone communication is crucial not only to enhance independence and access information but also as a safety device. For individuals with hearing and speech impairments, the Americans with Disabilities Act of 1990 mandated that all states provide public access services or relay services for individuals who are deaf or hard of hearing, or who have speech disabilities. For individuals who are deaf, the text telephone (TTY) is the most common mode of telecommunication services. The TTY, which was formerly called the telecommunication device (TDD), is a device that enables people to send and receive phone calls. A telecommunication relay service (TRS) is required by law in all states and is a free service. The TRS consists of the operator at the relay center reading the typed message from the sender to the person who is receiving the phone call, so the message goes from written to voice form via the operator. The person receiving the message can respond conventionally; the operator then types the message and sends it to the sender, whose TTY translates the message (Smith & Tyler, 2010). Although the telecommunication system provides phone access for people who are deaf, it certainly is not private. Recent developments in technology, for example the voice carry over (VCO), enable individuals to use their voice to communicate their message and still have access to the use of the TTY to receive the printed message.

Cellular telephones, personal digital assistants (PDAs), and the like are transforming personal communications. For people with and without disabilities, they afford an opportunity for portable communications in ways barely imagined only a decade ago. Whether the mobile devices are used as vocal communicators, text messengers, or for Internet access, the tools ensure that the user is "wired" to his or her communication partners and the world (see Personal Perspective 6.2 about the use of text messaging for individuals who have hearing impairments). Recent products have been devised for AAC users to interface their speech generating devices (SGDs) with mobile phones and PDAs. Wireless devices also are available for wheelchair users who communicate with AAC devices to connect with household and mobile phone systems. Given these developments, there is hope that accessibility features will be built into products as communication technologies continue to emerge.

Internet Access

Access to the Internet and the World Wide Web (WWW) is imperative in today's society. Services such as e-mail, e-commerce, electronic-based research, and telecommunication are important tools in daily living activities at home, school, and work across all age groups. As more schools and libraries become wired and businesses rely on the Internet, all individuals will need access to this invaluable resource if they are to compete and interact successfully in today's market. Internet access is increasingly becoming an issue as more people with a variety of needs seek to use this great resource. Particularly, accessibility issues focus on the ability to see the graphics, to hear audio features, to navigate complex and unorganized sites, and to use adaptive technology.

As stipulated in the 1998 Rehabilitation Act Amendments, federal agencies have to make their electronic and information technology accessible to people with disabilities. Section 508 was enacted to eliminate barriers in information technology, to make available new opportunities for people with disabilities, and to encourage development of technologies that will help achieve these goals. The law applies to all federal agencies when they develop, procure, maintain, or use electronic and information technology (Section 508, 29 U.S.C. 794d).

Universal design features focus on the importance of ensuring accessibility. As noted in Chapter 2, universal design for learning means that the instructional activities are accessible and the learning goals are achievable by all people regardless of their ability to read, write, hear, see, speak, comprehend, move, and remember. For example, activities should be designed to be accessible for individuals with sensory impairments, cognitive impairments, and communication difficulties. WWW page design can include universal design features with some thoughtful planning before development. In the area of basic page design, consistent layout, contrasting backgrounds, use of HTML, and large buttons are all examples of ways to make the page accessible to a variety of individual needs. Graphical features also should be considered. Alternative text information should be available for all graphics to indicate that a graphic is present. Providing captions for video and scripting audio can address multimedia features that may be inaccessible for individuals with sensory disabilities. Also, tables and figures, which may be difficult for screen reading software to read accurately, should be used on a limited basis (University of Washington, 1997). Certainly, access to online courses and electronic communication is an area that warrants consideration by instructors when they design their courses and course assignments. Again, Web-accessibility issues must be addressed to ensure that all students have equal access to course content. All students must be able to use this instructional tool effectively.

"Bobby" (CAST) is a Web-based tool that examines pages for accessibility for people with disabilities. Questions about the free service can be directed to bobby@cast.org. Once a site is examined, and depending on the findings, the designer can receive an official seal of approval for prominent display on the Web page. Also, DO-IT (Disabilities, Opportunities, Internetworking, and Technology) at the University of Washington provides a list of Internet resources for accessible Web design (www.washington.edu/doit/Resources/web-design.html). Finally, the National Center for Accessible Media (NCAM) provides guidelines for accessible digital media (http://ncam.wgbh.org/invent_build/web_multimedia/accessible-digital-media-guide). The final section of this chapter focuses on listening and print access issues and devices.

LISTENING AND PRINT ACCESS

In this section, we provide a personal perspective by Tony "Mac" McGregor, who talks about life growing up as a person who is deaf, the challenges he has encountered, and his suggestions for educators (see Personal Perspective 6.2).

Listening Aids

HEARING AIDS

As we all know, hearing aids are small battery-operated devices that amplify sound. Hearing aids can help individuals with hearing loss access oral communication; in some cases, hearing acuity can become within the normal range. Hearing aids are designed to be worn behind the ear, in the ear, or in the canal (Smith & Tyler, 2010). Hearing aids amplify all sound within an environment; therefore, they work best in quieter environments where background noise is minimal. Hearing aids do not necessarily improve the clarity of sounds, and sometimes hearing aids produce noise, such as acoustic feedback.

The cochlear implant, which replaces the cochlea in the ear, is an electronic microprocessor that is surgically placed in the hearing mechanism and helps some individuals who are deaf to receive and understand some sounds (Smith & Tyler, 2010). Since its approval in 1990 by the U.S. Food and Drug Administration, controversy from the Deaf community helped to create a debate about the merits of the cochlear implant in terms of its potential to be the "cure" of deafness and its threat to the existence of the Deaf culture. However, such debate has lessened as people have come to realize that the cochlear implant is not the cure for deafness but is more of an assistance for certain clients and has not caused the demise of Deaf culture.

PERSONAL FREQUENCY-MODULATED TRANSMISSION DEVICE

A frequency-modulated (FM) transmission device or auditory trainer enables students with hearing impairments to listen to their teacher via a student receiver or hearing aid. FM transmission devices consist of two basic components, a wireless transmitter with a microphone and a receiver with a headset or earphone. The speaker (teacher, for example) "wears" the transmitter unit (about 2 × 3 inches), which is easily clipped to a belt or shirt pocket, and the user wears the receiver unit (also about 2 × 3 inches). The microphone is only about 1½ inches long and is easily

PERSONAL PERSPECTIVE 6.2

Tony "Mac" Landon McGregor attended the Regional Day School Program for the Deaf (RDSPD) in Dallas, Texas. At the end of his sophomore year, he took and passed the Gallaudet University entrance exam and received a first-of-a-kind prep-college program diploma (Model Secondary School for the Deaf). He attended Gallaudet for a short time; and then, transferred to The University of Texas at Austin (UT-Austin) in the summer of 1978. At UT-Austin, Tony "Mac" received his B.A., B.F.A., M.Ed., and Ph.D. degrees. He was the first Deaf student to receive four degrees from UT-Austin. During his doctoral studies, he majored in multicultural special education, focusing on art education for children with disabilities. His dissertation focused on the life of a Diné Deaf rug weaver living on the Navajo reservation. In the early 1990s, Tony "Mac" was heavily involved in establishing a national organization for Native American Deaf individuals (now called the Intertribal Deaf Council). For several years, he worked as a resident artist-in-education at the Austin Museum of Art in Austin, Texas. For 30 years, he had been involved in many fine art festivals and shows, marketing his artworks across the United States. Additional information on Tony "Mac's" life and artworks can be found in *Deaf Artists in America: Colonial to Contemporary*, authored by D. M. Sonnenstrahl, Ph.D.

During the 2006–2008 school years, Dr. McGregor taught English and reading, and provided in-class support services to middle and high school Deaf students at the San Marcos Consolidated Independent School District's Regional Day School Program for the Deaf (RDSPD). The following year, he taught Deaf children at North East Independent School District's (NEISD) Garner Middle School in San Antonio, Texas. Now, he teaches at Jackson Middle School in NEISD. One of his ways to give back to the Deaf community is helping Deaf children express their feelings and needs in order to succeed in life as he did.

What Types of Assistive Technology Devices and Services Do You Think Are Important for Individuals Who Are D/Deaf[1] to Be Able to Access Information in their Daily Lives?

Assistive technology devices such as Teletype Devices for the Deaf (TTYs or TDDs), signalling systems (e.g., telephone ring signaller, door knock, or door bell signaller, baby cry signaller, and smoke alarm device with attached strobe light), and televisions with captioned decoders are essential to individuals who are deaf to where they can access information and receive warnings. In most medical, educational, legal, and general settings, American Sign Language (ASL)/Signed English Interpreting services and statewide Relay Interpreting Services (telephone) are of great assistance.

How Can Service Providers (Educators, Speech-Language Therapists, and the Like) Assist School-Age Students Who Are Deaf in Accessing Information in an Educational Setting?

Service providers can assist students with hearing loss in accessing information by setting up a K–12 curriculum that will promote an understanding of what is happening in the real world. Exceptional children's books can also help illustrate how deaf people perform different routines in their daily lives. In addition, educators can invite deaf people to be guest speakers to discuss their use of AT devices and services. It is ideal to start educating children about AT devices and services at the earliest age possible. Many families, including parents who can hear, are not aware of what is available for deaf people; and service providers familiar with Deaf culture and services can help. Also, Deaf and hard-of-hearing teachers are good models for children and can give parents and

[1]D/deaf—Capital "D" indicates affiliation with Deaf culture; lower case "d" refers to deafness (Smith & Tyler, 2010).

others invaluable information about how AT works because they use them in daily life and know what it is like using AT devices.

How Can Service Providers Work More Effectively with Families in Promoting the Use of Assistive Technology to Facilitate Independence?

Service providers such as the Texas Public schools (Special/Deaf Education departments), the Texas School for the Deaf, local social services, and Texas' Department of Assistive and Rehabilitative Services (DARS) can help promote the use of AT to facilitate independence through (1) family involvement, (2) shared resources of AT devices and services within the local community, and (3) home visits. All of these can tell families where AT devices can be obtained and how they operate. Similar service providers are available in other states as well.

What Are Your Experiences with Assistive Technology? How Have Your Experiences Changed, as You Have Gotten Older?

I recall obtaining a large Western Union telephone teletype (TTY) machine at the age of 12. How my family learned about TTY was that my first Deaf teacher, who graduated from Gallaudet University in Washington, DC, told them of its existence. Since then, I have seen many changes in the appearances of TTYs as well as costs over the years. For example, TTYs have become much smaller and cheaper. Also, there is a larger availability of AT devices and more choices are provided. Laws such as the Closed Captioned TV Act of 1993 (requiring TVs to be closed-captioned) and the Telecommunications Act of 1996 (requiring computers and Instant Messaging to be accessible to people with disabilities) have helped the Deaf community.

The Video Relay Interpreting (VRI) and the Video Phone (VP) are the newest AT services for the Deaf and hard-of-hearing people. With these two services, Deaf people can use video capabilities through the computer to communicate with Relay agents who use American Sign Language (ASL). Also, hard-of-hearing people can speak for themselves using voice carry-over while Relay agents can sign what hearing people are saying. To access these services, Deaf people need TV monitors, VRI/VP equipment, computers, and a private cable company that will install and make electronic connections.

Since the early 1990s, most deaf people used regular state-wide relay services, where TTYs relay information to an operator, who will relay the message to the person who can hear. However, that has changed rapidly. More and more Deaf and hard-of-hearing people prefer to use VRI services when they need to talk to hearing people and use the Video Phone (VP) to converse with other deaf people. In the last fifteen years, many technological changes have taken place on a daily basis since VRI and VP technology were invented.

Personally, I do not use TTY or Texas Relay Interpreting Services anymore because it is too time-consuming especially when I am emotional or dealing with a crisis. I prefer to use ASL and use Sorenson Video Relay Interpreting services all the time. I also use a T-Mobile sidekick to phone-text my employers, colleagues, or friends. My Sidekick also has AOL and T-Mobile services for E-mail messaging and Instant Messaging (IM). And, I use the sidekick often when I am travelling.

Today, Deaf and hard-of-hearing people can enjoy going to theatres where films are open-captioned, similar to subtitles for those who do not speak the language used by actors on the screen. Also, there are amplifier systems that hard-of-hearing people can use to hear voices clearly. In addition, many hard-of-hearing or oral deaf people are using Communication Real-time Translation (CART). CART is the instantaneous translation of spoken words into print using a stenotype machine, computer, real-time software, and a projector that displays the text onto a screen. CART equipment is used mostly at large conventions, conferences, and educational classrooms. AT devices and/or technology today are drastically different and much better than what they were 40 years ago.

(continued)

What Are Some Challenges in Your Life as Someone Who Is Deaf in Accessing Information in the Community, School, Recreational and Social Activities, Work, and So Forth?

Deafness made me strong and aggressive. I wanted the same opportunities that hearing children had. When I faced struggles, I always found ways to overcome them. One obstacle I remember in high school was that the school district and day school for the deaf would not let me go to a magnet high school that emphasized studio arts. Interpreting costs for classes at the magnet high school prevented me from going; it was the biggest reason why I decided not to finish high school and move on to Gallaudet University's preparatory program.

Costs of ASL/Signed English interpreting in some situations continue to be a challenge. At UT-Austin, I was lucky not to have problems of obtaining interpreters for my classes; similarly, I did not have this issue when working as a teaching assistant for students who could hear. The interpreters I had were CODAs (children of Deaf adults); they were skilled in ASL and were knowledgeable about Deaf culture. Another challenge was the lack of pay TDDs on campus; thus, it was rather difficult to make phone calls from campus. One year, a group of Deaf students on campus got together with the leadership of Walter Kelley, a doctoral student at the university, and battled the University's administration for the pay TDDs to be placed in different buildings on campus.

Today, more and more Deaf and hard-of-hearing people gain employment because of AT; the public is increasingly aware of deafness and has become more culturally sensitive of Deaf needs. New businesses and companies have emerged to help bridge the gap between the Deaf and hearing worlds. AT is a critical key for Deaf and hard-of-hearing people to maintain and lead successful lives.

Here Is Your Chance to Tell Our Readers Anything Else That You Think Is Important for Them to Know About AT

I think it is extremely important that all children with disabilities, including those who are Deaf and hard-of-hearing, be more computer- and technology-literate to utilize most AT technology devices. Educators, Deaf and hearing alike, should help prepare students for the future. AT is here and we should use it to foster productive, quality lives. For example, as a Deaf educator in my own classroom at the North East ISD, I have a Video Phone (VP) with a TV monitor where I can contact parents or administrators regarding Admission, Review, and Dismissal conferences and student evaluations. My students see me using the VP to communicate with those who can hear and this naturally teaches them how to use one. I usually tell my students: "Anything is possible but they will have to be assertive, meet others to learn something new, and pay attention to what is out there to be able to survive." My favorite motto is "If there is a will, there is a way," written by one of my much-admired Deaf artists, Francisco de Goya of Spain.

Source: Reproduced with permission from Psycho-Educational Services.

clipped to clothing (e.g., tie, lapel). The transmission device allows teachers to move about the classroom and maintain communication with students who have hearing impairments without also having to have full face view for lip-reading (Smith & Tyler, 2010). Like any other assistive technology device, the FM transmission device is not without issues. Specifically, the FM transmitters may have low power output, which potentially could interfere with the ability of individuals to use them in high-noise areas. Also, depending on how the device is connected, it may not be possible to control the volume. On the other hand, using the device, that is, evaluating the use of the device on the user's ability to benefit from classroom instruction, is of paramount importance.

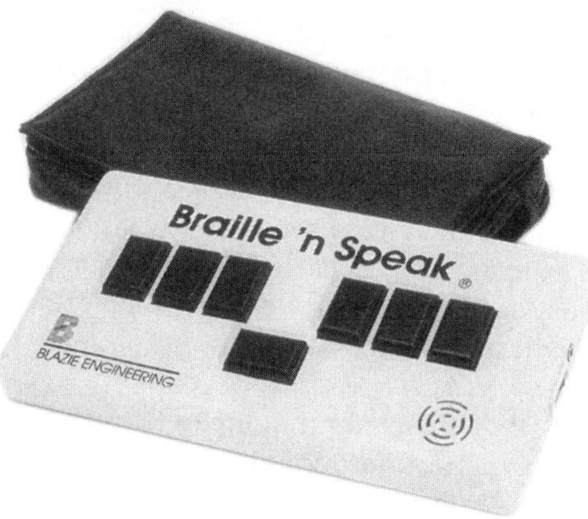

FIGURE 6.4 Braille 'n Speak
Source: Courtesy of Blazie Engineering.

NOTE-TAKERS

Depending on the needs of the individual, there are a variety of note-taking devices from which people can choose to help them take notes efficiently and effectively. For example, abbreviation expansion is a tool that can be used with a word processing program. Users can create their own abbreviations for frequently used words, phrases, or standard pieces of text, thus saving keystrokes. For example, a student in a science class who has to frequently type out "photosynthesis" in taking notes might create the abbreviation "ph." The user types in the abbreviation (e.g., "ph"), presses the spacebar on the keyboard (or, depending on the particular program, points and clicks), and the abbreviation is expanded (e.g., "photosynthesis"). Abbreviations are recorded easily by executing a few simple commands and may be saved from one writing session to another. Abbreviation expansion is an important part of many word processing programs and is available as "memory-resident add-on" programs, operating simultaneously with the word processing program.

The Braille 'n Speak (Blazie Engineering; see Figure 6.4) is another note taking tool that can be used by individuals with visual impairments. It operates using refreshable Braille cells, which are an alternative format to the embossed paper used with conventional Braille. The individual inputs information in Braille, and the information is stored electronically. It can be transferred to a computer for editing purposes or read back by screen reading software. Voice output is also included in Braille note-takers.

Print Aids

As discussed in Chapter 1, IDEA (34 CFR §300.172, §300.210; Section 300.172, Final Regulations of IDEA 2004) includes provisions that require state and local education agencies (SEAs and LEAs) to ensure that all students with disabilities can access the general education curriculum, which includes textbooks and core instructional materials (i.e., accessible instructional materials [AIM]). SEAs are required to adopt the National Instructional Materials Accessibility Standard (NIMAS) to ensure that students with print disabilities can access print materials. As part of the legislation, print must be presented in specialized formats to accommodate the different types of print disabilities; formats include Braille, large print, audio, and digital text. Descriptions of aids that fulfill the intent of this legislation are discussed in the following sections.

MAGNIFICATION AIDS

Magnification aids focus on size, spacing, and contrast. Magnification aids range from simple to more complex and include optical aids, nonoptical aids, and electronic aids (Cook & Hussey, 2002). Because more than 90% of people with visual impairments have some degree of usable vision, optical aids can be used to promote access (Cook & Hussey, 2002). For individuals who can benefit from enlarged print, such as those who have low vision or who have reading disabilities, optical aids may be an appropriate technology solution. Optical aids include magnifying glasses and magnifiers on stands. These devices are simple tools and readily available. Magnifiers on stands are particularly useful if the individual is doing a task that requires the use of both hands.

Nonoptical aids consist of enlarged print, high-intensity lamps, and contrast objects (Cook & Hussey, 2002). For instance, some forms of print come already enlarged such as books and newspapers for individuals with low vision. High-intensity lamps can provide contrast on reading materials and objects, such as brightly colored objects in the environment, making them stand out against backgrounds and become more visually distinguishable.

A closed circuit television (CCTV) device is one of the most common examples of an electronic aid. A CCTV includes a camera, a video display, and a unit that manages how the material is presented (zoom feature, scanning table). Individuals place their reading material on the scanning table, the camera captures the image, and the lens projects the image, which is shown on the video display. The scanning table can be easily moved forward and backward and from side to side to allow maximum visibility of the material. The use of color, contrast, and type size permit users with varying acuity abilities to access and read the material. In addition, the use of foot pedals can further enhance the usability of the device for individuals who have upper extremity disabilities.

TACTILE AIDS

Access to print through the use of touch by individuals with visual impairments can be accomplished through the use of technology that produces print in a tactile format.

Braille is the tactile aid most widely used by individuals with severe visual impairments (Cook & Hussey, 2002). Braille consists of characters that have six or eight dots and can be read letter by letter, by word signs, and by contractions. Braille is produced by embossing the characters on heavy-duty paper. A brailler can be used to produce written language; naturally, the receiver of the document must be able to read Braille. For individuals who read Braille, computer-generated text is transformed into embossed Braille output through the use of a translation program (Alliance for Technology Access, 2001). For example, the Index Everest Braille Embosser is a high-speed Braille embosser that includes speech feedback (see Figure 6.5).

SCANNER/OCR/SPEECH SYNTHESIS

Often, individuals wish to access print from a variety of sources such as textbooks, newspapers, or magazines. Simply picking up the material and reading it may not be an option for individuals with visual impairments and in some cases for individuals with cognitive disabilities, because they may not possess the visual acuity or the reading skills to access the text, respectively. A system for accessing print includes the use of a scanner, optical character recognition (OCR) software/hardware, and speech synthesis. OCR systems might be thought of as "reading machines" because they provide a way of inputting print (e.g., a page in a book, a letter) into a computer, and speech synthesis/screen reading software "reads" the print (output). A scanner, using a camera, captures the print. The OCR system, which may be either

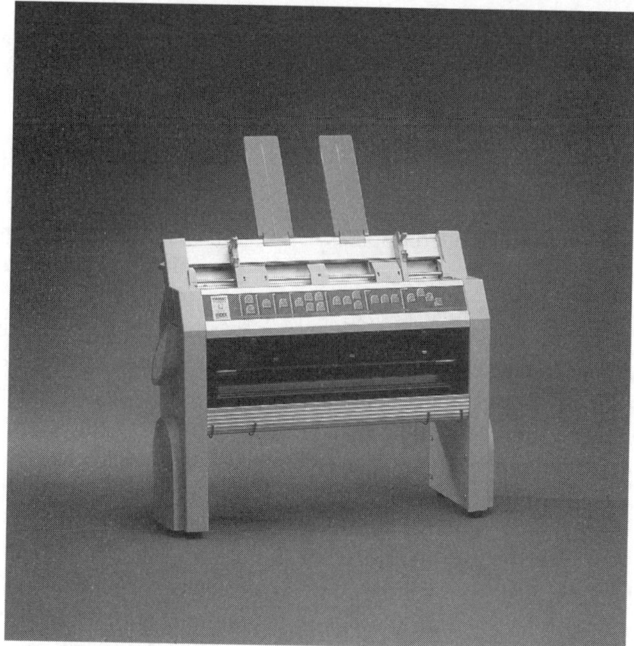

FIGURE 6.5 Index Everest Braille Embosser
Source: Courtesy of Synapse.

software or a piece of hardware plugged into a personal computer, translates the print into a format that can be read and spoken by the computer or translated into Braille. This system is helpful for school and work activities. For example, a middle school, high school, or postsecondary student might be required to read a chapter for homework. Because of a severe reading disability, this setting demand task is challenging for the student. However, by scanning the text into the computer, the student can hear the chapter material read aloud and thus be able to access the print. In a similar way, an employee can use this technology at work to access print related to his or her work environment.

Caution must be exercised with this technology, however. First, OCR systems do not always read text with 100% accuracy or even read 100% of the text at all (tables, for example, may be lost in translation). Second, although the user can access print and hear the material read, understanding the material and knowing the vocabulary that is used within the context might require additional instruction or explanation from the teacher or employer. Access to print does not guarantee comprehension of the text.

There are two primary ways text can be scanned. First, text can be scanned using a full-page flatbed scanner where a page of text is placed face down on the device (much like a copy machine). Or text can be scanned using a handheld scanner, where the individual moves the scanner's camera across or down a page of text. Full-page scanners provide access to entire pages, whereas the handheld scanner may or may not accommodate a full page. If it does not, then the user must manually manipulate the scanning process. The flatbed scanner is usually heavier and more expensive than the handheld scanner, which is portable and can plug into a laptop computer. Thus, the type of scanner should be selected depending on the needs of the user (Cook & Hussey, 1995).

There are two types of OCR systems: stand-alone or PC-based. In the stand-alone system, all the components are built into one device, including the scanner, OCR software/hardware, and the speech synthesizer. Some stand-alone systems are portable and can be used in the library or at work; others are desktop units. The PC-based components consist of a full-page (desktop) or handheld scanner, an OCR board and/or software, and a speech synthesizer. Some companies have added other features, such as highlighting words as they are spoken back by the system, and being able to alter the rate at which the text is read. This feature could help students develop reading fluency, which is a skill that contributes to comprehension. Systems aimed at developing access to print can facilitate word recognition and fluency skills, but comprehension skills also must be developed to aid student understanding of class content.

Several OCR systems are available and used in many settings. First, the newer version, Kurzweil 3000 (Lernout & Hauspie, Inc.), uses a stand-alone scanner, can be used to scan and display print as it appears in the document including the color graphics and pictures. The Kurzweil then reads the document out loud while highlighting the text. With adjustable reading rates and highlighting, fluency and word recognition are addressed. The student can also use the highlighting feature to identify the main ideas or supporting details. Notes and highlighted text can be saved into a separate document for later study.

Second, the WYNN™ Literacy Software Solution (What You Need Now [WYNN]; Freedom Scientific: www.freedomscientific.com; Arkenstone Products) was designed with assistance from students with learning disabilities in reading and from special educators. Several types of software are available that are intended to help students with print disabilities and English language learners tackle the process of reading. The software contains scanning, OCR, and speech synthesis capabilities. Used with a PC platform, text is represented in auditory and visual formats and includes highlighting, bookmarks, ruler guides, and annotations. WYNN includes color-coded tool bars that are labeled with pictures and words. Users can highlight text by chunks, thus focusing on groups of words rather than on word-by-word reading. Some of the features include scanning a page, customizing the document page (spacing, margins, type size), accessing a dictionary, adding voice, and decoding words.

Finally, the OPENBook software (Freedom Scientific; Arkenstone Products www.synapseadaptive.com) allows individuals with visual impairments, print disabilities, and dyslexia to read and edit scanned images from books, magazines, newspapers, and other documents. Once text is scanned, OPENBook software transforms print into electronic text, which is read aloud through speech synthesis options. Features include dictionary, thesaurus, spell check; page insertion and deletion; book marking; and page layout navigation to move from one component to the next. Possible applications are uploading electronic text onto iPods and other MP3 players, for example, to allow portable text access.

Application of a small-scale OCR/speech synthesis system is available in Wizcom's Quicktionary™ Reading Pen (www.wizcomtech.com/eng/catalog/a/q2). This portable, pocket-sized "reading pen" (smaller than a TV remote control) uses a miniaturized optical scanning system to enable the user to scan single words and a full line of print on a page (e.g., textbook, magazine) and have the word read aloud by means of a built-in speech synthesizer. The device offers definitions for scanned words, auditory spelling of the word, and a save feature to keep a record of scanned words. The portability of this device allows users to take the pen to various environments (school, library, work) to assist with words that are unknown because of word-recognition or vocabulary issues. In addition, different types of electronic pens allow access to print for students with dyslexia and who are English language learners, and scanning capabilities in some instances for taking notes that can then be downloaded onto a computer.

ELECTRONIC BOOKS (E-BOOKS)

Digitally recorded books for individuals with visual impairments and dyslexia are available from a number of sources, including the Library of Congress (see www.loc.gov/library/libarch-digital.html) with digital collections to access print, pictorial, and audiovisual materials; Recording for the Blind & Dyslexic (RFB & D www.rfbd.org) with DAISY formatted digitally recorded audiobooks; and commercial companies with a wide variety of popular types of fiction and nonfiction books. For example, Amazon.com's Kindle™ and Barnes & Noble's Nook™ are available to wirelessly download books, magazines, and newspapers, and department stores feature e-books for individuals of all ages. Organizations such as the Reading Rights Coalition (see www.readingrights.org) and the Digital Accessible Information System (DAISY; see www.daisy.org) Consortium are working with companies such as Amazon to ensure that e-books are accessible to people with disabilities.

Thus, individuals with print disabilities, including those with learning disabilities, visual impairments, cognitive disabilities, and physical disabilities, can benefit greatly with electronic books as their means to access print. In addition, electronic books are quite popular among mainstream consumers. Digital books for different platforms (e.g., PC, Mac) and mobile phones make this print option widely available for many individuals with and without disabilities on portable devices. For instance, RFB & D offers users the ability to download audio textbooks and works with educational institutions (K–16) to help improve access to text in today's classrooms. One of the appeals of this type of technology is that individuals who have disabilities and *need* these devices for access to information purposes can now easily become part of the mainstream who use these devices for entertainment and educational purposes.

Summary

In this chapter, we have focused on AT devices that can be used to help individuals with different types of disabilities access the wealth of information found across a variety of environments. Access to the computer is one of the most critical dimensions in today's society if individuals are going to be "players" in this technology age. A variety of input and output device options were presented, including ways to adapt the conventional keyboard and alternative input and output options to meet more access challenges. Certainly, telecommunications is another major area individuals must be able to access. Simply using the telephone is a task that most of us take for granted. For individuals who are deaf or hard of hearing, access is now available and has become a legal mandate. Also, Internet access is yet another area that enables people to be competitive, informed, and part of the market economy. Universal design features can ensure that all individuals can enjoy the options offered by Internet service. Finally, access to information presented orally and in print is another important consideration. Numerous devices are available that can promote access for individuals with mild to severe challenges. Clearly, access to information has been greatly improved and enhanced for individuals with disabilities through the electronic age in which we live.

SCENARIO APPLICATIONS

Scenario 6.1

Visit the Microsoft Web site or the Alliance for Technology Access (www.ataccess.org) to select information about computer accessibility. Prepare a short presentation on your topic including a demo or video from the Web site that portrays computer accessibility. Identify the functional limitations of individuals with specific disabilities that would most benefit from the accessibility features.

Scenario 6.2

Conduct an online search of switches and scanning software (a couple of Web sites have already been offered in this chapter). Identify characteristics and types of switches and scanning formats and techniques. Make a list of the devices and software and determine the requisite abilities and person-specific characteristics that are necessary to use these devices. Share this information with the class.

Scenario 6.3

Select either input or output devices and conduct an online search to locate examples of devices that promote access at the input or output level. Prepare a list of your devices, identify the features, rate them on the simple to complex scale found in Chapter 2, and provide specific examples of individuals with disabilities who might benefit most from your device selections.

Scenario 6.4

Review the information found on the Web design accessible tools (e.g., "Bobby") pages. Then, locate a Web page with information that can be used for educational purposes in a classroom and decide whether that Web page is accessible for individuals who have sensory or motor disabilities. Make recommendations for improving the Web-based platforms. Share your findings in class.

Scenario 6.5

Summarize the information presented in the listening devices and print aids sections. Identify devices, their purpose, and individuals who might benefit from using the devices. Consider the setting demands, tasks, and requisite abilities for which these devices might be used and the person-specific characteristics, functional capabilities, and limitations that would influence the selection of devices. See Chapter 2, Table 2.3.

For Discussion

1. Describe the features of input devices and explain considerations for selecting the devices to meet individual needs.
2. Describe the features of output devices. Explain how these devices might be used in a home, school, and work setting.
3. Describe your thoughts about how universal design features can be more widely accepted and employed. Describe potential barriers to universal design and possible solutions.
4. Describe the features of devices that promote access to listening and print.
5. Explain the telecommunication issues encountered by individuals with disabilities and how the electronic age has helped to address some of these issues. Propose ideas for solving other issues that the electronic age has not solved or cannot solve.
6. Explain different types of switches and scanning and provide examples of when they can be used.
7. Given the information presented in Personal Perspectives 6.1 and 6.2, imagine how the lives of these individuals might have looked without the technology they described as critical for their success and independence.

References

Alliance for Technology Access. (2001). *Computer resources for people with disabilities* (4th ed.). Alameda, CA: Hunter House.

Angelo, D. H. (1997). AAC in the family and home. In S. Glennen & D. DeCoste (Eds.), *The handbook of augmentative communication* (pp. 523–545). San Diego, CA: Singular.

Bryant, B. R., Bryant, D. P., & Rieth, H. J. (2002). The use of assistive technology in postsecondary education. In L. C. Brinckerhoff, J. M. McGuire, & S. F. Shaw, *Postsecondary education and transition for students with learning disabilities* (pp. 389–429). Austin, TX: Pro-Ed.

Church, G., & Glennen, S. (1992). *The handbook of assistive technology.* San Diego, CA: Singular.

Cook, A. M., & Hussey, S. M. (2002). *Assistive technologies: Principles and practices.* St. Louis, MO: Mosby.

King, M. L., & Rental, V. M. (1981). Research update: Conveying meaning in written texts. *Language Arts, 58,* 721–728.

Lewis, R. (1993). *Special education technology.* Pacific Grove, CA: Brooks/Cole.

Rehabilitation Act Amendments of 1998. Section 508 (29 U.S.C. § 2).

Smith, D. D., & Tyler, N. C. (2010). *Introduction to special education: Making a difference* (7th ed.). Upper Saddle River, NJ: Merrill/Pearson Education.

University of Washington. (1997). *World wide access: Accessible Web design.* Seattle, WA: Author.

7 INTEGRATING ASSISTIVE TECHNOLOGY ADAPTATIONS INTO ACADEMIC INSTRUCTION

The second edition of this chapter was written by Robin Lock. The first edition of this chapter was written by Diane Pedrotty Bryant and Ae-Hwa Kim.

Chapter at a Glance

Objectives

1. Describe the components of designing, implementing, and evaluating academic instruction.
2. Explain the features of instructional software, types of software, and guidelines for evaluating software.
3. Describe how Instructional Technology and Assistive Technology adaptations can be used to improve basic skills.
4. Describe Instructional Technology and Assistive Technology adaptations that can be used in reading.
5. Describe Instructional Technology and Assistive Technology adaptations that can be used in writing.
6. Describe Instructional Technology and Assistive Technology adaptations that can be used in mathematics.
7. Explain what to evaluate when using Instructional Technology and Assistive Technology adaptations.

MAKING CONNECTIONS

Many students with disabilities have difficulties acquiring basic reading, writing, and mathematics skills. You have already learned about many assistive technology devices that improve these students' access in school. Instructional technology (IT) and AT adaptations increase opportunities to build a foundation for higher-level learning. Think about how IT and AT adaptations have helped you learn in elementary, middle, and high school. The purpose of this chapter is to discuss assistive and instructional technology from an academic standpoint. We provide (a) an introduction to integrating technology adaptations into academic instruction, as well as guidelines for (b) designing instruction, (c) implementing instruction, and (d) evaluating instruction using technology. We begin this chapter with Personal Perspective 7.1 by a student who uses assistive technology to tackle the academic demands of school. As you read, think about how AT makes a difference in his life and the importance of AT to him.

PERSONAL PERSPECTIVE 7.1

The following is an interview with a student who attended a learning lab at a major university.

Please Tell us a Little Bit About Your Challenges Learning Academic Subjects

Without a computer, I could not write a report and writing essays would be impossible. I have trouble taking notes in school because I am a slow writer. I have trouble remembering the order of words and what I want to write when writing with pencil and paper. I have trouble decoding words and sequencing sounds when I read. I have difficulties when given many directions at one time.

For What Reasons Do You Use Speech Recognition?

Some of the reasons I use speech recognition are:

- Putting thoughts on paper
- School work and for writing paragraphs, reports, essays, and summaries
- Chatting with grandparents and friends on AOL instant messenger
- Writing e-mails
- Writing thank you notes and letters

Basically for everything I have to write.

I write better with speech recognition in school and at home because I can get my thoughts down on paper and I'm able to write more. I also write better because I can say what I want to write and I don't fall behind. I use a lot more vocabulary in what I write and I write longer sentences. I have an extensive vocabulary and now I can use it when I write.

Are There Other Technologies that You Use to Help You in Your Academic Studies?

I use a calculator, desktop computer, and a laptop computer. I use a Plantronics USB headset microphone for speech recognition on my laptop computer and my desktop computer at home. I have a watch that can hold telephone numbers that I can't remember. The calculator is for doing mathematical equations, and I have a laptop computer to use in all my classrooms with speech recognition installed on it. I also use various types of software for the computer such as:

- **Text Aloud MP3:** I use it to proofread papers that I have written. When I do research, I paste the text into the program and then I can have it read to me.
- **Inspiration:** a program for mapping ideas for writing assignments.
- **Microsoft Word:** for spelling and grammar.

Technology is the reason I am now succeeding in school. I'm even doing this e-mail with my speech recognition.

If You had a Chance to Tell Teachers About Assistive Technology, What Would You Tell Them?

I would first tell teachers that it is a tool, not a toy. I would also tell them that it helps me in a lot of ways. I believe that it helps me learn how to read and write and it helps me do better and to succeed in school.

Source: Reprinted with permission from Psycho-Educational Services.

INTRODUCTION TO INTEGRATING TECHNOLOGY ADAPTATIONS INTO ACADEMIC INSTRUCTION

Over the past 20 years, national and state legislative mandates have emphasized the need to raise both academic standards and access to the general education curriculum for all students including those with disabilities. As you read in Chapter 1, legislation that dealt with the education of children with disabilities has evolved to include the Assistive Technology Act of 2004 (P.L. 108-364). The AT Act changed the focus of state and federal funding from the development of state assistive technology infrastructure to personal assistance to people with disabilities in need of AT including those in educational settings. As the No Child Left Behind Act (NCLB, P.L. 107-110) emphasized greater accountability for all student learning, changes to The Individuals with Disabilities Improvement Act of 2004 (IDEA) (P.L. 108-446) aligned both laws to increase support and improve outcomes for children with disabilities. AT plays an integral role in this effort by improving access to the general education curriculum, protecting students' rights to equal access, and increasing their opportunities to successfully learn in the classroom with specific AT support.

For students with disabilities in the preschool, elementary, middle (or junior high school), and high school classroom, access to the general education curriculum and/or a functional curriculum that meets the student's needs reflects the surest route to a quality education. Both AT adaptations and IT provide useable and successful adaptations and opportunities to promote learning and access. Computer technology has taken a "giant leap forward" in enabling children with disabilities to achieve their developmental and educational goals (Judgen, 2001). The benefits of technology may be even greater for individuals with disabilities as compared to their counterparts without disabilities (Burgstahler, 2003). Behavioral, curricular, and instructional adaptations can be recommended by IEP teams for access and academic instruction. Technology has evolved tremendously in terms of ease of use, increased capability, and decreased cost (Stover & Pendegraft, 2005), making AT and IT integral components of a quality education for individuals with disabilities. This chapter focuses on both IT and AT adaptations, including remedial software, stand-alone tools, and compensatory aids. Moreover, although instruction for students with disabilities encompasses the full range of academic subjects, this chapter concentrates on reading, writing, and mathematics.

Assistive Technology and Instruction

Reading, writing, and mathematics constitute the basic academic curriculum taught in the school years and provide the foundation for further learning in social studies and science. Mastery of the knowledge and skills in these subjects is critical to student success. As students progress into more advanced subject areas, basic skill development in all three of these areas affects the ability to succeed and points to the need for AT support. Both AT adaptations and IT provide students with new ways to learn (Lee & Vail, 2005) by reducing their cognitive load and enhancing students' mental energy and thinking capacity (Brown, 2005).

The role of assistive technology in support of students with disabilities is clearly seen in the use of software programming that compensates for reading or writing difficulties and enables the learner to more successfully master higher-order learning tasks (Lange, McPhillips, Mulhern, & Wylie, 2006). Technological tools that make the process of writing easier and more productive will motivate and support the student with disabilities (Graham, Harris, & Larsen, 2001). It is important to remember that AT used in isolation is seldom effective, and it does not take the place of quality instruction in the areas of reading, writing, and mathematics. Graham et al.

(2001) point out that the impact of AT adaptations diminishes if the student fails to develop the basic knowledge and skills to effectively progress.

Instructional Technology and Instruction

Hand in hand with the use of AT adaptations is the critical utilization of IT as a learning platform for individuals with disabilities. Educators must consider the integral role that IT plays in the academic development of children with disabilities. IT increases access to the general education curriculum by adapting the curriculum, improving instructional delivery, providing practice opportunities, and increasing motivation (Twyman & Tindal, 2006). Although AT does not teach the student content-related skills, IT provides the student with learning opportunities to address literacy performance and boost performance in skill development (Englert, Zhao, Collings, & Roming, 2005). IT uses teacher-mediated instruction often in a student-directed format that allows for guided practice and feedback along with monitoring and evaluation to provide more opportunities for mastering knowledge and skills, particularly in the areas of reading, writing, and mathematics (Keel, Dangel, & Owens, 1999).

Integrating AT adaptations and IT into the classroom continues to be a major challenge for general and special education teachers. McLaren, Baush, and Ault (2007) note that the lack of a common knowledge base concerning assistive technology affects teachers' communication. As they struggle with the "hows" and "whys," they may fail to work collaboratively to use assistive technology to enhance student outcomes. McLaren et al. suggest that school districts as well as preservice teacher preparation programs provide similar training for general and special educators using a shared vocabulary and that support for learning about new AT be made readily and easily available. For example, teachers may lack training as to how technology works. They may need continued technical support to use technology effectively. Also, although teachers may understand how to make the technology function, they may not have the experience to integrate the AT adaptations into instruction (Lemons, 2000). Some teachers have not developed the skills to evaluate the effectiveness of IT and AT adaptations. They may continue using the device or a particular IT program without making necessary changes so that its use is feasible or efficient. This frustrates both the teacher and the student. Working together and considering the student's needs is an effective way to utilize both AT and IT and can increase general education access.

DESIGNING INSTRUCTION

Designing instruction focuses on the student, the curriculum and instruction, and IT and AT adaptations. Teachers use a variety of resources to decide what they teach, how to teach, and the resources used for instruction. AT adaptations for students with disabilities are mandated in the student's Individualized Education Program (IEP). Teachers must plan how they can best integrate IT and AT adaptations into their instruction.

Students

To be effective, instruction should be planned around the personal/social and academic needs of students. Teachers must spend some time considering their students' experiences and academic levels. Understanding a student's levels of performance as documented through psychoeducational assessment in the areas of cognitive, social, motor, sensory, and language domains provides specific knowledge about functional capabilities and limitations. The IEP and other documents provide the teacher with instructional information, including both what to teach and how to accommodate the student's individual differences. Furthermore, the IEP will delineate specific AT adaptations that must be included in the student's classroom accommodations.

Students with high-incidence disabilities such as learning disabilities, speech/language disorders, or emotional disorders will, of course, have different needs in terms of both IT and AT adaptations. However, they may share some common features, such as the need for specific direct instruction and independent drill, practice, and repetition. Students with high-incidence disabilities also benefit from peer tutoring and learning cognitive strategies to become self-regulated learners (Raymond, 2008). Using IT and AT adaptations in conjunction with these strategies enhances access to general education and improves learning outcomes.

Students with low-incidence disabilities also have some common learning characteristics in the classroom. According to Hamill and Everington (2002), there are three major areas that teachers must address for students with low-incidence disabilities. These include (a) cognitive and learning, (b) motivation and behavior, and (c) physical and medical impairments. For children with low-incidence disabilities, difficulties with acquisition of new learning, retaining that new skill, and then generalizing it to other settings proves challenging. Teachers must create an environment that maximizes success to avoid failure expectation, dependence on others, and acquiescence. Finally, medical and physical issues often affect these students' ability to control their environment. Utilizing IT and AT adaptations helps to design an instructional setting in which students can reach their full potential.

Curriculum, Instructional Planning, and AT Adaptations

Curriculum is a plan for the selection and organization of learning experiences to change and develop behaviors. The IEP stipulates the curriculum from an academic and life skills perspective to determine what is taught. Differences exist in the curriculum of elementary versus secondary schools according to state standards. Textbooks are typically designed to match these standards. All of these factors influence the curriculum that students experience.

Instructional planning includes the way in which the teacher operationalizes the curriculum. Teachers make decisions about how much to teach in a lesson, the manner of instruction, and the amount of practice or repetition the student will experience. Through the lesson plan, the teacher determines the specific instructional activities as well as number of children included in any given lesson throughout the day. Decision-making questions such as the following can aid in the development of valuable lesson plans:

1. What are the student's IEP goals and short-term objectives?
2. How will the instruction be delivered?
3. What teaching techniques will be used?
4. Will the groups for instruction be large or small?
5. How will materials and adaptations be integrated into the instruction?
6. What evaluation methods will be used to determine student progress?

When the teacher is planning a lesson that will include IT or AT adaptations, factors such as the ability to successfully use the device, the ease of operating the device in the classroom, the need for other devices such as computer access to make the lesson successful, and methods for evaluating the impact of the device on the student's learning all come into play.

In this chapter, we focus on remedial and compensatory IT and AT adaptations. Remedial adaptations use techniques that attempt to correct a problem after other strategies have proven ineffective (Rivera & Smith, 1997). Remedial strategies may include using additional instructional

Designing Instruction	Implementing Instruction	Evaluating Instruction
• Student • Curriculum • Adaptations • Classroom	• Delivery • Grouping	• Environmental factors • Use of adaptations • Monitoring student progress

FIGURE 7.1 Integrating Instructional Technology and AT Adaptations into Instruction

materials; employing a multisensory approach that incorporates visual, tactile, or auditory learning; or, in the case of this chapter, using instructional software and AT adaptations. Compensatory adaptations attempt to avoid a problem by offering a solution to promote access. For example, a calculator can enable a student without basic math fact memory to learn and perform whole-number computation.

The IEP team, in conjunction with the teacher and student, continues to evaluate the success of IT and AT adaptations as instruction progresses. As the teacher sees the IT and AT adaptations in action, additional supports can be identified and implemented. The teacher designs instruction that embraces IT and AT adaptations to promote student learning. In the next section, we explain how to evaluate instructional software for remediation; provide a description of reading, writing, and mathematics curriculum; and review representative examples of IT and AT adaptations for remedial or access purposes. Figure 7.1 provides information about the factors to consider for integrating IT and AT adaptations into instruction.

Instructional Software

Instructional software falls under the category of IT and includes text and graphics such as pictures or animation that supply the student with a variety of activities to promote learning to lead to increased mastery. Instructional software is a tool used during a lesson that can help to improve basic skills. However, it does not take the place of quality direct instruction. Whether the software is used for remediation or for problem-based learning, students must first be provided with specific instruction grounded in best practice. In addition, not just any software will add to a student's mastery of a skill. Quality instructional software should contain simple, easy-to-follow directions, models, examples, positive corrective feedback, extra practice opportunities, an appropriate reading level, pacing options, and documentation of student progress (Bryant, Smith, & Bryant, 2008) to increase access to the curriculum.

In addition to the technical features just described, instructional software must be based on research-based practices. The Center for the Improvement of Early Reading Achievement (CIERA), funded by the National Institute for Literacy (NIFL), identified five research-based components of effective reading programs. The five include (a) phonemic (phonological) awareness, (b) phonics, (c) fluency, (d) vocabulary, and (e) comprehension. Teachers must consider how software addresses these elements. For example, if software is aimed at reinforcing decoding skills, then practice activities should revolve around phonemic (phonological) awareness such as blending or segmenting. The teacher's guide or directions that accompany the instructional software may include explanations of how the software, lessons, and activities are research-based.

Teachers must be able to evaluate software before purchasing it. Considerations such as the tie to research-based practices are critical. Teacher should also consider how software fits with

Table 7.1 Types of Instructional Software

TYPE	PURPOSE	STRENGTHS
Instructional Practice	• Reinforcement of skills previously taught • Practice • Feedback	• Provides multiple practice opportunities • Can be individualized • Provides corrective feedback • May provide branching to easier skills
Simulation	• Decision-making and cause–effect situations	• Gives students opportunities to make decisions and to witness the results of those decisions • Provides opportunities to analyze situations and apply problem-solving skills
Games	• Fun, gamelike situation • Animation and sound to simulate a game format	• May be motivating • May reinforce skills

their curriculum and the integrity of the instructional design of the software (Bryant & Bryant, 2003). School district technology specialists can often help teachers to make informed decisions about the research-based practices included in a particular piece of instructional software and whether it appropriately fits the curriculum. Table 7.1 presents a look at the types of instructional software that are available. Also, because the use of educational software is such an important component of many academic programs, guidelines for evaluating and selecting software are shown in Figure 7.2 as further considerations when designing instruction. We recommend that the consumer carefully examine software components in light of individual student needs and review any available evidence of the effectiveness of specific software programs. The most effective software does not necessarily have the most "bells and whistles."

Reading

Achievement in reading remains a major factor for success in all facets of our society (Vaughn & Bos, 2009). Much information is presented through text, and the ability to read and understand the written word is a necessity in today's society (Bryant, Ugel, Thompson, & Hamff, 1999). IT software and other AT adaptations are being viewed as resources for improving the literacy skills of students (Englert et al., 2005).

According to Vaughn and Bos (2009), reading involves two overarching concepts: (a) decoding and reading words rapidly and (b) understanding the text through active engagement and interpretation by the reader. They identify decoding strategies as methods that readers use to decipher unknown words. Active engagement means that the reader does not passively obtain the content from the written word but predicts, summarizes, questions, and clarifies the text through his or her own experiences.

The rapid improvement in technology in terms of both IT and AT adaptations over the past few decades has led to widespread acceptance of technology as a tool used during quality instruction. Raskind and Higgins (1999) found that speech recognition software actually served to remediate and improve students' reading and spelling abilities. Computer-assisted instruction (CAI) has increasingly been used to improve literacy skills in students with disabilities (Lee &

A. Basic Information

Name of software____

Publisher____

Cost____

Hardware Requirements____

B. Software Description

Software grade level(s)

____

Software instructional area(s)

____

Reading level of software text (if applicable)

____

Purpose

____

____Tutorial ____Drill and practice ____Simulation ____Support

Instructional objectives ____ yes ____no List stated objectives

____

____

____

How is information presented? (check all that apply)

____Speech ____Music ____Graphics (pictures) ____Text (words) ____Animation

How do the visuals look? (check all that apply)

____Screen is too busy. ____Graphics enhance rather man distract from purpose.

____Print is legible. ____Print size is age-appropriate.

What is the quality of the sound? (check all that apply)

____Sound is clear/audible. ____Speech is audible.

____Sound is distracting. ____Rate of speech is appropriate.

Overall impressions/concerns ____

C. Instructional Design

Directions are clear, easy to read, and short. ____yes ____no

Examples or models are provided. ____yes ____no

Pacing is appropriate. ____yes ____no

Practice opportunities are provided. ____yes ____no

Error correction is provided. ____yes ____no

FIGURE 7.2 Guidelines for Software Evaluating & Selecting

Source: Adapted from *Teaching Students with Learning and Behavior Problems* (3rd ed.), by D. P. Rivera and D. D. Smith, 1997, Boston: Allyn & Bacon and *Teaching Students with Special Needs in Inclusive Classrooms,* by D. P. Bryant, D. D. Smith, and B.R. Bryant, 2008, Pearson/Allyn & Bacon.

Difficulty level can be individualized. ____yes ____no

Reinforcement (visual and/or auditory) is present. ____yes ____no

A record keeping/evaluation option is available. ____yes ____no

Overall impressions/concerns____

D. Software Content

Appropriate to stated objectives ____yes ____no

Factual and accurate ____yes ____no

Free of gender, cultural, or racial bias ____yes ____no

Relates to school's curriculum ____yes ____no

Relates to student's IEP ____yes ____no

Sufficient scope and sequence ____yes ____no

Overall impressions/concerns____

E. Technical Considerations

User Demands (respond to all that apply)
Academic____

____Physical/motor____

____Computer knowledge____

Technical vocabulary____

Problem solving____

Functions (check all that apply)

____Save work in progress? ____Print in progress? ____Alter sound/level?

____Return to main menu at any point in the program? ____Change pace?

Teacher Demands

Amount of instruction to students for using____

software ____

____

____Installation

procedures ____

Level of student monitoring

____

Preparation needed before using software

____

Overall impressions/concerns

____

FIGURE 7.2 *Continued*

Vail, 2005). In addition, software has been improved to address the fundamental aspects of research-based reading programs, including activities to increase word identification, vocabulary, fluency, and comprehension skills. In the next section of this chapter, examples of IT and AT adaptations are presented, but these examples are not endorsements of any particular product or vendor. Teachers must make their own determinations about the appropriateness of software and AT adaptations based on their students' needs.

PHONOLOGICAL AWARENESS

Phonological awareness is knowing and demonstrating how spoken language can be reduced to smaller units (words, syllables, phonemes) within an alphabetic system (Podhajski, 1999). According to Bryant, Wiederholt, and Bryant (2004); Chard and Dickson (1999); and Torgesen and Mathes (2000), problems with phonological awareness include

- recognizing or producing words that rhyme;
- blending or segmenting syllables or onset rhymes;
- recognizing the beginning, medial, or ending sounds in words;
- segmenting or blending a word's individuals sounds; and
- using sounds to identify new words changed by substitutions or deletions.

The software described next provides a summary of some activities that can be used to develop students' rhyming, blending, segmenting, and phonics skills to improve their phonological abilities.

Simon S.I.O. (Don Johnston, Inc.) (Ability Level: Grades PK–2 • Interest Level: Grades PK–8) helps beginning readers develop phonics skills through the use of a personal tutor to deliver individualized instruction and corrective feedback. Students engage in a variety of activities in two levels and master letter-sounds and word families. Students increase fluency by building new words, recalling learned words, practicing guided spelling, discriminating between words, and reading controlled texts. Thirty-three levels allow the student to practice a variety of phonological awareness skills. Two challenge activities increase the student's proficiency in using his or her newly enhanced skills. The program contains a built-in data collection system to monitor progress. See Figure 7.3 for a screen shot from Simon S.I.O.

The Card Reader (Drake Educational Associates) is a card reader system that features audio cards with a strip of magnetic tape running along the bottom edge. It is sometimes called the language master. The Card Reader unit and cards are purchased separately. This unique audiovisual aid features preprinted cards that provide practice in phonics, sight word development, onsets and rhymes, vocabulary development, and much more. The system includes both the Card Reader audio recording and playback unit. The cards are purchased separately. The student plays the card through the unit and listens to the recording while reading along with the words. The student then records the words on the student track and compares these to the teacher's recording. The student listens and records the cards as many times as necessary to master the word. The card reader machine is individualized and allows the student to work at his or her own pace without direct teacher supervision.

Destination Reading (Houghton Mifflin Harcourt) uses a "teach, practice, apply" methodology to promote learning for students through active engagement in individualized lessons. The program provides a comprehensive and versatile curriculum that is data driven, focusing on explicit instruction for specific skills. The program includes the use of electronic whiteboards for whole-group instruction and also provides individualized tutorials. Destination Reading targets the components of research-based reading instruction, including phonemic

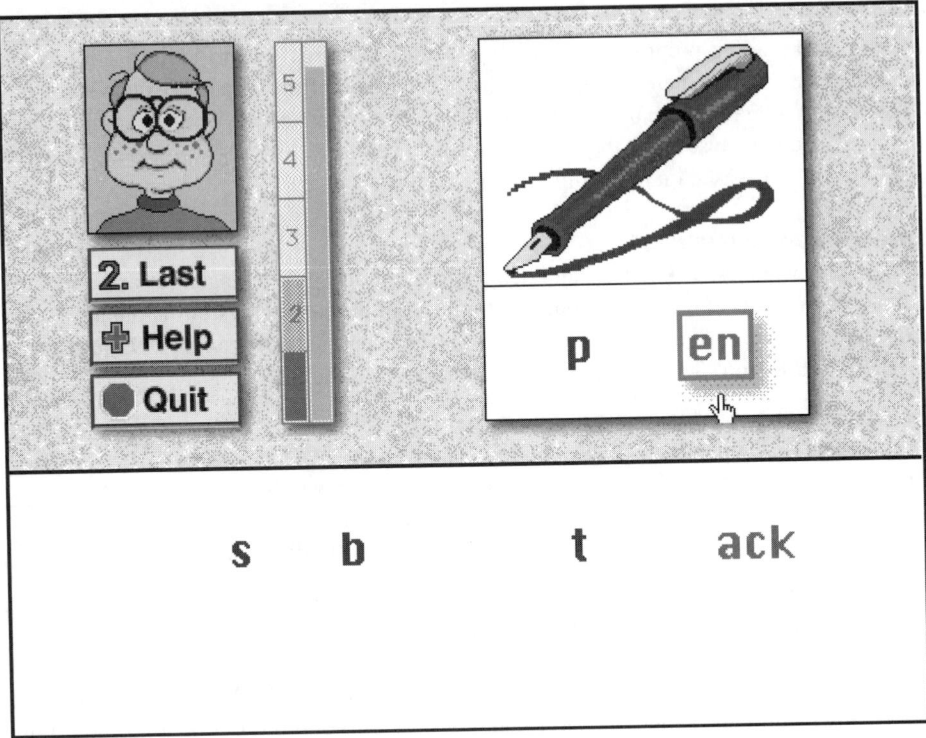

FIGURE 7.3 Simon S.I.O.
Source: Copyright © Don Johnston, Inc., Volo, IL. Used by permission.

awareness, phonics, word study, fluency, vocabulary, and comprehension. Phonemic awareness is addressed through song, rhyme, and manipulative activities. Phonics begins with letter-sound correspondence and progresses as the student masters each level. This comprehensive program not only provides instruction in phonemic awareness and phonics but includes all facets critical to student progress.

WORD IDENTIFICATION

Word identification is often referred to as the process used to figure out unfamiliar words (Hargis, 1999). Instruction in word identification includes the ability to recognize sight words and employ specific strategies to decode unknown words (Vaughn & Bos, 2009). The ability to identify words recognized by sight or through decoding strategies affects a student's success as a reader. Through the use of instructional software and AT adaptations, students can be provided with a variety of activities to hear and practice word identification skills.

Wordmaker (Don Johnston, Inc.) (Ability Level: Grades K–3 • Interest Level: Grades K–8) uses varied activities to engage students in a systematic and interactive approach to teaching word attack and spelling skills. Students increase decoding skills by manipulating letters, onsets, and rhymes to learn new patterns in meaningful contexts. Activities provide the opportunity for students to generate word walls of phonetically irregular and sight words. The program helps students to apply their new skills to unknown words through the transfer activities. A built-in data collection system allows for both formative assessment and decisions about instruction and intervention.

Bailey's Book House (Edmark, Inc.) provides students with activities to explore letters, words, rhymes, sentence building, and stories. The software addresses a variety of skills including mastery of simple prepositions, learning three-letter rhyming words, working with the alphabet, making up rhymes, exploring self-expression, creating stories, and exploring adjectives. There are two activities related to word identification skills. The Letter Machine helps students to learn the alphabet by pressing a letter key and seeing an animated figure that matches that letter. For example, after the student presses the letter "d," a picture of a dinosaur appears on the screen. In the Three-Letter Carnival, the student sounds out words of animals and objects grouped by names that rhyme or groups them by names that begin with the same letter. The software has a spoken language feature that supplies students with both the written and spoken words in the program, so no reading skills are required to begin this program. The software includes the ability to customize lessons and to track and assess student development.

The Edmark Reading Software Program (Houghton Mifflin Harcourt Learning Technology) (Ability Level: Grades K–3 • Interest Level: Grades 1–6) is available in two levels, both sold separately. Level One teaches 150 words from the Dolch Word List and also introduces "s," "ed," and "ing" endings. The software has 227 step-by-step lessons. Students learn about top-to-bottom and left-to-right reading, pairing spoken and written words, matching words and sentences to pictures, and reading simple sentences. In Level Two, students learn 200 new words, review those learned in Level One, and work with compound words. The program provides 345 lessons that progress in difficulty and offer students a variety of ways to succeed. Both programs feature prereading skills, word recognition, picture/phrase exercises, word review, and words in context and stories. A complete management system tracks student performance. The program is single-switch and touch-screen compatible.

VOCABULARY

Vocabulary knowledge is an essential component of reading ability (Bryant et al., 2008). Deficits in vocabulary development affect reading comprehension (Carnine, Silbert, Kame'enui, & Tarver, 2010), the ability to use context clues in the text, and the understanding and use of vocabulary on a deeper level. Typically, students with reading difficulties do not possess an extensive vocabulary because they have not had multiple exposures to vocabulary development activities through reading experience (Simmons & Kame'enui, 1990). Students with disabilities require many specific opportunities to build their vocabulary knowledge base, including activities to understand both the literal and implied meanings of words and to develop the ability to use vocabulary in a variety of ways. IT provides a direct method to immerse the student in vocabulary knowledge development to improve reading skill.

WordWise Software (Attainment Company) combines 588 pictures, words, speech, and print features to create a language enrichment package. Students can record words and compare them to the computer pronunciation. It can also be used to create an individual word list to build vocabulary. All 588 illustrations are realistic and appropriate for any age. The software includes instructions and allows for a multiple-choice option. A new feature presents the written word with or without a picture. The teacher can easily create a personalized word file for each student, or choose from seven preselected lists including community, house, people, outdoor, actions, and adjectives. The pictures can be printed out in large, medium, or small size and in color or black and white to create custom picture books.

Words Around Me (Edmark, Inc.) is a vocabulary development program in English and Spanish for students with unique learning needs from ages PreK to adult. The program engages students in activities that identify 275 common vocabulary words and 186 plurals. Students learn to associate spoken words with photographs, drawn images, and animations that illustrate the word. Five different activities, including word identification, plurals, categorization, sameness, and difference, as well as four review games provide a variety of opportunities for reinforcement. The software contains a flexible management system that allows the teacher to customize the program to the individual student's age and ability.

Words & Concepts (Laureate Learning Systems, Inc.) offers a complete, integrated approach to vocabulary development and concept training. These programs are flexible, easy-to-run, based on sound learning principles, and fun to use. These programs include 40 core nouns in six integrated language activities to strengthen comprehension and increase understanding of word relationships. Most of the activities have three levels of difficulty, and the program can work exclusively on one level or move between levels to customize the experience. Vocabulary is built through engaging the student with three different pictures that appear on the screen, and the user is asked to choose one by name. ("Find the hat.") *Words and Concepts* introduces nouns to build vocabulary, categorization skills, word functioning and association, and the concepts of *same* and *different* to enhance comprehension.

Merriam-Webster® Speaking Dictionary & Thesaurus (MWS-1840) (Franklin Electronic Publishers) helps students to build their vocabulary through learning exercises and fun-filled games built into the *Merriam-Webster Speaking Dictionary & Thesaurus*. The Speaking Electronic Dictionary teaches a new word each time. Students can work on grammar, solve crossword puzzles, expand their vocabulary, and improve spelling skills. The Franklin's talking thesaurus and renowned phonetic spell-correction feature allows the student to enter words by how they sound; the large eight-line display screen offers visibility.

Finally, the *Speaking Language Master*™ (Franklin Electronic Publishers) is a reference tool for students with limited vocabulary. It Includes 130,000 words; 300,000 definitions; 500,000 thesaurus entries; and a grammar guide. The headphones can be connected for use in the classroom. Students can create their own lists of words to study. The device also uses Franklin's Dynamic Phonics Guide! so students can hear how letters in a word sound, which relates to word identification and spelling. The device is helpful for students who need assistance with vocabulary (audio and visual output provide ways to access the information) and English language learners who are learning new reading vocabulary.

FLUENCY

Fluent readers are individuals who read with automaticity or quick, effortless, and accurate reading of words (Vaughn & Bos, 2009). Struggling readers lose the meaning of the passage as they name the words. Research has shown that fluency instruction can be an effective means of enhancing understanding of the text (Meyer & Felton, 1999). IT plays an important role in providing students with specialized practice for developing fluency skills through research-based activities such as listening to others read text aloud, reading books aloud and silently at an independent reading level, and using guided oral reading.

Start-to-Finish® Library—Strengthen Reading Fluency and Comprehension (Don Johnson, Inc.) (Ability Level: Grades 1.5–5.5 • Interest Level: Grades 5–12) utilizes a wide selection of age-appropriate narrative chapter books written at two readability levels. The two readability levels are levels second through third and fourth through fifth grades. The program uses three media formats, including a paperback book, an audio recording, and a computer book that includes highlighted text. Students practice reading fluently and increase their comprehension using multiple text and electronic supports, while accessing the curriculum's required topics, genres, and literature. A comprehension check and a fluency passage to practice appear at

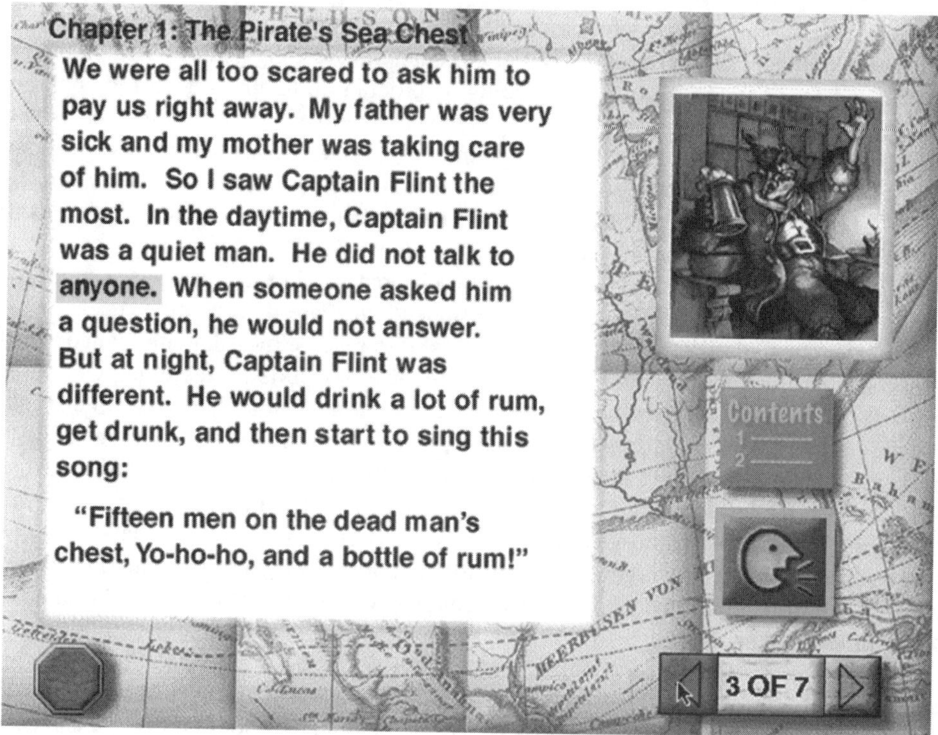

FIGURE 7.4 Start-to-Finish Story
Source: Copyright © Don Johnston, Inc., Volo, IL. Used by permission.

the end of every chapter. A fluency guide helps the teacher to match the student's level and interests to particular texts, instructions on choosing the correct titles for students, information about lab and classroom implementation, examples of reading routines and strategies, student evaluations, fluency practice reports, and a data collection method to make instructional decisions. Progress on chapter-by-chapter checks for comprehension can be viewed in graph format. Figure 7.4 provides a screen of a *Start-to-Finish* story.

READING COMPREHENSION

Reading comprehension is the ultimate goal of reading and is a major challenge for many students with learning disabilities (Boon, Fore, & Spencer, 2006). It is an active process in which the reader constructs meaning from the text through prior knowledge. Students with literacy problems benefit from both remediation and AT adaptations that compensate for the difficulties they experience with literacy (Lange et al., 2006). Although a student may be able to read words aloud, without comprehension the task is meaningless. Decoding words does not always lead to comprehension of the passage (Bryant et al., 2008). Instruction in reading comprehension skills is imperative for struggling readers. The following software represents the variety of available IT used to improve reading comprehension.

Read:OutLoud Universal Access (Don Johnston, Inc.) (Ability Level: Grades 3–9 • Interest Level: Grades 3–12) is an accessible text reader that gives below-grade-level readers access to the general curriculum. *Read:OutLoud* contains a feature that allows students to add e-text to their assignment folders for easy access. The program also enables students to browse and capture Web pages for later use. A variety of supported reading guides based on research-based comprehension strategies are included in the program to remind students to apply these strategies to their comprehension tasks. eHighlighters allow the student to use color coding to create a hierarchy of facts that resembles an outline. *The Franklin Dictionary* is also included in this software program for use by students in the setting of grades 3 through 12. *Read: OutLoud* contains a progress monitoring feature that allows the teacher to evaluate student achievement in the area of reading comprehension as well as other reading skills.

ClassMate Reader (HumanWare) (Ability Level: Grades 3–12 • Interest Level: Grades 3–12) is a new portable text reader designed to help students increase their reading speed, comprehension, and vocabulary development. The ClassMate reads aloud and simultaneously displays and highlights text on its full-color screen. The device is portable and can be used anywhere. The *ClassMate Reader* has a touch screen and navigation buttons with a speaking dictionary. The student can also add bookmarks, voice recording, or highlighting to the text. The device can be configured to the student's exact preferences, including font type, text size, color, line spacing, letter spacing, and the scrolling speed of text. Files are stored on a removable secure digital flash memory card and play various electronic book formats. With 1 GB storage capacity, this secure digital card can store hundreds of books. The *ClassMate Reader* uses a multisensory, multimodal approach, combining both sight and hearing by the simultaneous use of text and audio.

The Stories & More Series (Edmark, Inc.) is a series of classic children's books with interactive activities. The program focuses on reading comprehension skills for students with disabilities. The software contains initial activities to activate the student's prior knowledge and engage the student in predicting story outcomes. Students explore stories that are accompanied by two prereading activities to set the stage for the story. Once the prereading activities are completed, the student reads the story in its original book form with text and illustration(s) on each screen page. The student can also choose to have the book read aloud by the computer, along with words that highlight when read. Once the story is completed, the student completes story immersion and follow-up activities. Students analyze and think about what they have read, including setting the stage for the story, making predictions about the story, putting story parts into the correct sequence, creating a poster about the story, and drawing a personal conclusion from the story. The *Stories and More Series* comes in two different levels.

Writing

Writing is the process of translating thoughts into the written word through text generation and transcription of language into writing (Polloway, Patton, & Serna, 2008). Transcription processes include the mechanical aspects of writing, such as handwriting and spelling, whereas text generation involves the composition process. Students with physical disabilities may benefit in terms of spelling accuracy, readability, legibility, and mean lengths of consecutive correct word sequences (Mirenda, Turoldo, & McAvoy, 2006). In addition, student with learning disabilities benefit from IT and AT adaptations in the drafting, revising, and publishing processes (Graham et al., 2001).

TEXT GENERATION

The text generation writing process consists of five phases: (a) prewriting, (b) drafting, (c), revising, (d) editing, and (e) publishing (Bryant et al., 2008). Prewriting includes all the activities a writer does to prepare for writing. Activities such as selecting a topic, planning the content, and gathering and organizing the information are all a part of prewriting. In the drafting stage, the writer focuses on getting thoughts on paper in an initial attempt. Next, the writer moves on to the revising stage, in which a review of the product results in changes and additions to the content. Editing reflects the time when the writer focuses on correcting mechanical errors such as misspellings. Finally, in the publishing stage, the writer shares the piece. In the following sections, we look at how instructional and assistive technology can improve the mechanical aspects as well as the transcription process of writing.

TRANSCRIPTION OR MECHANICAL ASPECTS

The mechanical aspects of writing involve skills in the areas of spelling, handwriting, punctuation, and capitalization. Students should develop accurate and quick handwriting skills and should become proficient in spelling words for successful writing (Graham, Harris, MacArthur, & Schwartz, 2004). Problems in the areas of spelling, capitalization, and punctuation are not unusual for students with disabilities, and incorporating IT and AT adaptations into the instructional delivery may assist these students (Johnston, Beard, & Carpenter, 2007). Without mastery of the mechanical aspects of writing, student must spend more time and effort on these skills in order to create written products. Difficulties in spelling words, handwriting, or punctuation result in problems with acquiring the higher-level writing processes involved in text generation (Graham, 1999; McCutchen, 1996). In this section, we describe the various types of instructional software and AT devices that can be used to facilitate the writing process.

HANDWRITING

Students experiencing difficulties with handwriting may benefit from a variety of AT adaptations including some low-tech methods. Simply stabilizing the paper on a clipboard or using a slant-board may improve the student's ability to write more efficiently. Students may use pencil grips to improve their ability to grasp and to lessen strain during the writing process. In addition, raised-line paper provides tactile cues that help to define the appropriate space for writing. Alternative keyboards and keyguards may be needed for students with dysgraphia or other types of fine-motor control problems. These are described in another chapter of this book.

The Slant Board (Adaptables) helps students with problems in handwriting. It can be used as a document or large manual holder, provides an angled writing surface with several different positions, and can be adjusted from 12 to 21 inches in height.

Stage Write Raised Line Paper (Therapro) is a six-stage series of handwriting papers that begin with clearly defined writing spaces and perceptual cues that become less intense in the later stages as the student gains mastery. The thick, colorful dark blue baselines are raised, providing not only visual cues, but also tactile cues. All lines are separated by 3/8", except for 1/4" separation in Stage Five. All packages come with suggestions on how to use the paper.

WORD PREDICTION

Word prediction software supports the writing process by providing the student with related words to complete a thought. This technology was originally developed for students with physical impairments to lessen the number of keystrokes needed to write. For students with writing difficulties, particularly in the area of spelling, word prediction software analyzes the structure and content of the sentence and then provides a list of possibilities to complete the sentence. The student selects the appropriate word from this list. Word prediction programs often include speech synthesis to read the text and the list of words aloud as well as a spell-check feature. The

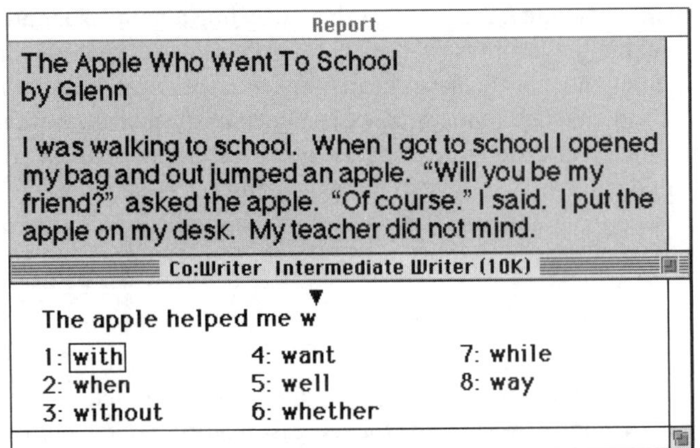

FIGURE 7.5 Co:Writer

Source: Copyright © Don Johnston, Inc., Volo, IL. Used by permission.

speech synthesis feature allows students to listen to what they have written to check for content (Lange et al., 2006).

Co:Writer (Don Johnston, Inc.) adds word prediction, grammar, and vocabulary to word processors. Flexspell is included in this program to give students who spell phonetically word prediction to aid in the writing process. The software brings up a list of possible words when the student starts to type. Grammar support corrects errors and helps students to practice basic written language skills. Figure 7.5 shows a screen shot from the word prediction software in Co:Writer.

WordQ 2 (Quillsoft) can be used with word processing programs to predict words by displaying a list of correctly spelled words. The correct word can be chosen by a mouse click or a single keystroke. Once the sentence is complete, WordQ 2 can read it back and allows the writer to correct words or punctuation. The word production software is self-adapting and matches the student's age and writing level. The user can expand, focus, or limit the word prediction vocabulary as well. Finally, a temporarily disappearing word prediction box allows the user to move through the document without distraction.

SPELLING

In a survey of elementary school teachers, Graham and Harris (2005) found that some 26% of students experience spelling difficulty. Spelling continues to represent an important area of instruction for students with disabilities (Polloway et al., 2008). From an assistive technology perspective, both software and AT devices can help improve spelling skills and also support the student in the selection of correctly spelled words during the writing process. The word processor, which is described shortly, provides a spell checker through software packages such as Microsoft Office and is an example of an AT adaptation used to improve spelling in a written document. We review software programs that focus on improving the student's spelling skills.

Show Me Spelling (Attainment, Company, Inc.) teaches functional spelling through 600 spelling words paired with corresponding speech with pictures. It is appropriate for any age and for a wide range of ability levels. Two modes are available, including the instruction and quiz modes. In the instruction mode, the teacher can create a spelling list by selecting words from the word bank or choose from dozens of preselected lists. The program difficulty can be adjusted by offering students helpful spelling hints, such as showing the next letter. Students can then select the "Show Me" option that introduces a short animated movie to present the correct spelling. A "celebration" movie appears when a student spells a word correctly. The quiz mode allows the teacher to implement a pre- and posttest strategy to evaluate student progress. The program easily saves students' word lists and quiz scores.

Spelling Blaster (Knowledge Adventure) uses phonics-based activities to introduce spelling rules and patterns for more than 1,700 words to build spelling skills. The program displays multiple word-attack strategies in seven spelling activities correlated to state and national standards. Printable materials including word searches and crossword puzzles are available for practice away from the computer. The program includes more than 140 spelling lists and crossword puzzles. "SpellTrack" technology allows the teacher to monitor deficit areas.

SYNTAX

Instruction in syntax is a critical feature in written language. Syntax refers to the order of words in a sentence as well as the rules that govern that order. Students face difficulty in the drafting, revising, and editing stages of writing without knowledge of the rules of syntax as well the ability to efficiently use them. Several software programs are reviewed here, focusing on improving a student's knowledge of syntax.

LanguageLinks®: Syntax Assessment and Intervention (Laureate Learning Systems, Inc.) helps students to master syntax and become better communicators through a comprehensive, evidence-based approach to syntax assessment and intervention. These programs provide activities for 75 different grammatical forms and include 750 stimulus pictures through six different modules. The first level introduces possessives, noun plurals, determiners, and pronouns. The second level adds several verb forms. The third level adds noun/verb agreement. The remaining levels continue to increase the student's knowledge of syntax.

WORD PROCESSORS

Research has demonstrated that word processors help students to compensate for a variety of writing difficulties (Twyman & Tindal, 2006). There are several ways in which word processors can be used as an AT adaptations to facilitate the writing process. First, word processors allow corrections to be made easily and often provide highlighting features for mistakes in spelling and grammar. This allows the student to focus on the content rather than the mechanical aspects of writing. The highlighting feature strengthens students' ability to edit their work and serves as a visual reminder that editing must be completed. Second, word processors with desktop publishing features allow the student to create written products with a minimum of errors. Using the "cut," "copy," and "paste" features encourages students to draft, revise, and edit to form a more complete result.

Kurzweil 3000™, which is also discussed in Chapter 6, is a comprehensive reading, writing, and learning software solution that can access virtually any information, whether it is printed, electronic, or on the Web. Because the Kurzweil 3000 is also content independent, teachers in elementary schools, middle schools, high schools, and colleges alike use it to help students succeed in the classroom regardless of curriculum or lesson plan. The Kurzweil 3000 features writing toolbars that help the student with writing and editing skills. As students type, the software speaks each letter or word, so they can quickly recognize and correct spelling mistakes. The Check Spelling As You Type feature underlines misspelled words in red. The audible spell checker and customizable word prediction further assist students with creating and modifying reports, essays, and papers without teacher intervention.

Write:OutLoud (Don Johnston, Inc.) is a talking word processor and writing software program built specifically for students in grades 3–12. The program uses auditory feedback plus purposeful revising and editing tools to support the quality of writing. It also provides productivity reports to track data, compare documents, and monitor overall progress. Equipped with a text-to-speech function, *Write:OutLoud* can speak words or sentences as well as whole passages. The program also highlights word by word as students write enabling them to hear what they have written and to correct inaccuracies.

SEMANTIC MAPPING

Semantic mapping software helps students to generate and organize information or ideas in the writing process. Research has supported computerized graphic organizers as an effective tool for improving both writing and reading skills (Kim, Vaughn, Wanzek, & Wei, 2004). This type of technology-based instruction has the potential to enhance student achievement, improve time on task, and increase student motivation as well as increase skills (Boon et al., 2006).

Inspiration (Inspiration Software, Inc.) is a visual learning tool that enables students to organize ideas. It provides functions for organization such as diagramming, concept map development, templates, and worksheets. This program helps students to create semantic webs, graphic organizers, and outlines in the planning stages of writing. Inspiration is easily manipulated to allow students to reformulate the plan as they learn more about their subject or draft. Figure 7.6 shows a diagram that was created using Inspiration software.

WRITING PROGRAMS

Research continues to explore the efficacy of software programs that teach and reinforce the writing process. There are programs that purport to accomplish the goal. These programs often target primary-grade students in the early stages of written language development. They may also be used for remediation with older students.

WYNN Scan and Read Literacy Software (Freedom Scientific, Learning Systems Group) uses a bimodal approach with simultaneous highlighting of the text as it is spoken to transform printed text into understandable information. WYNN provides programming for both literacy and writing skills. In the area of writing, WYNN's four color-coded, rotating toolbars use a simple point-and-click interface. The toolbars emphasize file management, visual and auditory presentation

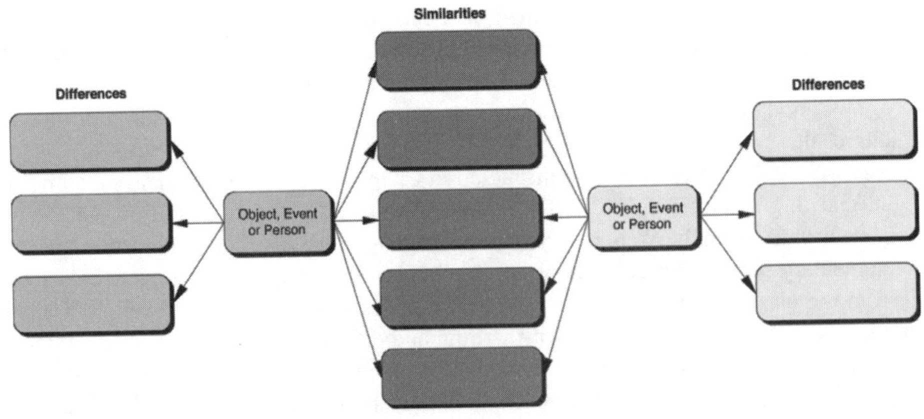

FIGURE 7.6 Brainstorming Format for a Compare-Contrast Paper Using Inspiration
Source: Diagram from Inspiration® by Inspiration Software, Inc.

of text, traditional study tools, writing aids, and Internet use. The program includes dictionaries, a thesaurus, a listing of homophones, word prediction ability, a highlighter, an outliner, voice notes, and text notes.

ULTimate KidBooks (CAST) allows teachers and others to create electronic books using images and text from any source. The resulting electronic books feature multiple representations of information and provide the student with several means of control. Multiple images can appear on each page with associated picture descriptions. All text can be highlighted and read aloud either word by word or sentence by sentence. Text and graphics from a textbook can be entered, allowing students typically excluded from content subjects because they cannot use the textbook to have necessary supports to engage in the learning experience.

Stanley's Sticker Stories (Edmark, Inc.) addresses a variety of skills in reading, writing, vocabulary, spelling, and creativity. Students create their own animated storybooks, alphabet and number books, letters, and signs. Tools, large buttons, and Stanley's spoken aids help make it easy to use animation, sound effects, and music to bring stories to life. Special features include spoken help to assist readers and nonreaders, as well as record and playback options that allow nonwriters to express ideas independently. The Sticker Spelling Book allows students to see and hear the spelling of each of more than 300 stickers, animate characters with the click of a button, and click on Stanley to get fun ideas for stories.

Mathematics

"The need to understand and be able to use mathematics in everyday life and in the workplace has never been greater and will continue to increase" according to the National Council of Teachers of Mathematics (NCTM, 2000). With 5% to 8% of school-age children being diagnosed with a mathematics disability (Geary, 2004), it remains critical that educators find a variety of research-based interventions to address the needs of these students. Geary further reports that problems in learning arithmetic combinations suggest a developmental difference involving memory or cognition problems in these students. These issues will affect the student's ability not only to memorize basic calculation facts but also to engage in more advanced mathematical operations such as solving word problems. Bryant, Bryant, and Hammill (2000) reported that in a rank ordering of mathematics difficulties in students with learning disabilities, teachers described certain tasks as problematic across ages. In addition, because students with mathematics disabilities spend much of their instructional time concentrating on the computation aspect of mathematics, their exposure to other facets such as time, measurement, and practical problem solving may be limited (Vaughn & Bos, 2009). The next sections review a variety of IT that will expand students' experiences with all aspects of mathematics.

NUMBER CONCEPTS

Number concepts, or "number sense," consist of a variety of early number development skills including numeration, place value, numeral recognition, counting, and an understanding of quantity. For many students struggling with mathematics, a lack of emphasis and time spent on the development of number concepts continues to impair their mathematics reasoning (Bryant et al., 2008). This lack of time for instruction and practice is reflected later as the student fails to progress. Irish (2002) determined that the number of computer-assisted mathematics instruction sessions per week significantly increased both the level of mastery and the rapidity of the change. The development of these basic mathematics skills remains critical for students to succeed and develop the ability to use mathematics in daily life.

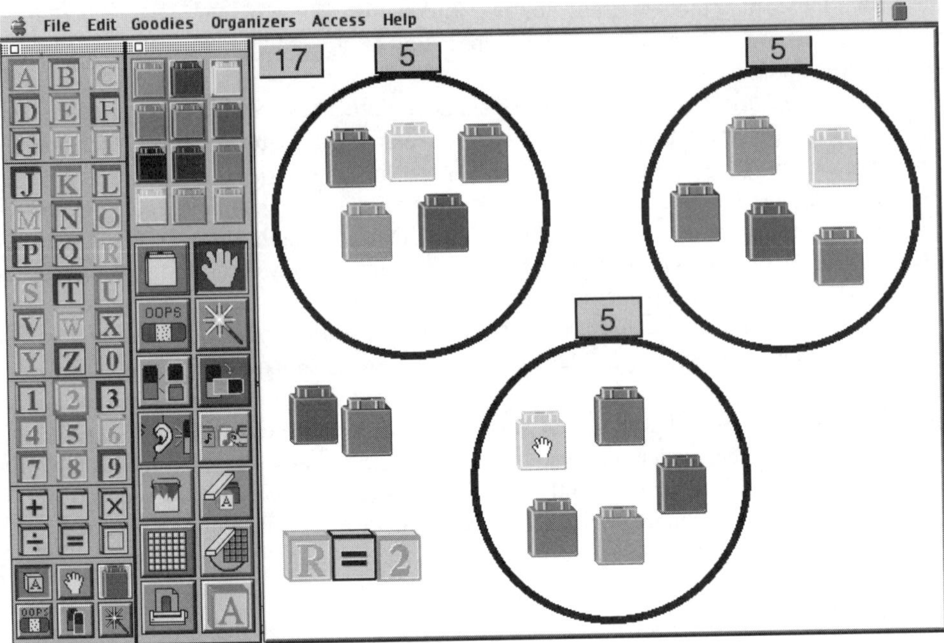

FIGURE 7.7 Pictorial Experiences with Math Concepts in Unifix® Software. Unifix® is a registered trademark of Philograph Publications Ltd.

Unifix® Software (Didax Educational Resources) provides a visual representation to help make the connection between concrete hands-on experiences and abstract math concepts. The program includes on-screen Unifix Cubes, counting bears, and counting people. It provides sounds for patterning, reinforcement, and song making. Unifix Software allows work in progress to be saved for later and prints in color or black and white for portfolios and take-home projects. The program includes on-screen activities or produces worksheets and includes a complete teacher's manual and 100 free Unifix Cubes. The software features built-in access for single switch users. Figure 7.7 provides a screen shot of how students use Unifix Software.

COMPUTATION

Students with mathematics disabilities have problems both in the memorization of facts and in their use of computational operations such as addition (Polloway et al., 2008). The process of solving whole-number computation involves symbols, multiple steps, and a level of abstraction that proves difficult for many students with disabilities (Bley & Thornton, 2001). A lack of fluency or automaticity with the basic facts impedes the progress of many of these students. Students with mathematics disabilities need time and repetition in a variety of ways to develop an understanding of all the complex steps required in computation activities. IT and AT adaptations provide a critical link for students to master these basic mathematics skills.

Calculator Tutor Software (Attainment Company, Inc.) is a big talking on-screen calculator that helps students who struggle to use a calculator. The Calculator Tutor Software includes a large on-screen talking calculator and exercises that vary in complexity. Addition, subtraction, multiplication, division, percentages, and decimals are covered. The hint feature helps the beginning learner to make more informed decisions. A quiz option with scoring reports lets the teacher keep track of student progress. The Calculator Tutor Software works especially well with touch screens and is single-switch compatible.

Access to Math (Don Johnston, Inc.) is a talking math worksheet program. Access to Math provides teachers with math worksheets for addition, subtraction, multiplication, and division. Students complete math worksheets on or off the computer. Speech feedback, color coding of number columns, and grid support are features that are provided by this program.

Big:Calc (Don Johnston, Inc.) is a talking calculator, which can be used alone or with other programs. Students can hear numbers, allowing them to access math. There are six different calculator styles: phone pad, number line, giant calc, keyboard, business calc, and pyramid. Students can solve math problems ranging from simple addition and subtraction to currency and numbers involving decimals and negative integers. Switch and touch-screen access are also available with this program.

MindTwister Math (Edmark, Inc.) provides students with practice in the essential math facts and encourages problem-solving skills such as visualization, deduction, sequencing, and estimating. Using a multiplayer game format, students practice a wide range of skills including rounding, decimals, and reading graphs. MindTwister Math improves computation proficiency, increases math-fact fluency, and strengthens mental math skills.

MathPad and *MathPad Plus* (IntelliTools, Inc.) are electronic number processors that encourage students to do arithmetic directly on the computer. *MathPad Plus: Fractions and Decimals* offers the same functionality as MathPad and allows student to do addition, subtraction, multiplication, and division using fractions and decimals. The programs feature a toolbar, worksheets, and problem list features. Teachers can enter problems from worksheets or textbooks so students can work on the same problems as their peers. The programs support switch or overlay access.

GEOMETRY

The *NCTM Standards* (2000) list geometry as a crucial content ability for all students across the grade levels. Students need the opportunity to experience geometry in a variety of concrete manners. IT often provides them with an additional method for visualizing the more abstract features geometric relationships.

Cosmic Geometry (Edmark, Inc.) allows students to explore the attributes of shapes and solids, constructions and transformations, 2D and 3D coordinates, and the relationships among length, perimeter, area, and volume. While moving through a 3D maze, assembling robots, creating tessellating patterns, and making movies of geometric constructions, students develop a strong real-world foundation for geometry. Virtual Manipulatives help students make the connection between concrete and abstract concepts. Grow Slides automatically advance topics and problems.

ALGEBRA

Algebra is an area sorely neglected in math instruction for youngsters with learning and behavior problems (Rivera & Smith, 1997). The *NCTM Standards* (2000) identify algebra as a mathematical area that must be addressed beginning in elementary school in order to form the foundation for further learning of more complex facets in the upper grades. Algebraic elements such as the identity and commutative properties of addition and multiplication are important concepts for students to understand. Some IT addresses these mathematical properties and encourages students to gain expertise in manipulating them through software programming.

Mighty Math Astro Algebra (Edmark, Inc.) reinforces the concepts and problem-solving skills in basic algebra. Students learn to graph functions, translate word problems into solvable equations, and represent algebraic expressions using the program's Virtual Manipulatives. The program provides hundreds of problems in more than 90 space missions. Students travel with four crew members, who help them strategize, calculate, and check their work. They play with the basic building blocks of algebra using features such as Capture Satellites and Meteoroids and Unusual Outer-Space Treasures. They learn about functions, graphing, ratios and proportions, slope and intercept, fractions, decimals and percents, exponents, problem solving, and reasoning. A step-by-step calculator, a talking reference database, and progress record function are included.

TIME, MONEY, MEASUREMENT

Time, money, and measurement are skills emphasized in the *NCTM Standards* (2000). They represent abilities directly reflected in everyday life and critical for success. Students with mathematics disabilities seldom receive the intensive instruction they require in order to master these skills. A variety of instructional software is available to increase the amount of time and the intensity of the instructional process for students needing to learn about time, money, and measurement.

MatchTime (Attainment Company, Inc.) helps students who are learning to tell time. It has four progressively difficult levels. The program uses a preset sequence of multiple-choice matching exercises in which students simply find the clock that matches the large sample clock in Levels 1 through 3. In Level 4, the concepts of "earlier" and "later" are introduced. Level 1 concentrates on matching the hour hand; Level 2 introduces 15-minute intervals. Level 3 provides activities using all the minutes, and Level 4 progresses to clocks that are up to four hours earlier or later than the example. Both digital and analog clocks are used. The program provides extensive record-keeping methods to monitor student progress. Spoken cues are provided in all exercises.

The *Coin-u-lator* (PCI Education) is a handheld, coin-counting calculator that allows individuals of all abilities to add and subtract various denominations of coins while it teaches the different values of each coin. It can add or subtract any combination of coins and bills up to $99.99, and it has two different coin games. The Coin-u-lator is a battery-operated device with an easy-to-read LCD screen that clearly displays the status of the counting while unique sounds and an animated voice send immediate auditory feedback to the user. The device features four "Coin" buttons and one "Dollar" button that depict realistic money. When the coin buttons are pressed, the value of the coin is displayed on the LCD screen. Students can add and subtract the amounts and play two different coin-counting games.

Destination Advantage-Math (Houghton Mifflin Harcourt) provides a comprehensive program for students across grade levels. It provides step-by-step explicit instruction in math reasoning, conceptual understanding, and problem-solving skills. In Destination Advantage-Math grades 2 to 3, students apply mathematics concepts through measuring time, money, and temperature. Destination Advantage-Math uses animation and audio support to engage students in the learning process and can be used individually or with the whole class. The program provides individualization and performance monitoring.

WORD PROBLEMS

Word-problem solving is an essential component of mathematics and should be taught across all grade levels (NCTM, 2000; Rivera, 1997). Students with mathematics disabilities experience a variety of difficulties when trying to solve word problems. They may not understand what the problem is describing, how to set up the solution, or how to select the appropriate information to include in the solution, or they may be thrown by the different varieties of word problems. Rivera (1997) identified difficulties with vocabulary, sentence structure complexity, extraneous information, reading problems, computational skill deficits, a lack of multistep problem representation, and confusion over word problem types as typical challenges for students with mathematics disabilities. The NCTM (2000) recommends that the emphasis for mathematics should be placed on the development of problem solving and reasoning. The use of research-based instructional software in the area of problem solving that provides opportunities for learning for students with mathematics disabilities can be a positive addition to the instructional plan.

Mighty Math Number Heroes (Edmark, Inc.) focuses on basic math concepts and problem-solving skills. With the help of Fraction Man, Star Brilliant, and other math superheroes, student practice math concepts, computation, fractions, geometry, and probability. They build shapes and play games applying math logic. Number heroes includes two calculators that display the steps for solving a problem and convert between fractions and decimals.

For examples of software in various academic areas, readers should search online for vendors listed in the various areas to get an idea of available software. We do not endorse any particular vendor but merely provide examples of various tools that teachers can review. Again, we advise using a software evaluation tool to closely scrutinize software as part of the instructional decision-making process when designing instruction.

IMPLEMENTING INSTRUCTION

Implementing instruction focuses on how the teacher groups students and the way in which instruction is delivered. The grouping of students plays an integral role as the teacher explores ways to intensify direct instruction. Research-based interventions stipulate the methods and amount of time the student has for supplemental instruction, modeling, review, and additional targeted practice. Instructional delivery includes the pacing, the amount of material to be covered, and the number of repetitions of key elements of the lesson as aided by research-based strategies and materials and accommodations. IT and AT adaptations play an integral role in implementing instruction to promote learning and access to the curriculum. In this section, we describe groupings that promote the use of IT and AT adaptations.

Grouping

Grouping for instruction should be a primary consideration as the teacher plans and implements instruction (Bryant et al., 2008). Whole-group instruction entails the presentation of a lesson to the entire class simultaneously. This type of instruction can be direct, explicit, read-alouds, or other types of presentation. Whole-group instruction provides little opportunity for individualization. For students using AT adaptations, the teacher must ensure that the student is using the device correctly during the lesson. For example, whether the student is using a high-tech note-taking device or a low-tech advance organizer, the teacher must frequently observe the student's use of such technology. The teacher must also monitor the student's use of IT such as software for semantic mapping to make certain that the student is engaged with the lesson. Merely sitting at the computer during the lesson without actually being able to use the software to participate in the lesson is not effective implementation of instruction.

Small groups provide the opportunity for students to engage with others with the same ability level or, at other times, to be included in mixed-ability groupings. As with whole-group instruction, the teacher must be vigilant in checking with the student using an AT adaptation to provide guidance as needed. For example, using a large-print calculator makes a difference for a student in mathematics calculation when the student actually uses the device. IT in the small-group setting may increase the opportunities for the student with disabilities to interact successfully in a mixed-ability group. Using word-prediction software may enable that student to successfully act as the scribe in a cooperative learning group, thus giving them the chance to engage in every role rather than being relegated to a lesser one. The teacher must plan for the use of IT or AT adaptations regardless of the size of the group. Issues such as electrical outlets, access to desks and other furniture, and equipment such as computers or tape recorders are elements of instruction that must be planned for in order to successfully include technology in lessons.

Instructional Delivery

Instructional delivery is a critical component for improving students' access and learning opportunities. Just as with traditional instruction, lessons that utilize IT and AT adaptations must address the most appropriate instructional delivery issues for students with disabilities. Ulman (2005) describes some instructional delivery elements for IT. Use software programs with stated objectives, and match those objectives to your student's learning needs. Understand the prerequisite skills that are needed in order for the student to successfully operate the program. Find out how the student is "reinforced" during the program and determine if that fits your student's needs. Determine the amount of time it takes to totally complete the software and whether a student can save and return to a specific spot at a later time. Examine the independence level of the program and decide if your student is ready to work alone with the program. Check out the pace of the software and ascertain whether it can be changed for different students. Establish whether this program actually meets your student's needs or if it is simply filling time. Look at the flexibility of the program in terms of sound and graphic sequences. Some of these may be too stimulating or distracting for certain students. Finally, examine the screen design and verify whether it is appropriate for your student.

EVALUATING INSTRUCTION

The final part of this chapter focuses on the effectiveness of IT and AT adaptations. Lesson plans should contain specific evaluation related to the instructional objective, and the teacher should examine the usefulness of IT and AT adaptations in the lesson. The evaluation information explored at the end of the lesson should incorporate an assessment of environmental factors, use of adaptations, and monitoring of the student's progress using the technology in the lesson. In Table 7.2, we provide an academic version of the Adaptations Framework known as ADAPT. As shown in Table 7.2, each letter of the word ADAPT signifies specific questions for teachers to consider and ways to make and evaluate AT adaptations. In our example, the student is expected to learn new science vocabulary. Examine the information for each letter of ADAPT to learn more about ways teachers can go about identifying possible AT adaptations to help students access the curriculum and be successful.

Knowledge about how well the person uses the technology and its impact on skills development is critical (Layton & Lock, 2008). Evaluation of technology is a critical feature that has been emphasized repeatedly in this book. Evaluation is essential to determine how students are responding to instruction. Combining lesson plan progress monitoring and evaluation of the effectiveness of IT and AT adaptations helps to provide a comprehensive picture of student progress. Finally, evaluation is a major feature of the Adaptations Framework; the multidisciplinary evaluation team discussed in Chapter 3 should carefully review student performance in light of the effectiveness of adaptations.

Table 7.2 ADAPT Framework

A What am I requiring the student to do?

The student will learn three new vocabulary words linked to the science lesson's concept.

D Determine the prerequisite skills of the task.

- The student will be able to listen and respond as the teacher presents the science concept.
- The student will be able to use the smart board in her cooperative learning group to learn about the science concept.
- The student will be able to select color-coded buttons on her computer to locate information electronically.
- The student will be able to use the turn-taking routine with her computer partner.
- The student will be able to copy the word into her computer.
- The student will be able to select pictures that illustrate the words.
- The student will be able to use the Franklin Electronic Dictionary to get a definition for the word.
- The student will be able to use aspects of the word processor and printer.

A Analyze the student's strengths and struggles.

Strengths

- The student listens during lessons.
- The student can work in the cooperative group.
- The student understands the color-coded system of the computer.
- The student follows the turn-taking routine.
- The student can copy words on the computer.
- The student can use the software on the computer.

Struggles

- Social skill deficits
- Some vision problems but does not wear glasses
- Oral language skills are deficient.
- Illegible handwriting
- Needs help with sequencing the complete science concept

P Propose and implement adaptations from among the four categories.

- Instructional material is adapted using the computer, the student's electronic science notebook where she places the words and pictures for each science concept, and her use of software to produce her assignments rather than handwritten products.

T Test to determine if the adaptations helped the student accomplish the task.

- The notebook displays 100% completion for each vocabulary word.
- The student can answer questions about each vocabulary word with 70% accuracy.

SUMMARY

In this chapter, we focused on integrating IT and AT adaptations into the design, implementation, and evaluation of instruction with an emphasis on academic instruction at the elementary, middle, and high school levels. The student is at the heart of this chapter. Remedial and compensatory strategies to improve student functioning can be greatly enhanced through the use of IT and AT adaptations. Instructional software requires careful consideration and selection to ensure that it meets student needs through research-based interventions. AT adaptations accommodate the student and provide them with devices that help to increase learning. By designing instruction that incorporates both IT and AT adaptations for students with disabilities, the teacher improves classroom performance. Teachers utilizing IT and AT adaptations must also consider effective implementation of instruction, including grouping arrangements and instructional delivery. Finally, evaluation is an integral component of the successful use of IT and AT adaptations. Careful monitoring of AT use and student progress informs instructional decision making concerning the effectiveness of IT and AT adaptations to remediate, promote access, and improve independence.

SCENARIO APPLICATIONS

Scenario 7.1

Although students with the same disability diagnosis may have some similar needs, AT is, by its nature, customized to the individual. Refer back to the various software you read about in this chapter. Do an online search for the software to learn more about specific features. Identify how different types of instructional software and AT adaptations may enhance learning for a student depending on the setting-specific demands and the person-specific characteristics. Identify the task and requisite abilities that a student would need in order to be successful with a variety of instructional software and AT adaptations.

Scenario 7.2

Teachers plan to deliver the most effective instruction to their students. Think about how students with disabilities are affected by various grouping arrangements. How do IT and AT adaptations figure into the teacher's implementation of a lesson? Describe the advantages and disadvantages of a variety of IT and AT adaptations when designing and implementing instruction.

Scenario 7.3

IT and AT adaptations are only productive if they actual create opportunities for learning for the student using them. What are some of the critical evaluation issues presented in this textbook? Name some other points that you think are important when evaluating student use of IT and AT adaptations in a lesson.

For Discussion

1. Explain the challenges teachers might encounter when integrating AT adaptations into instruction.
2. Identify questions to consider when designing lessons and possible answers for the questions.
3. Describe the components of designing, implementing, and evaluating academic instruction.
4. Explain the features of instructional software, types of software, and guidelines for evaluating software.

5. Describe the basic skills for reading, writing, and mathematics and difficulties students might exhibit in these areas.
6. Compare and contrast the AT adaptations that were described in reading. Describe how the adaptations might help students with different functional limitations in reading.
7. Compare and contrast the AT adaptations that were described in writing. Describe how the adaptations might help students with different functional limitations in writing.
8. Compare and contrast the AT adaptations that were described in mathematics. Describe how the adaptations might help students with different functional limitations in mathematics.
9. Describe how a classroom might be set up to support technology adaptations.
10. Develop your own case study and lesson plan.
11. Describe how you would evaluate the effectiveness of AT adaptations in a classroom or other environmental setting.
12. Develop speaking points for talking with the classroom teacher of the student in Personal Perspective 7.1 to explain the importance of supporting the student in using AT.

References

Bley, N., & Thornton, C. (2001). *Teaching mathematics to students with learning disabilities* (4th ed.). Austin, TX: Pro-Ed.

Boon, R. T., Fore, C., & Spencer, V. G. (2006). Teacher's attitudes and perceptions toward the use of Inspiration 6 software in inclusive world history classes at the secondary level. *Journal of Instructional Psychology, 34*(3), 166–171.

Brown, C. A. (2005). Computer software genres that help students think! Electronic Classroom. *Kappa Delta Pi Record, 42*(1), 42–44.

Bryant, D. P., & Bryant, B. R. (2003). *Assistive technology for people with disabilities*. Boston: Allyn & Bacon.

Bryant, D. P., Bryant, B., & Hammill, D. D. (2000). Characteristic behaviors of students with LD who have teacher-identified math weaknesses. *Journal of Learning Disabilities, 33*(2), 168–177.

Bryant, D. P., Smith, D. D., & Bryant, B. R. (2008). *Teaching students with special needs in inclusive classrooms.* Upper Saddle River, NJ: Allyn & Bacon/Pearson Education.

Bryant, D. P., Ugel, N., Thompson, S., & Hamff, A. (1999). Instructional strategies for content-area reading instruction. *Intervention in School and Clinic, 34*(5), 293–302.

Bryant, B. R., Wiederholt, J. L., & Bryant, D. P. (2004). *Gray diagnostic reading test* (2nd ed.). Austin, TX: Pro-Ed.

Burgstahler, S. (2003). The role of technology in preparing youth with disabilities for postsecondary education and employment. *Journal of Special Education Technology, 18*(4), 7–19.

Carnine, D. W., Silbert, J., Kame'enui, E. J., & Tarver, S. G. (2010). *Direct instruction reading* (5th ed.). Upper Saddle River, NJ: Merrill/Pearson Education.

Chard, D. J., & Dickson, S. V. (1999). Phonological awareness: Instructional and assessment guidelines. *Intervention in School & Clinic, 34*, 261–270.

Englert, C. S., Zhao, Y., Collings, N., & Roming, N. (2005). Learning to read words: The effects of Internet-based software on the improvement of reading performance. *Remedial and Special Education, 26*(6), 357–371.

Geary, D. C. (2004). Mathematics and learning disabilities. *Journal of Learning Disabilities, 37*, 4–15.

Graham, S. (1999). Handwriting and spelling instruction for students with learning disabilities: A review. *Learning Disabilities Quarterly, 22*(2), 78–98.

Graham, S., & Harris, K. R. (2005). *Writing better: Effective strategies for teaching students with learning difficulties*. Baltimore: Brookes.

Graham, S., Harris, K. R., & Larsen, L. (2001). Prevention and intervention of writing difficulties for students with learning disabilities. *Learning Disabilities Research & Practice, 16*(2), 74–84.

Graham, S., Harris, K. R., MacArthur, C., & Schwartz, S. (2004). Writing instruction. In B. Wong (Ed.), *Learning about learning disabilities* (3rd ed.). San Diego, CA: Academic Press.

Hamill, L., & Everington, C. (2002). *Teaching students with moderate to severe disabilities: An applied approach for inclusive environments*. Upper Saddle River, NJ: Merrill/Pearson Education.

Hargis, C. H. (1999). *Teaching and testing in reading: A practical guide for teachers and parents*. Springfield, IL: Charles C. Thomas.

Irish, C. (2002). Using peg-and keyword mnemonics and computer assisted instruction to enhance basic multiplication performance in elementary students with learning and cognitive disabilities. *Journal of Special Education Technology, 17*(4), 29–40.

Johnston, L., Beard, L. A., & Carpenter, L. B. (2007). *Assistive technology access for all students.* Upper Saddle River, NJ: Merrill/Pearson Education.

Judgen, S. L. (2001). Computer applications in programs for young children with disabilities: Current status and future directions. *Journal of Special Education Technology, 16*(1), 29–40.

`Keel, M. C., Dangel, H. L., & Owens, S. H. (1999). Selecting instructional interventions for students with mild disabilities in inclusive classrooms. *Focus on Exceptional Children, 31*(8), 1–16.

Kim, A., Vaughn, S., Wanzek, J., & Wei, S. (2004). Graphic organizers and their effects on the reading comprehension of students with LD: A synthesis of the research. *Journal of Learning Disabilities, 37*, 105–118.

Lange, A. A., McPhillips, M., Mulhern, G., & Wylie, J. (2006). Assistive software tools for secondary-level students with literacy difficulties. *Journal of Special Education Technology, 23*(3), 13–22.

Layton, C. A., & Lock, R. H. (2008). *Assessing students with special needs to produce quality outcomes.* Upper Saddle River, NJ: Merrill/Pearson Education.

Lee, Y., & Vail, C. O. (2005). Computer-based reading instruction for young children with disabilities. *Journal of Special Education Technology, 20*(1), 5–18.

Lemons, C. J. (2000). *Comparison of parent and teacher knowledge and opinions related to augmentative and alternative communication.* Unpublished master's thesis, The University of Texas at Austin.

McCutchen, D. (1996). A capacity theory of writing: Working memory in composition. *Educational Psychology Review, 8*, 299–325.

McLaren, E. M., Baush, M. E., & Ault, M. J. (2007). Collaboration strategies reported by teachers providing assistive technology services. *Journal of Special Education Technology, 22*(4), 16–29.

Meyer, M., & Felton, R. H. (1999). Repeated reading to enhance fluency: Old approaches and new directions. *Annuals of Dyslexia, 49*, 283–306.

Mirenda, P., Turoldo, K., & McAvoy, C. (2006). The impact of word prediction software on the written output of students with physical disabilities. *Journal of Special Education Technology, 23*(3), 5–12.

National Council of Teachers of Mathematics. (2000). *Principles and standards for school mathematics.* Reston, VA: Author.

Podhajski, B. (1999). *TIME for Teachers—What teachers need to know about what children need to know to learn to read: A trainer's manual for professional development of K–3 educators. (1st ed.).* Williston, VT: Stern Center for Language and Learning.

Polloway, E. A., Patton, J. R., & Serna, L. (2008). *Strategies for teaching learners with special needs* (9th ed.). Upper Saddle River, NJ: Merrill/Pearson Education.

Raskind, M. H., & Higgins, E. L. (1999). Speaking to read: The effects of speech recognition technology on the reading and spelling performance of children with learning disabilities. *Annals of Dyslexia, 49*, 251–281.

Raymond, E. B. (2008). *Learners with mild disabilities: A characteristics approach* (2nd ed.). Boston: Allyn & Bacon/Pearson Education.

Rivera, D. P. (1997). Mathematics education and students with learning disabilities: Introduction to the special series. *Journal of Learning Disabilities, 30*(1), 2–19, 68.

Rivera, D., & Smith, D. D. (1997). *Teaching students with learning and behavior problems* (3rd ed.). Boston: Allyn & Bacon.

Simmons, D. C., & Kame'enui, E. J. (1990). The effect of task alternatives on vocabulary knowledge: A comparison of students with learning disabilities and students with normal achievement. *Journal of Learning Disabilities, 23*, 291–97.

Stover, D. L., & Pendegraft, N. (2005). Revisiting computer-aided notetaking technological assistive devices for hearing-impaired students. *Journal of Educational Strategies, 79*(2), 94–97.

Torgesen, J. K., & Mathes, P. G. (2000). A basic guide to understanding, assessing, and teaching phonological awareness. Austin, TX: Pro-Ed.

Twyman, T., & Tindal, G. (2006). Using a computer-adapted, conceptually based history text to increase comprehension and problem-solving skills of students with disabilities. *Journal of Special Education Technology, 23*(2), 5–16.

Ulman, J. G. (2005). *Making technology work for learners with special needs. Practical skills for teachers.* Upper Saddle River, NJ: Allyn & Bacon/Pearson Education.

Vaughn, S., & Bos, C. S. (2009). *Strategies for teaching students with learning and behavior problems* (7th ed.). Upper Saddle River, NJ: Merrill/Pearson Education.

8 ASSISTIVE TECHNOLOGY DEVICES TO ENHANCE INDEPENDENT LIVING

Chapter at a Glance

Objectives

1. Explain what "independent living" means.
2. Describe ways in which assistive technology adaptations can be used to promote independence in daily living activities.
3. Describe switches and scanning and provide examples of when they can be used.
4. Describe environmental control unit systems and provide examples of how they are used in homes, work, and school.
5. Explain how assistive technology adaptations can be used for management purposes.
6. Describe the role of federal legislation in promoting independence and identify environmental accessibility issues that must be addressed.

MAKING CONNECTIONS

Think back to Chapter 2 and the purpose of assistive technology, that is, to promote independence. Based on the content you have read so far, consider ways in which assistive technology enables people to be independent. Identify in your own life how you live independently of others and the impact of losing your independence.

The purpose of this chapter is to discuss issues and related AT of independent living for individuals with disabilities. We do so by (a) introducing the concept of independent living, (b) describing devices for daily living, (c) discussing electronic aids to daily living, (d) describing devices to manage one's environment, and (e) examining issues and AT to enhance mobility.

INTRODUCTION TO INDEPENDENT LIVING

Individuals with disabilities have a right to live independently and experience full integration into society. Being able to live independently is fundamental to life. For example, independent living skills are identified in the adaptive areas (e.g., communication, self-care, home-living, social, community use, self-direction, health and safety, leisure, work) of the most recent conceptualization of intellectual disability (formerly called mental retardation) (Schalock, Luckasson, & Shogren, 2007). Skills such as caring for one's personal needs, engaging in recreational activities, and being able to go to work are activities that empower people and make them independent of others. Notably, for a number of years the Independent Living Movement has stimulated political action calling for social justice to promote acceptance of and action toward independent living for individuals with disabilities. The first center for Independent Living was established by disability activists in 1972 at the University of California at Berkeley. Although it is beyond the scope of this text, we urge readers to examine the historical perspective, advocacy efforts, and current activities by visiting Web sites that provide detailed information, such as www.independentliving.org/docs5/ILhistory.html, www.ilusa.com/articles/mshreve_article_ilc.htm, and http://bancroft.berkeley.edu/collections/drilm.

Assistive technology is intended to promote independence and enable users to access their environments and the associated tasks. Maintaining control over and having choices is a critical feature of independent living. Individuals with disabilities now have more ability to engage in independent living with the increased availability of AT devices and services.

Independent living means "control over one's life based on the choice of acceptable options that minimize reliance on others in making decisions and in performing everyday activities" (Frieden, Richards, Cole, & Bailey as cited in Nosek, 1992, p. 103). Individuals who possess independent living skills are more empowered than those who lack these abilities. Independent living skills involve mobility (in the home and within the community, including the use of public transportation), activities of daily living (grooming, eating, dressing), use of personal assistants (i.e., attendants), communication, work, and use of leisure time (Nosek, 1992).

In many cases, people with disabilities lack opportunities to exercise choice and control over many parts of their lives. When people do not have these opportunities, they may remain or become helpless and dependent on others. Making choices and having some control in one's life is very important for achieving quality of life for persons with disabilities (Gardner, 1990; Schalock & Kiernan, 1990). For example, some adults with disabilities live in group homes, which provide treatment and supervision (O'Brien, 1991). Typically, professionally approved caretakers manage their daily schedules, activities, meals, and bedtimes. Unfortunately, choice and environmental control may be limited (O'Brien, 1991). If independence is the ultimate goal for individuals with disabilities, then procedures and support systems must be in place to promote independent living skills and the ability to make choices (Mithaug & Hanawalt, 1978). We suggest that as readers progress through this chapter, they spend time reviewing AT devices for independent living on www.abledata.com/abledata.cfm. We begin by providing a Personal Perspective by Dr. Peg Nosek (Personal Perspective 8.1). We believe that Dr. Nosek's reflections convey the spirit of this chapter.

PERSONAL PERSPECTIVE 8.1

Dr. Margaret (Peg) A. Nosek received a Ph.D. in Rehabilitation Research and a Master of Arts in Rehabilitation Counseling from The University of Texas (UT), Austin, and a Master of Arts in Music from Case Western Reserve University. She is currently a professor and executive director of the Center for Research on Women with Disabilities in the Department of Physical Medicine and Rehabilitation at Baylor College of Medicine. She is an internationally recognized authority on women with disabilities and independent living for persons with disabilities. She has done considerable research and writing on developments in public policy that affect the ability of people with disabilities to live independently in the community. She is recognized as one of the first to apply scientific methodologies to the study of the health of women with disabilities and the independence of people with disabilities. More than $6 million has been awarded by the National Institutes of Health, Centers for Disease Control and Prevention, National Institute on Disability and Rehabilitation Research, and various private foundations to support her research, with another almost $5 million funding for projects she has done in collaboration with other researchers. Dr. Nosek's accomplishments are reflected in her 54 articles published in refereed academic journals, 18 chapters in academic textbooks, over 100 presentations at national conferences of scholarly organizations, and many presentations at international conferences outside of the United States. Dr. Nosek is the recipient of numerous awards for her research and advocacy by local, state, and national organizations. As a person with a severe physical disability, she has been both a pioneer and an activist in the disability rights movement, including vigorously supporting passage of the Americans with Disabilities Act. The President's Committee on Employment of People with Disabilities has honored her as a "Disability Patriot."

Tell Our Readers About Your Memories of Your Childhood Years and how Assistive Devices Played a Role in Your Development

I was diagnosed at the age of two with spinal muscular atrophy, which is a progressive neuromuscular disorder that results in slow loss of muscle function. As a child, I began walking with a waddling gate. Walking became more difficult for me as I grew older; I started using a wheelchair for mobility in the fourth grade, at which time I was also diagnosed with scoliosis. Because of a lack of arm strength, I was never able to propel the chair independently. This limited my ability to move around my environment and explore. I think it is absolutely critical for kids to be able to explore so they can learn about boundaries. A lot of kids aren't mobile right from the start. I was lucky because I could get around during my early years, but I was not mobile at a critical time in my life, adolescence. I even had to be carried in and out of my own house. I started acting out a little in order to draw people toward me because I couldn't get around. I used humor so that people would like to be around me. I didn't get my first electric wheelchair until I was 25. That's why I love seeing little kids in power wheelchairs. It's an equalizer, a liberator. For the first time I could go somewhere without people knowing where I was going. I could take off and explore my city. If I was at a party and someone was boring me, I could actually leave. I didn't have to wait for someone interesting to come up to me and talk. I could go find them. Having mobility impacted my personal life, my social life, and my self-esteem. I could actually take risks—it was exhilarating!

You have Been a Strong Advocate for Many Years for Disability Rights. How Do You See Assistive Technology Fitting into the Advocacy Discussion?

In my opinion, assistive technology equals liberation. Imagine life without it—I would be dead or severely limited or bed-bound. But many people are unserved or underserved. People who are

(*continued*)

poor, people who don't have insurance, older people, people who don't speak English and don't have access to this kind of information all have problems getting AT devices and services. To me, it's very important for people to accept their disability and to get connected to the service delivery systems. I count my blessings that I'm connected and have good doctors. I see so many people who refuse to use a wheelchair or hearing aids. I remember my grandmother who had developed serious mobility impairments from arthritis and could have benefited from using a wheelchair. But she said, "I'm no cripple." And she said that as I was sitting right next to her in my chair. This attitude has to change. It's okay to use a wheelchair. It's okay to use hearing aids. They're not a stigma.

You have Done Considerable Research on Women with Disabilities. Describe Briefly Any Relationship, if there is One, Between Women's Issues and the Use of Assistive Technology Devices

There's a huge connection. Technology developed in response to the needs of veterans injured in war so they could get back to work. A lot of technology is developed for men's needs and industrial applications. There are no effective bladder management systems for women—catheterization or diapers, that's it. Women's bladder and menstrual needs are not considered. You can't even get a seat cushion to keep your legs together. There are no gender differences in seat cushions—never been considered. There are also technology issues related to pregnancy and child raising. In a wheelchair, you can't lean over very easily, not to mention when you're pregnant. That makes it hard to lift a baby out of a crib. You have to ask someone else in the family to do it. Applications of AT for child raising are simply not there. "Through the Looking Glass," a research and training center for parents with disabilities in California, has worked to address the needs of women with disabilities and child raising (see http://lookingglass.org/index.php). There are a lot of low-tech tricks that women have made up to help them care for children, and TLG has helped disseminate this information.

You Live in One of the Largest Cities in the United States, Houston. Describe Some of the Most Complicated Issues Surrounding Transportation Needs for People with Disabilities in Urban Settings. How Do These Issues Differ with Regard to Rural Issues, and how Does Assistive Technology Play a Role in Each Setting?

In Houston, there are a lot of miles between Point A and Point B, so the transportation system faces many problems in serving everyone, especially people with disabilities. It was such a feeling of conquest when I first rode in one of their accessible buses, because we had to fight hard to get it to happen. When we first approached the transportation system, the city was adamant that they would not spend the money to create accessibility to the mainline buses. But at the very first meeting after we filed a lawsuit the city backed down, and the next thing you know they bought 400 buses with lifts. They also have a door-to-door system for those who can't use buses. Like I said, the first time I rode the bus I felt like a conquering hero. I also felt like a neighbor for the first time. I just had an unbelievably warm feeling of inclusion. That said, sometimes the lifts break down and buses just go by if a driver doesn't want to take the time to pick you up.

As for rural areas, when I graduated from UT, I moved to the Davis Mountains of west Texas to live with Justin Dart and his family for four months. I was completely dependent on him and his truck for getting anywhere. In rural areas, like large urban areas, life depends on being able to get around. If there is any public transportation at all, it probably includes only a door-to-door service for people with disabilities. Such systems have an even greater problem dealing with large distances, and breakdowns can be devastating. In Fort Davis there were no accessible services when I lived there. It was an interesting, and a bit of a frightening, experience.

Assistive Technology Encompasses Highly Technological Devices but also Includes Very Simple Devices. Describe for Our Readers how Your Home is Set up to Foster Independence in Daily Living and the Role Assistive Devices Play in Contributing to Your Independence on a Daily Basis.

We always lived in inaccessible houses while I was growing up in Ohio. I had to be carried in and out of my parents' house. This really affected my feelings of self-worth and personal development. My father did not want a ramp because he feared it would lower the resale value of the house. I felt restricted and dependent. Later, when I attended UT at the age of 25, I lived in the dorm and later in cooperative housing, and both were completely accessible to me with no more than an automatic door button and a widened door to the bathroom. When I graduated I lived in an apartment, then bought my own house. I looked for a house with a minimum of steps near an accessible bus line that would be reasonably modifiable, with wider doors and ramps, for instance. I've outfitted the house with lowered light switches, a toilet seat extension, handheld shower, rope on the door for opening and closing, and lots of other gadgets. I have sticks with rubber tips in every room that I use to turn pages, move pencils around, and pull things close. I also have lamps that I just have to touch to turn on and off. When I was younger, one of the hardest challenges I faced was to do something so that I could turn over by myself at night. My dad and an occupational therapist helped me rig up some pulleys and rope suspended from the ceiling over my bed that could be used with my wheelchair's joystick and power supply to lift up my knees so I could wiggle around and get comfortable. That was a great help for many years.

As a Leader in The Disability Movement, You Undoubtedly have Strong Opinions with Regard to the Timely Acquisition of Assistive Devices for People who Need Them. What have You Seen as Barriers to Device Acquisition and are You Optimistic Concerning the Future in This Area?

There are several barriers, the first of which deals with the importance of connecting with an agency that can purchase or provide devices. It's also important to get an accurate evaluation. We really don't have a good system to determine how people can be assessed. There is a lack of laboratories to try things out—no place you can go to try out keyboards to use with your computer. We need a place where people with disabilities can go to get matched with the technology that exists in the marketplace. Also, policies are ridiculous—it's often an all or nothing package. With my van, for example, I wanted a simple lift, but I had to get a whole package that cost $16,000 and included a kneeling system and other features that I knew I didn't want or need. Many of the components that have broken down are not under warranty any more and I can't afford to get them repaired. Now I don't use them, and I didn't need them to begin with. All I needed was a lift but I had to buy the whole package because of the liability policies of the state rehab agency that paid for it.

Another major issue involves funding. Medicare and some insurance plans are limited and won't pay for some devices, for example. And organizations are restrictive also. For instance, the Muscular Dystrophy Association will pay for a manual chair but not a power chair. So we need to work hard to get funding issues taken care of. After lack of information, I think funding is the single biggest barrier. (For an updated explanation of this funding issue, see www.mda.org/publications/quest/extra/jul09/restored.html.)

Finally, we need to make professionals more aware of AT issues. I count my blessings that I had a doctor who knew about the latest AT and could help me get set up with a nice compact, quiet ventilator for my wheelchair. Not all professionals are that well connected. We need to work on information dissemination for professionals.

(*continued*)

Finally, as a Person who has Numerous Degrees and has Spent a Number of Years in our Educational System, what Would You Want to Share with Prospective or Current Teachers About Assistive Technology Use by their Students in and Out of the Classroom?

AT is a way of thinking. It has to do with acceptance of disability as a given and something that can be accommodated. It has to do with creativity and inventiveness. AT is a great equalizer that provides people with the opportunity to participate.

The role of the teacher is to help students learn how to think, how to be creative, how to solve problems. "Low functional fixity" means you are creative and look at objects and think about a multiplicity of applications. "High functional fixity" means you only see one or two uses for the object; you're more rigid in how you look at an object and how it can be used. For example, take a brick. Some people only see a brick as something you use to build a house. But others see a brick as something that can be used to hold a door open or that can serve as a counterweight or something that can be used to raise a table a few inches so a wheelchair can fit underneath it. Teachers need to be flexible and have low functional fixity so that, for example, they can figure out ways their students with disabilities can do science experiments on their own and participate in field trips.

Also, remember that it's not good enough to assign one student to another student with a disability to do things for them while they just sit and watch. Every student needs to participate and be as independent as possible. And when the limits of independence have been reached, they need to learn how to work together with others to get their needs met.

Source: Reproduced with permission from Psycho-Educational Services.

DEVICES FOR DAILY LIFE

Independent living involves performing the activities and tasks associated with daily life. Very often individuals with physical disabilities, sensory impairments, autism spectrum disorders, and cognitive challenges find some of these activities challenging; assistive technology devices help promote independence and provide choices for decision making across environments and setting demands. For example, most AT devices for individuals with physical disabilities focus on adapting the reach necessary to do a task, adapting devices for grasping and manipulation, making two-handed activities into one-handed activities, and increasing the pressure exerted by one's hands (Cook & Hussey, 2002). To be independent to the maximum extent possible, people must be able to care for their own needs at home and school in the areas of eating and food preparation, dressing, grooming, and safety. Examples of devices are explained for different activities related to daily life for home, school, work, and leisure. We refer the reader back to Chapter 2 to review the Adaptations Framework process. As with any type of AT device, the tasks at hand, the strengths and limitations of the individual, and the features of devices must all be carefully considered before deciding which devices might be most appropriate to promote independence for individuals with different types of disabilities.

Eating and Food Preparation

There are many types of simple AT adaptations that can be used to promote independence. For example, to enable people to manage eating, handles on utensils can be built up or handles can be angled to facilitate grasping and manipulation. Suction devices can be added to the bottom of plates to prevent them from moving and to provide stability, and sides of dishes can be built up

FIGURE 8.1 (A) Utensil Grips; (B) Large-Handled Utensils
Source: Photo courtesy of Psycho-Educational Services

for easier scooping. Drinking devices include cups with covers to prevent spilling and handles to help with grasping. Preschool and school-age students are taught how to use these devices as part of their total curriculum in self-help to foster independence in eating across the lifespan.

Food preparation can be accomplished through a one-handed can opener, mechanical "reachers" to get items off shelves, jar openers, and bowls with suction devices to prevent spilling. Other devices are available that help with daily household tasks. For instance, North Coast Medical (www.ncmedical.com) provides a variety of functional adaptations for activities of daily living (ADLs). Their adaptations or devices include an adjustable gripping tool to grasp plugs and tops on jars; doorknob turns, which can be adapted with easy-to-open handles that are pushed down to turn the doorknob; a key turner with a large handle for improving leverage; and long-handled brooms and dustpans to minimize bending. We refer the reader to their Web site, as one example of a company that specializes in devices, to see actual examples of ADL devices.

Other helpful kitchen devices for individuals who have low vision or who are blind include color-coded measuring devices and speaking liquid level indicators, respectively (Independent Living Aids). Additional devices include high-contrast cutting boards, spatulas with a pinch design (enabling more effective food flipping during cooking), Braille and talking scales and measures, and the use of Braille Dymo™ tape to label microwave ovens, stoves, and canned goods. New devices are also becoming available that will help individuals who are blind or visually impaired to identify canned and labeled goods via barcode, thus possibly reducing the need to label everything purchased. Figure 8.1 provides examples of AT devices for eating.

Finally, for individuals with intellectual disabilities and ASD, visual prompting systems such as pictorial cues using charts and video prompts using DVD players, computers, or handheld devices have been used to teach multistep tasks (e.g., making a sandwich, brushing teeth). Studies have shown that students with ASD can successfully use picture cues to do daily living skills (e.g., Lancioni & O'Reilly, 2001). Other studies have demonstrated that video technology helps students with daily living skills (Charlop-Christy, Le, & Freeman, 2000). Finally, another study found that a combination of picture cues and video technology produced the best effects when teaching cooking-related tasks independently (Mechling & Gustafson, 2008).

Dressing, Grooming, and Personal Needs

There are many adaptations for clothing that can be made to promote independence in dressing. For example, hook-and-loop tape instead of ties on shoes helps fasten shoes; other devices help

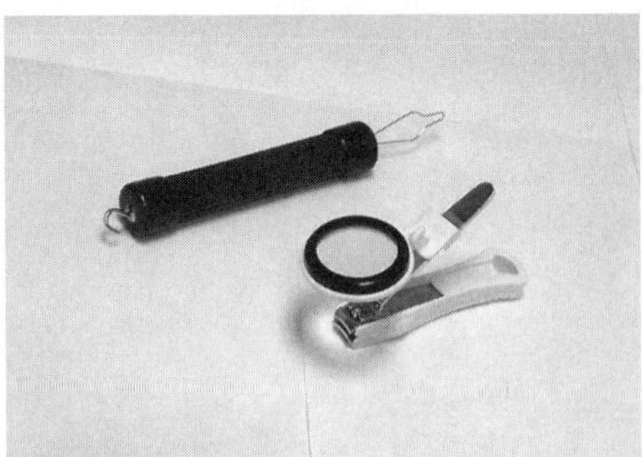

FIGURE 8.2 (A) Zipper Pull; (B) Grooming Clippers
Source: Photo courtesy of Psycho-Educational Services

individuals who have limited range of motion for bending, limited fine-motor control, or only the use of one hand to put on socks and pantyhose. Adapted button hooks (hooking device that helps pull the button through the button hole) and zipper pulls assist with dressing.

To promote independence in the grooming area, modified handles (length and built-up) can be used for toothbrushes, combs, and brushes. For bathing, handheld shower heads, shower chairs, wall grab bars, and scrub sponges with handles can be used by individuals with motor challenges. For individuals who have low vision, the bathroom should include high-contrast colors rather than the typical white found in many showers and bathtubs. Colored towels and mats and contrast on shower chairs help individuals discern items needed for grooming. Figure 8.2 provides examples of AT devices for dressing and grooming.

Finally, individuals with physical disabilities in particular may require adaptations in the bathroom to help them tend to their personal toileting needs, which is an essential daily living activity, as independently as possible. Depending on the individual's needs or limitations and strengths, toileting adaptations may be necessary for individuals to access the facilities, tend to themselves, and transfer on and off the toilet. For example, a variety of commodes that can be adjusted in seat height or include a higher backrest can provide alternatives to the typical toilet. Also, a variety of toilet seats, such as a padded seat, a raised seat, and a seat with a supportive frame, can provide options for individuals depending on their abilities to maneuver, position themselves, sit upright, and so forth. Items such as bottom wipers and something as simple as wipes can assist individuals in tending to their personal needs with dignity and independence. Also, an alarm system can also be installed near the toilet for the individual to use if assistance is needed. Finally, grab bars can provide support as an individual transfers on and off the toilet.

Safety

Home safety is always a concern for any individual. For example, *alerting devices* can be used for individuals with hearing impairments. A flashing light or vibration can signal the doorbell or fire alarm. The U.S. Fire Administration (see www.usfa.dhs.gov/citizens/disability) has published documents that provide emergency procedures, barrier free safety, and safety checklists for individuals with sensory and mobility impairments. For home appliance operation, some companies (e.g., Whirlpool, GE) provide instructions in Braille or on audiocassettes for ovens, refrigerators, and laundry appliances (Smith & Tyler, 2010). To keep people safe when answering the door, people who are blind often find that door intercoms enable a greater sense of security by eliminating the need to open the door to find out who has knocked or rung.

Community safety is yet another concern. One example of how community officials are trying to ensure more safety for pedestrians occurred in San Francisco. Noteworthy for individuals who are blind, in 2007, the city of San Francisco and the blind community signed an agreement for the city to install accessible pedestrian signals (APSs). An APS provides information in verbal messages, vibrating surfaces, and/or audible tones associated with the typical "Walk" signal to assist individuals with visual impairments, for example, to decide when to cross the street safely. Access to pedestrian signals and the associated safety factor enhances independence for individuals who have visual impairments. Reports on guidelines for best practice are available for communities nationwide to assist in the installment of such devices (Harkey, Carter, Barlow, & Bentzen, 2007a; Harkey et al., 2007b).

Mounting Devices and Page Turners

In order to promote independence, individuals must be able to use their adaptations across environments and tasks. Very often adaptations or devices must be mounted to furniture or wheelchairs. Mountability refers to the ability to attach devices to surfaces. For example, a computer, communication device, or tray might need to be mounted on a wheelchair, or switches may need to be mounted on hardware close to the user's face or hand or on a surface with a sticking device to prevent slipping. Devices such as switches to turn appliances on and off might need to be mounted to a bed or table. Mounting systems, such as those sold by Tash, Inc., and Able Net, Inc., ensure that the adaptations are accessible for individuals to use as needed.

Page turners can be used at home, school, and work for individuals who can read various types of text but have motor challenges that impede the ability to turn the pages. Page turners promote independence because individuals can read the material at their own rate and activate the turning device when they are ready for more text; individuals do not have to rely on others to do this task. For instance, the GEWA Page Turner BLV-6 (Zygo Industries, Inc.) provides the user with control of the page-turning process whether in the sitting or lying position. The Page Turner can also be operated with multiple or single switches and by environmental control units (see the discussion on environmental control units).

Leisure

Leisure activities, such as reading, sewing, and card playing, are another area in which individuals with disabilities should have access and independence to choose what they wish to engage in for recreation. For instance, books on tape (e.g., novels) from the Recording for the Blind and Dyslexic (RFB&D) can provide access to reading material for those who need AT adaptations to access print. A variety of categories, such as textbooks and novels, are available to rent. A special tape player can be purchased from RFB&D to accommodate the tapes (see www.rfbd.org). The National Library Service (NLS) for the Blind (see www.loc.gov/nls) is another resource that provides popular reading; NLS loans playback equipment.

Built-up handles on scissors can help with sewing and cutting for those with fine motor difficulties, and holders for cards and pool cues can aid in playing card games and shooting pool (Cook & Hussey, 2002). For instance, North Coast Medical offers Lo Vision® playing cards for individuals with as little as 5% normal vision. The cards contain numbers, letters, and suit symbols that are enlarged, and each suit is color-coded. Braille dominoes, a volley beep ball, Braille bingo boards, and large-print bingo cards (Independent Living Aids) enable individuals who are blind and who have low vision to participate fully in games played by children and adults alike.

In the area of entertainment, there are several adaptations that can be used to enable individuals with sensory impairments to access the entertainment world. For example, for individuals who are hard of hearing or deaf, closed-captioned television programs are now available. As a part of the Americans with Disabilities Act, televisions must now include built-in decoding capability. More and more broadcasts include closed-captioned programming, including, for instance, news stations such as CNN, sporting events, prime-time shows, and public-service programs. For individuals with visual impairments, access to some forms of television and other forms of entertainment, such as movies, is becoming increasingly available through audio description (Smith, 2010). Audio description involves the verbal description of the onscreen story and is made available during the silent portions of the show through earphones and a small FM receiver (Smith, 2010). Thus, the entertainment world is becoming increasingly accessible for individuals with sensory impairments. Technology devices enhance and expand opportunities for leisure activities.

ELECTRONIC AIDS TO DAILY LIVING

Electronic aids to daily living (EADLs), also called environmental control units (ECUs), help people with disabilities operate electrically powered devices, such as appliances, and foster independent living in home, school, and work. Certainly, EADLs are commonly used for individuals to access entertainment devices such as TVs, DVDs, lighting (e.g., Clapper Plus with Remote Control), and stereos. These enabling devices give individuals control over their environment and promote independence. EADL systems can range from simple applications, such as turning a light on and off, to more complex systems that manage appliances, heating and cooling, and security alarms found in "smart homes" (Church & Glennen, 1992). Typically, individuals with physical challenges, such as gross- and fine-motor difficulties, who need an alternative way to manage common devices and appliances use EADLs.

Generally speaking, EADLs operate in this manner:

- An *input device* controls the EADL: a keypad, keyboard, joystick, switches, and voice control are examples of input devices.
- A *control unit* receives the message from the input device and translates the message into an output signal that goes to the device. Transmission options for sending messages include ultrasound, infrared, radio control, and AC power signals.
- The *device,* such as a lamp, receives and responds to the output signal.

It is helpful to understand the capabilities of the different types of input devices and transmission options so decisions can be made about the needs of the user, the environmental demands, and the most appropriate EADL match. Questions for decision makers to consider when thinking about EADLs are included in Table 8.1.

Input Devices

Input devices consist of direct selection, switches and scanning, and voice control (Angelo, 1997). *Direct selection* means that the user chooses any device to control; pressing a keypad is a way in which the user can choose the device to activate. For example, four devices (e.g., 1. lamp; 2. television; 3. DVD; 4. fan) might be connected to the EADL system. The user wishes to turn on the fan, so number 4 is pressed on the keypad; this is direct selection, where the device is selected and the action happens. Depending on the user's abilities, the keypad can be pressed simply by using a finger, or the action may involve technology such as a head stick, mouth stick,

Table 8.1 Questions for Decision Makers to Consider for Electronic Aids to Daily Living Devices

- What does the user want to be able to do with the EADL?
- What type of input device most appropriately matches the needs of the user?
- What type of feedback (visual, auditory) is most appropriate for the user and the environment?
- In what locations will the EADL be used?
- What are the user's cognitive and positioning abilities?
- What services are available (funding, maintenance, training)?

joystick, or ocular eye gaze monitor (Church & Glennen, 1992). The same idea can be applied to a computer-controlled EADL where the user moves through the menus until the EADL system is highlighted; then the user gives commands to the devices by pressing individual keys. This is a good input choice for someone who spends a lot of time at the computer (Angelo, 1997).

Switches and scanning are other types of input devices. Recall the discussion about switches and scanning in Chapter 6. A switch may be a good choice when the user needs an alternative type of input device (see the discussion about switches in Chapter 6); scanning works well for users who have the cognitive abilities to respond to multiple choices. For example, a switch can be used to activate an appliance. Several switches can be used to activate different appliances. Switches can also be paired with a scanning array, such as a linear presentation of the appliances. By activating a switch, each appliance can be scanned in a linear fashion (horizontally or vertically); the user activates the switch when the appliance of choice (e.g., fan) is highlighted. There are also scanning arrays that offer branching options so that if the fan is highlighted, the branching feature offers more choices: on, off, slow, medium, high speed. Items for selection, such as appliances, are usually arranged in the scanning array in order of preference and frequency of use, thus allowing the user independence, choice, and decision-making opportunities.

Voice control involves the user's speaking commands into a microphone for the EADL. The EADL interprets the message and activate the appliance. Voice control is a voice recognition system, which involves training the machine to recognize the user's voice (Angelo, 1997). This input device is a good choice for users who may not be able to use upper body extremities to activate the EADL with other types of input devices such as keypads, joysticks, or switches. Actual words are not essential to activate the system; rather, the machine is trained to recognize the user's voice, pitch, loudness, and articulation (Cook & Hussey, 2002). Therefore, in order for the input device to be effective, the user must be consistent in oral expression and operate in an environment where background noise will not interfere with the system.

Transmission Options

There are four transmission options for output signals: ultrasound, infrared, radio control, and AC power signals. *Ultrasound* involves high-frequency sound waves that are not discernible to the human hearing range. A frequency is emitted through the input device, and the control box activates the appliance. Ultrasound can only be used with appliances that are in same room as the input device (ultrasound transmitter). *Infrared* transmission involves infrared pulses being sent from a remote control to the control box. Because the remote control is portable, it can be used from various locations in the room as long as the device is pointed directly at the control box and there is nothing in the way to interfere with the transmission. Devices that have built-in infrared controls, such as televisions and DVD players, can only be operated with infrared signals (Lewis, 1993). *Radio control* (electromagnetic) uses the same radio waves that are used in toys, garage door openers, and radios. The advantage to this transmission device is that the user does not have to be in the same room as the control box when activating the radio control signal. Finally, *AC power signals* take advantage of existing house wiring to transmit signals to activate appliances. The input device can be a remote unit or part of the control box (Angelo, 1997).

Use of EADLs at Home, School, and Work

EADLs can be used in the home to activate appliances and telephones. For example, Zygo Industries, Inc., offers the GEWA Prog, which is based on infrared transmission and operated using a handheld transmitter. Input device options include either a keypad or switches and scanning techniques. The GEWA Prog can work from as far away as 100 feet and does not have to be aimed directly at the control box (receiver). The GEWA Prog with its INFRA-LINK system for lighting switches, wall sockets, opening windows, intercoms, alarm systems, and elevator controls can be used in the "smart home" concept. Lights, TVs, VCRs, and computers can all be connected to the GEWA Prog.

Sicare Pilot (Tash, Inc.) is a voice-activated device for environmental control at home and work. It can also be operated using a switch or single switch and scanning. Sicare Pilot converts spoken commands into signals that control numerous devices and appliances, such as computers, televisions, and lights, within multiple environments. Sicare Pilot uses both infrared and radio transmission and provides both visual and auditory feedback to the user. For individuals with visual impairments, at least one thermostat is needed that has large print and tactile markings. There is also a need for more innovation in the thermostat area for those wanting electronic thermostats; presently access by individuals who are blind is difficult at best. For telephone control, GEWA Infra-Link Speaker-Telephone offers user access to the phone with the use of a single switch to answer the phone or dial a number. Thus, this environmental control device provides complete access to users who might otherwise not be able to use telephones, both at home and at work.

A school application is the final example of environmental control. The PowerLink® 3 Control Unit coupled with the AirLink Cordless Switch (AbleNet, Inc.) enables students to access and participate in school activities that involve electrical devices. For instance, using the cordless switch, the student can activate a device independently, such as a tape recorder, through the PowerLink 3 Control Unit (see Figure 8.3). This process allows the student access to school tasks and participation with peers. See Figure 8.3 for an example of a PowerLink.

FIGURE 8.3 PowerLink

Source: Photo courtesy of Psycho-Educational Services

ACCESS TO MANAGEMENT DEVICES

For individuals to be independent, they must demonstrate management skills for daily life activities at home, school, and work, and they must possess some degree of organization. The first step in being able to manage oneself in daily life and organization is access to information. This section focuses on AT adaptations, which involve visual and auditory feedback, that help individuals with disabilities access information to enhance their abilities to manage their daily activities.

Time and Money

There are many adaptations that can assist people in managing daily life tasks related to time and money. Time and money management are two major areas that require people to have tools that promote access to information and thus promote independence. In the area of time management, access to time is the first step. For individuals who have low vision or who are blind, a variety of calendars, clocks, and watches with enlarged numbers or tactile and auditory cues such as Braille numbers on watches and talking clocks are available (Independent Living Aids). For individuals who are hard of hearing, access to alarm clocks as a wake-up device can be accomplished through clocks that produce loud sounds. For instance, the Big Number Very Loud Desktop Alarm Clock (Independent Living Aids) produces a sound up to 90 decibels. To help with remembering time-sensitive "things to do," such as being somewhere by a certain time, the TimePAD (Attainment Company, Inc.) can provide up to five recorded messages, which can be activated by a timer.

Money management involves being able to access information related to money and numbers. Calculators are a useful tool to help with money management. Calculators with big keys such as the Big Display Calculator and the Talking Calculator, which speaks each entry and calculation (Attainment Company, Inc.), can help individuals who can benefit from vision aids, calculation assistance, and access to the keypad. The Large Print Check and Deposit Register (Independent Living Aids) enables individuals with low vision to manage their checkbooks and to write checks. Also, the Note Teller™ Talking Money Identifier (Independent Living Aids) is a portable talking money identifier that will verbally announce the denomination of all bills from $1 to $100. It automatically turns itself on when a bill is inserted and off when a bill is removed. It is available in English and Spanish.

Organization

Promoting organizational skills enables people to tackle the daily tasks of home, school, and work. There are many assistive technology adaptations that can help people manage their daily routines and access information. The use of a personal digital assistant (PDA) can promote remembering and organizing personal information. PDAs are available as handheld units and allow the user to store and access personal information. Information input and access occur via a keyboard or keypad and are displayed on an LCD display. Pocket-size PDAs (e.g., StepPAD, Memo Talker, Voice Organizer™, Voice It™) enable the user to enter and access information by speaking into the device. Stored data are spoken back in the user's own voice. Some of the features of digital managers include calendars, daily schedules, timing devices, memo files, address books, and telephone directories. The use of PDAs by individuals with sensory and mobility impairments can be facilitated through the use of accessibility software (e.g., speech recognition software).

MOBILITY

We begin this section by providing Dr. Ann Corn's Personal Perspective 8.2 to set the stage for understanding issues related to mobility for individuals with visual impairments.

PERSONAL PERSPECTIVE 8.2

Anne Corn has served as a professor of special education, ophthalmology and visual sciences at Vanderbilt University in Nashville, Tennessee. She has been a teacher of students with visual impairments and since 1976 she has prepared teachers and researchers in this field. Her experiences as an advocate for those with mobility impairments have taken several foci. She has conducted research and written curricula for people with visual impairments to become efficient nondrivers; she has given lectures on driving for those with low vision using bioptic telescopic lenses, and she has developed and coordinated a program that prepares orientation and mobility instructors for blind and visually impaired children and adults. In addition, she has served on committees related to mobility impairments and public transportation, and in the mid-1980s she was a member of the Urban Transportation Commission of Austin, Texas.

In Your Book, Titled *Finding Wheels,* You Briefly Discuss Your Mobility Experiences as a Child With Low Vision. Can You Summarize Those Experiences for us?

I had what may be considered pretty typical travel experiences for a child growing up in New York City. I walked, or took a city bus to elementary school (in poor weather) using landmarks. I took my first bus to visit my aunt around fifth grade. I went with friends into Manhattan by junior high. I knew all of the subway stops by the colors of the lighting and tiles at each station and I had memorized the order of the stops. I used these methods because I couldn't read the numbers (e.g., 42nd) as the train was coming into a stop. When I began to take a bus into unfamiliar areas, I needed to ask drivers to let me know when we arrived at a certain stop. At times drivers were helpful; other drivers were annoyed because I could obviously see and they thought I was giving them a hard time. Then again, there were New York City bus drivers who just didn't care. In those situations, I just asked for assistance from other passengers. I also learned to read maps well for both the bus and subway routes.

When friends started to take driving lessons, I felt left out. One friend thought it would be a good idea for me to go with her when her father taught her to drive. I believe my friend (who is now a pediatrician) wanted me to feel included. I went but felt that I'd rather not be there.

Your Book Does a Nice Job of Chronicling Four Individuals' Experiences with Transportation Issues. Tell us how Orientation and Mobility Training Affects all Aspects of Mobility for People who are Blind or who have Low Vision

By the time you were 3 or 4 years old you could probably use your finger to point in which ways your parents should turn a car to go from the grocery store to your house. At some level you understood streets, roads, intersections, that some buildings had one story and some had more. You may have watched people cross streets, understood that there are stop signs and lights and that pedestrians and drivers do certain things to navigate or find their way. Consider if you've never seen how the physical world was put together. Consider if you were placed in the back seat of a car and never saw the car itself. The car may seem like a moving couch and the physical world outside would not truly exist. A congenitally blind child must learn about all of the ways in which people move, indoors and outdoors. They must develop concepts and learn of how their bodies can move in relation to objects. Remember that with vision, you can glance about your surroundings and know what is there. Those who are blind must learn to "put the pieces together." They must also be courageous enough to learn the skills that enable them to be independent travelers. Lessons in orientation can begin while a child is still in his or her crib and should progress until the child is an independent traveler. For adults who lose some or all of their vision, orientation and mobility instruction helps them to reclaim their sense of independence.

What has been Your Biggest Mobility Challenge and how did You Deal with it?

My biggest challenge was not being able to drive. Choosing my location of housing, relying on others' schedules, and trying not to impose on others who drove were true challenges. Now that I can drive, I live where I want to live rather than first starting with a map of grocery stores and bus routes to choose the location of my residence. I live in a semi-rural area where there are no buses. I guess I was never destined to live in New York City.

You Obviously Travel a Great Deal as Part of Your Professional Duties. What at Devices for Mobility have You Found to be Particularly Helpful?

I use an 8× monocular telescope as a pedestrian. I will use it for seeing street signs, time schedules in airports, menus at fast food restaurants, finding a store at a distance, and so forth. For driving I use a 4× behind-the-lens bioptic telescopic system. Also, for reading maps, I use a 20 diopter hand-held magnifier.

As a Leader in the Field of Vision, how have Your Personal Experiences with Mobility Shaped Your Message to Your University Students and Your Colleagues?

I believe a teacher of any student who experiences a mobility disability must consider how that person views his or her freedom and independence. For a person with a visual impairment, getting from place to place is so tied to one's life options, social life, and employability that their instructors are compelled to address mobility issues in a sensitive and proactive way. They must provide options whenever possible. For example, many children and youths with low vision, and some who are blind, do not receive orientation and mobility instruction, which is today a related service under IDEIA [the Individuals with Disabilities Education Improvement Act].

If You Could Snap Your Fingers and Invent a Device that Could Serve as a Mobility Aid, What Would it be?

I believe the driverless car is in the future. I don't need to invent it because in Spain they're already working on a prototype. This would help people with low vision and blindness—and probably many fully sighted persons as well.

Here's Your Chance to Tell Our Readers One Thing Above all Else that You Want Them to Know About Mobility Issues for People who are Blind or who have Low Vision

Every day of our lives we move about. We learn that moving about can be within one's home or within one's community. We can move to obtain a drink from the refrigerator or we can move from one city to another. Our choice of where we live, our choice of vocation or recreation, our relationships with others, and our sense of self are all tied to how freely we are able to move about. As a person with low vision, I keenly felt the restrictions of not being able to come and go, to be restricted by what my visual impairment imposed in the society in which I lived. While some people may be happy to be "couch potatoes" or to sit at home, others want to maintain an active lifestyle and derive the benefits of employment as well as make a contribution to society. It is through the educators', parents', and clinicians' efforts that a person with low vision or

(*continued*)

blindness can take an active part in life. Many years ago I heard a speaker who was blind talk to a group of professionals. He said that every day of his life he used social skills and mobility skills. Still, he saw that these two areas of unique learning needs for persons with visual impairments took a very low priority in the field of education. From my many years of experience as a person with low vision and as a teacher and teacher-educator, I wholeheartedly agree with this speaker's appraisal.

The Expanded Core Curriculum for Students with Visual Impairments is designed to meet the unique learning needs of students with visual impairments. It contains nine areas of instruction. Perhaps when this curriculum is readily accepted and valued by educators and parents, we will see more students receive instruction in the areas of orientation and mobility, visual efficiency, social skills, and independent living skills. Each of these is addressed within the curriculum and all contribute to a student's mobility and freedom.

For further reading:

The Expanded Core Curriculum for Students with Visual Impairments: www.tsbvi.edu/Outreach/seehear/winter01/core.htm

Corn, A. L., & Rosenblum, L. P. (2000). *Finding wheels: A curriculum for non-drivers with visual impairments to gain control of their transportation needs*. Austin, TX: Pro-Ed.

Legislative mandates have been passed over the years that have facilitated the use of AT devices and services (Bryant & Seay, 1998; Raskind & Higgins, 1998). For instance, Title II of Section 504 of the Rehabilitation Act stated that public entities have to provide appropriate auxiliary aids and services to a student with a disability in order for the student to participate in any publicly funded program (Day & Edwards, 1996). Section 504 requires that all aspects of the learning environment, including the classroom, school, and transportation, be accessible. Chapter 4 provides information about mobility for people with physical impairments. Here we provide general information about mobility issues for people with variety of disabilities, including those with cognitive and sensory impairments.

In 1990, Congress passed the Americans with Disabilities Act (ADA), which extended the benefits and protections of the Rehab Act to individuals with disabilities in the private sector. Although the law does not specifically discuss AT devices and services (Day & Edwards, 1996), AT is clearly an important tool in providing people with disabilities an opportunity to be successful in all areas covered by the ADA including employment, transportation (e.g., buses, trains), public accommodations (e.g., hotels, restaurants, banks, theaters), and telecommunications. Therefore, barriers to mobility for all people with disabilities, particularly individuals with physical disabilities or who have low vision or are blind, must be addressed.

Architectural barriers must be removed. Thus, we see wider doorways, elevators with timing mechanisms for wheelchair accessibility, accessible restrooms (doors, towel racks, sinks), cutaway curbs, and so forth. In classrooms, lower chalkboards and water fountains, adapted playground equipment, and wheelchair ramps are all examples of ways to promote access, address barriers, and create independence. Ramps (8.3% slope) in buildings and lifts in transportation vehicles help people who use wheelchairs to access buildings, public buses, and vans. These are but a few of the issues surrounding access to mobility for people with various disabilities.

In addition to addressing architectural barriers, more accessibility features are noted in public places. For example, accessible entrances, accessible passenger loading zones, accessible areas with signage that has Braille (e.g., men's room, exit signs), and accessible parking spaces promote more independence for individuals with visual impairments and physical disabilities. These environmental features promote not only accessibility but also mobility and safety.

In describing the nature of mobility needs for people who are blind or have visual impairments, the Committee on Vision for the National Research Council (1986) noted:

> There are two major elements of the mobility problem that result from blindness. First, the blind traveler with no pattern vision must avoid obstacles and detect drop-offs. The second problem, which is less obvious and equally serious, is navigation. Sighted travelers have many landmarks, most of which are known through vision, to guide their way. These landmarks not only identify the location but also are used in the memorial representation or cognitive map of the area. Deprived of vision, the blind person must use other types of landmarks and information to orient and navigate. (p. 20)

For individuals who have low vision or who are blind, orientation and mobility training is beneficial to promote freedom, movement, and independence. For instance, adults might use the long cane to help them move about their environments. Tactile maps help individuals identify key areas (e.g., elevators) and services (e.g., restrooms). Something as simple as uniform riser heights on stairs and tread widths can promote mobility (Smith & Tyler, 2010). Orientation and mobility have been used for decades to help people who are blind move about effectively in their environments.

Over time, a number of mobility aids have been developed to help people with visual impairments travel about. Such aids include long canes, guide dogs, and electronic travel aids (ETAs). To date, most ETAs have failed to provide needed improvements over traditional long canes and guide dogs, so their use has been minimal. It is hoped that a dialogue between consumers and engineers/developers will result in the creation of sophisticated yet practical devices to enhance the mobility needs of people who are blind or who have low vision. Clearly, the mobility issues of people with these conditions go far beyond technology. Many have to do with planning and preparation. Thousands of people who are blind travel to work, appointments, stores, and other places every day. They can even travel to foreign countries. A few simple tips and tricks make traveling easier for them (see Table 8.2 for travel tips).

There are also some visual impairments that result in different levels of functioning with different environmental conditions, those that fluctuate at different times of day, and those that are degenerative. For example, a person with retinitis pigmentosa may have good visual functioning during the day but have difficulties in the evening under lower levels of light. Those with diabetic retinopathy may have fluctuations throughout the day. Others with degenerative conditions may need to adapt to changes in their visual abilities over time.

Perhaps one of the largest differences in mobility for people who have low vision and those who are blind relates to constancy. The person who is blind experiences a constant need to function with other senses. Many people with low vision need to adapt to different environments or other changes throughout the day. Even when a visual condition is stable, they may move about without restrictions in one environment and encounter some difficulties in another. However, people with low vision, who can use their vision for getting about, will want to use their vision as a primary method of learning about their environment. Vision is immediate and provides information in the near, intermediate, and far distance.

People who are functionally or totally blind will use nonvisual methods for learning orientation—where they are in their environment; mobility—the methods of traveling indoors and outdoors; and way finding—how to plan and execute routes. Self-protective techniques, traveling with a sighted guide, using a cane, and using a guide dog are among the methods used during travel by those who are blind. Though used less frequently, electronic travel devices are available

Table 8.2 Travel Tips for People Who Are Blind: How to Make the Trip a Little Easier

Plan Your Trip in Detail

Learn about the city layout, rules of traffic, and the location of city landmarks with respect to your hotel, bus schedules, and the airport layout. Discover exactly where you will go to get a taxi or other transportation, and decide beforehand where you will go to eat. Carry a piece of paper with the addresses of all the places you want to visit written in the native language to make traveling easier. With precision planning, very little is left up to chance, and you can relax on your trip.

Make Reservations for Everything

You know to make reservations for your hotel and airplane, bus, or train travel, but you can also make reservations at museums, restaurants, and taxi services. When making reservations, tell everyone you have a visual impairment, and tell them exactly what type of help you may need. Ask if the museums allow touch tours to take place. That way, they know you are coming and can prepare for your arrival, and you know what to expect.

Buy Before You Go

Purchase your museum, airplane, train, and bus tickets and anything else you can buy and have delivered before you go. This will eliminate the hassle of standing in endless lines only to be told you have been waiting in the wrong line. You will also become aware of the individual feel of each ticket so it won't get confused with other tickets and receipts acquired in a day.

Bring a Cane

Though guide dogs are acceptable in most parts of North America and Europe, some countries do not have a general policy regarding the dogs; so you may not be allowed into individual businesses. A cane is allowed everywhere and is a readily acceptable symbol that you have a visual impairment, which helps in many instances. Other devices, like electronic travel aids, are also allowed everywhere.

Let People Help

Many people have a difficult time adjusting to the thought of a capable person who is blind. Therefore, many people all over the world want to help. Be gracious in accepting their assistance; after all, the sighted feel better about themselves when they are helpful.

Ask Questions

Depending on the culture, some people may ignore you completely. One way to overcome these difficulties is to learn a few words of the foreign language before you travel. Don't be shy about asking questions or asking for assistance.

Know About Flying

If you choose to fly on your travels, you may be asked to preboard, postboard, or demonstrate your ability to fasten or unfasten a seat belt. You may also be asked to move if you are seated in the emergency exit row. It is unlawful for airlines to require you to do any of these things, but still it occurs. Also, bring carry-on luggage to avoid having to navigate through crowds and obstacles.

Book Your Travel with an Experienced Agent

If you choose to use an agent, book with someone who knows what services are available for people who are blind. Braille labels on elevators and hotel doors, easily accessible stairways, tour guides who tell interesting verbal tales—all of these make traveling easier. By using the services of a good agent you will save a lot of grief and have a better time. Several tour companies (e.g., Campanian, AggieWorld) specialize in travelers who are blind or have visual impairments.

People with visual impairments can have just as much fun on trips as their sighted counterparts. All it takes is a little preplanning and a few accommodations. There are several Web sites that provide useful information, such as http://preparedfortravel.com/plan/travel_tips_for_the_blind_or_visually_impaired, and www.disabledtraveladvice.co.uk. Blindness should not stop anyone from seeing the world!

to provide information about environments that are not within reach of one's cane or foot. When orientation and mobility instruction is provided, most individuals are able to learn to travel independently in familiar and unfamiliar environments. In recent years, research has looked at using global positioning systems with blind travelers. Children who have never had vision must learn in a careful and systematic way how the physical world is structured. What is a roof of a house, what is an intersection, how does traffic flow? These are only a few of the concepts and mental mapping that a congenitally blind person needs to learn.

When people lose some or all vision after the early years, they retain visual images and concepts that are helpful during the rehabilitation process. However, losing one's vision and losing one's ability to move about and go spontaneously and without thought for movements and location can profoundly affect one's adjustment processes.

SUMMARY

Individuals with disabilities have a right to independence and full integration into society. Living independently involves access to the activities and tasks associated with daily life. Because some of these activities and tasks might be challenging, AT adaptations can be used to help people circumvent disabilities whenever possible. People must be able to care for their own needs at home and school in the areas of eating and food preparation, dressing, grooming, and safety. Electronic aids for daily living can help people with disabilities operate devices and foster independent living at home, school, and work. These enabling devices give individuals control over their environment and promote independence. Finally, as a result of legislation, individuals with disabilities are entitled to access transportation, buildings, public facilities, and so forth to promote mobility in and integration into the community.

SCENARIO APPLICATIONS

Scenario 8.1

Keep a list for one day of your activities of daily living. Think about a specific type of disability and the types of AT devices you would need in order to continue your level of engagement successfully. Share the list in class with a small group. Identify the commonalities and differences among the lists.

Scenario 8.2

Using the case study you developed in Chapter 2 (Discussion Scenario 2.1), design a "Smart Home" for your individual. Explain the input device and transmission option. Your design should include examples of adaptations for different rooms in the house. Present your design in class to the other students.

Scenario 8.3

Identify ways you manage your time and money and keep yourself organized. Go online and locate the devices presented in the Access to Management Devices. Determine the tasks for which the devices would be well suited and the requisite abilities that are needed to use the devices. Identify the features of the devices. Describe problems people with disabilities might encounter for which these devices could be used to help manage their lives independently.

Scenario 8.4

Conduct a tour of your college or school building, public facilities, or governmental buildings. Identify ways in which mobility has been made accessible for individuals with disabilities. Share your information with other students in the class. Interview an individual who is blind or who has a physical disability that necessitates the use of a wheelchair. Talk with this person about accessibility issues. Share this information in class.

Scenario 8.5

Maria is 16 years old and has identified intellectual disabilities considered to be in the moderate range. She is fully ambulatory and has no sensory impairments. However, Maria has difficulty remembering how to do tasks, especially those that are multistep. She tends to get confused in new environments. Her communication skills are affected by a limited vocabulary. She can read common signs found in various contexts (e.g., bus, ladies' room, exit). One of her IEP goals focuses on developing the ability to use transportation independently. You are a high school special education transition teacher who is teaching students with mild to moderate intellectual disabilities how to use public transportation to go to work. Apply the Adaptations Framework to develop a plan that includes AT for Maria to help her learn the transportation system successfully. Use AT ideas presented in this chapter and other chapters and refer back to Chapter 2, Table 2.3, to help develop your plan.

For Discussion

1. Explain what *independent living* means.
2. Describe ways in which assistive technology adaptations can be used to promote independence in daily living activities.
3. Describe switches and scanning and provide examples of when they can be used.
4. Describe electronic aids to daily living systems and provide examples of how they are used in homes, work, and school.
5. Explain how assistive technology adaptations can be used for management purposes.
6. Describe the role of federal legislation in promoting independence and identify environmental accessibility issues that must be addressed.
7. Think about an individual you know who has a developmental or acquired disability. Discuss the impact of the disability on that individual's independence and the measures that have been taken to foster independence.
8. Conduct an inventory of a classroom, workplace, or community facility to determine how assistive technology adaptations might be used in different environments.
9. Explain how an EADL system works, including input devices and transmission options.
10. Identify examples of EADL systems in catalogues and share how they work in school, the workplace, and the community.
11. Explain assistive technology adaptations that can be used to help individuals with management skills.
12. Compare and contrast mobility issues for individuals with different disabilities. Think about accessibility in terms of architectural barriers, transportation (public and private), recreational facilities, and so forth. Refer back to Personal Perspectives 8.1 and 8.2 when considering mobility issues for individuals with severe physical disabilities and visual impairments.

References

Angelo, D. H. (1997). AAC in the family and home. In S. Glennen & D. DeCoste (Eds.), *The handbook of augmentative communication* (pp. 523–545). San Diego, CA: Singular.

Bryant, B. R., & Seay, P. C. (1998). The Technology-Related Assistance to Individuals with Disabilities Act: Relevance to individuals with learning disabilities and their advocates. *Journal of Learning Disabilities, 31*(1), 4–15.

Charlop-Christy, M. H., Le, L., & Freeman, K. A. (2000). A comparison of video modeling with in vivo modeling for teaching children with autism. *Journal of Autism and Developmental Disorders, 30*, 537–552.

Church, G., & Glennen, S. (1992). *The handbook of assistive technology.* San Diego, CA: Singular.

Committee on Vision for the National Research Council. (1986). *Electronic aids: New directions for research.* Washington, DC: National Academies Press.

Cook, A. M., & Hussey, S. M. (2002). *Assistive technologies: Principles and practices* (2nd ed.). St. Louis, MO: Mosby.

Corn, A. L., & Rosenblum, L. P. (2000). *Finding wheels: A curriculum for non-drivers with visual impairments to gain control of their transportation needs.* Austin, TX: Pro-Ed.

Day, S. L., & Edwards, B. J. (1996). Assistive technology for postsecondary students with learning disabilities. *Journal of Learning Disabilities, 29*(5), 486–492, 503.

Gardner, J. F. (1990). Introduction: A decade of change. In J. F. Gardner & M. S. Chapman (Eds.), *Program issues in developmental disabilities* (2nd ed., pp. 3–17). Baltimore: Paul H. Brookes.

Harkey, D. L., Carter, D. L., Barlow, J. M., & Bentzen, B. L. (2007a). *Accessible pedestrian signals: A guide to best practice.* NCHRP Web-Only Document 117A.

Harkey, D. L., Carter, D. L., Barlow, J. M., Bentzen, B. L., Myers, L., & Scott, A. (2007b). *Guidelines for accessible pedestrian signals, Final Report.* Contractor's Final Report for NCHRP Project 3-62, NCHRP Web-Only Document 117B.

Lancioni, G. E., & O'Reilly, M. F. (2001). Self-management of instruction cues for occupation: Review of studies with people with severe and profound developmental disabilities. *Research in Developmental Disabilities, 22,* 41–65.

Lewis, R. (1993). *Special education technology.* Pacific Grove, CA: Brooks/Cole.

Mechling, L., & Gustafson, M. R. (2008). Comparison of static picture and video prompting on the performance of cooking-related tasks by students with autism. *Journal of Special Education Technology, 27*(3), 31–45.

Mithaug, D. E., & Hanawalt, D. A. (1978). The validation of procedures to assess prevocational task preferences in retarded adults. *Journal of Applied Behavior Analysis, 11,* 153–162.

Nosek, M. A. (1992). Independent living. In R. M. Parker & E. M. Szymanski (Eds.), *Rehabilitation counseling* (2nd ed., pp. 103–134). Austin, TX: Pro-Ed.

O'Brien, J. (1991). *Down stairs that are never your own: Supporting people with developmental disabilities in their own homes.* Paper prepared for The Center on Human Policy, Syracuse University, Syracuse, New York.

Raskind, M. H., & Higgins, E. L. (1998). Assistive technology for postsecondary students with learning disabilities: An overview. *Journal of Learning Disabilities, 31*(1), 27–40.

Schalock, R. L., & Kiernan, W. E. (1990). *Habilitation planning for adults with disabilities.* New York: Springer-Verlag.

Schalock, R. L., Luckasson, R. A., & Shogren, K. A. (2007). The renaming of "mental retardation": Understanding the change to the term "intellectual disability." *Intellectual and Developmental Disabilities, 45*(2), 116–124.

Smith, D. D., & Tyler, N. C. (2010). Introduction to special education: Making a difference (7th ed.). Boston: Allyn & Bacon.

APPPENDIX

Listing of Assistive Technology Vendors

The following listing provides examples of vendors that carry assistive technology products. Inclusion on this list does not constitute an endorsement by the authors or the publisher. Every effort was made to ensure that the URLs are accurate; however, readers should keep in mind that vendors may change their URLs or may no longer carry AT products. A version of this listing was provided in the first edition of this book and was produced by the Alliance for Technology.

AbleNet, Inc.
Web site: www.ablenetinc.com
AbleNet develops and markets products and services to meet the needs of children and adults with severe disabilities. Products include simple technology systems and related materials that allow users to actively participate in daily activities. Support services include workshops aimed at parents, teachers, therapists, and care providers nationwide.

Academic Software, Inc.
Web site: www.acsw.com
ASI publishes and/or markets several products.

Adaptivation, Inc.
Web site: www.adaptivation.com
Adaptivation designs products for individuals with disabilities to provide them a means of communication and control. There is also a line of wireless environmental controls. Adaptivation has many new assistive products coming soon. Call for the latest Adaptivation product catalog.

Antarq
Web site: www.antarq.com.mx
Offers personal computer technology for special education and rehabilitation for bilingual populations in Mexico, Central and South America, Puerto Rico, and the United States. Special equipment is available for visually impaired and deaf-mute individuals, individuals with cognitive and physical disabilities, and the professionals who work with them. The equipment can be applied to all age groups in education, professional rehabilitation, vocation, and independent living. All products have been selected, adapted, or produced to be applied and used by Spanish-speaking or bilingual (Spanish/English, Portuguese/English spoken) populations.

Apple Computer, Inc.
Web site: www.apple.com
"Apple is committed to helping persons with disabilities attain an unparalleled level of independence through a personal computer. Every Macintosh ships with rich, built-in features that support a positive user experience for disabled people." Through their participation in the Alliance, Apple is demonstrating their intent to be responsive to the requirements of consumers with disabilities and to work with them and the ATA developers of assistive technologies to ensure access by all to emerging Apple technology. Apple's Disability Resources Web site is located at: http://www.apple.com/education/k12/disability

Arkenstone, Inc.
Web site: www.arkenstone.org
Arkenstone is a nonprofit organization that has become the leading provider of reading machines for people with visual and reading disabilities.

Articulate Systems, Inc.
Web site: www.dragonsys.com
Articulate Systems has been the pioneer in voice user interface and voice communication technology for the Macintosh since 1986. Articulate Systems' product line includes the award-winning Voice Navigator II, which allows users to control their favorite Macintosh application by spoken commands. Articulate Systems' complete line of sound solution products encompasses voice recognition, voice recording, voice annotation, and voice messaging.

CAST, Inc. (Center for Applied Special Technology)
Web site: www.cast.org
Founded in 1984, CAST is a not-for-profit organization whose mission is to expand the opportunities for all people through the use of innovative technology. This mission is achieved through a combination of training, evaluations, and research and development. The ResearchWare products developed out of the needs determined through our research and evaluations of people with disabilities. ResearchWare includes ClickReader, ClickWriter, Talking Calculator, and much more.

Closing the Gap, Inc.
Web site: www.closingthegap.com
Closing the Gap is an information source working exclusively in the field of microcomputers and persons with disabilities. Their goal is to discover ways that microcomputer-related products are being used in special education and rehabilitation and to disseminate that knowledge as widely as possible. Their products include *Closing the Gap*, a bimonthly newspaper, and an annual international conference for special education and rehabilitation professionals.

Don Johnston, Incorporated
Web site: www.donjohnston.com
Don Johnston, Inc., has become a leader in the field of adaptive equipment and computer access. DJI develops, manufactures, and markets materials for persons who are nonverbal and who have physical disabilities. Many products are specifically used for training in the areas of augmentative communication, physical access, and control of the environment. The DJI catalog reaches schools, hospitals, training centers, and families around the world. DJI exhibits at major augmentative communication and computer conferences.

Freedom Scientific
Web site: www.screenaccess.com/
This company has numerous products both software and hardware to help individuals with a variety of disabilities, specializing in visual impairments and print disabilities.

FutureForms
Web site: www.futureforms.com
FutureForms can convert existing or create a new paper-based form in an electronic format. Forms and documents are maintained in their electronic form library for clients' safety and convenience. FutureForms has proven products and services that will allow an organization to increase productivity and reduce costs. They offer an additional tool to aid people with disabilities in gaining employment.

Gus Communications, Inc.

Web site: www.gusinc.com

The Gus! Multimedia Speech System for Windows is the world's most popular AAC software product. It converts any Windows-compatible computer into a dynamic display communication device. Digitized and synthetic speech (synthesizer included), 2 to 72 buttons/page, unlimited layers, scanning. Includes the Gus! Talking Keyboard, Gus! Abbreviations, and Gus! Mouse. Also the Gus! Touch Screen for Portable Computers. Works with any Windows-compatible portable computer for finger/touch access.

IntelliTools

Web site: www.intellitools.com

IntelliTools produces and distributes IntelliKeys, the high-quality alternative keyboard, and a host of software products for people with physical, visual, or cognitive disabilities. Software includes the award-winning series of creativity tools: IntelliTalk, a versatile talking word processor; Overlay Maker, a drawing program for designing custom overlays for IntelliKeys; IntelliPics, an easy-to-use multimedia authoring program; and ClickIt!, a powerful utility providing mouseless access to point-and-click software. IntelliTools also publishes a growing number of ready-to-use curriculum resources, including instant access to Edmark and Living Books software; Hands-On Concepts, an integrated early reading and math series; MathPad; and Exploring Patterns. IntelliKeys works with Macintosh and PC-compatible computers. All software is available for the Macintosh with a growing line of Windows products including Overlay Maker and IntelliTalk.

Laureate Learning Systems, Inc.

Web site: www.laureatelearning.com

Laureate is dedicated to the innovative use of computer technology for special education and rehabilitation. Laureate offers programs for language development, concept development and processing, augmentative communication, and instructional games. Laureate programs are easy to use, flexible, and above all, effective. Natural-sounding speech and colorful pictures motivate and guide the learner, making most of the programs appropriate for nonreaders.

LD Resources

Web site: www.ldresources.com

LD Resources creates HyperCard stacks that are simple, easy to use, and inexpensive. They have reference, entertainment, clip art, language learning, story-telling, and many other kinds of stacks ranging in price from $5 to $20 and aimed at a variety of ages and abilities. Free and shareware stacks can be found on most online services and in many Macintosh user group libraries. Their commercial stacks can be ordered directly from them. Their goal is to help make the people who use their products happier and more independent.

Little Planet Learning

Web site: www.littleplanet.com

Little Planet Learning develops and publishes curriculum-based software for early education. The Little Planet Literacy Series is a language arts series with current titles for kindergarten to third-grade levels. The series is the result of four years of joint research and development between Little Planet Learning and the Learning Technology Center (LTC) at Peabody College, Vanderbilt University. The LTC is internationally known for its research into how technology may be fully integrated into the classroom curriculum.

LS&S Group
Web site: www.lssproducts.com
The LS&S Group specializes in products for the visually impaired, with a large selection of CCTV and computer products.

Mayer-Johnson Co.
Web site: www.mayer-johnson.com
The Mayer-Johnson Co. is the originator of the Picture Communication Symbols. Their symbols are used in augmentative communication. Their products include educational materials and software. The software is used to make communication boards, educational materials, and overlays for different computer access devices and for speech output. Presently software is designed for Macintosh and Windows.

Microsoft: Accessibility and Disabilities Group
Web site: www.microsoft.com/enable
Microsoft has established the Accessibility and Disabilities Group to make computers easier to use for people with special accessibility needs. This group works to make Microsoft products and services more accessible as well as promote accessibility throughout the computer industry. It also supports the development of a rich variety of third-party accessibility aids.

PageMinder
Web site: www.pagemindering.com
PageMinder provides a welcome solution for individuals struggling with memory deficits, or trying to keep up with a complicated schedule. With the use of paging technology, customers receive text reminders for medication times, daily living skills, appointments, or other routine tasks. The system is portable, easy to use, and requires no initiation on the part of the user. It can be adapted for many languages.

Prentke Romich Company
Web site: www.prentrom.com/
PRC's company mission is to help people with disabilities achieve their potential in educational, vocational, and personal pursuits. To this end PRC provides quality language and assistive technology products and services to people with disabilities, their families, and professions. Products include augmentative communication systems, computer access technology, and environmental controls. PRC services include toll-free sales and service numbers, a trial rental program to ensure applicability prior to purchase, and a service loaner program so that a user is not without a device while it is being serviced.

Psycho-Educational Services
Web site: www.psycho-educational.com
This company offers the Functional Evaluation for Assistive Technology (FEAT) assessment tool among other tests.

RJ Cooper and Associates
Web site: www.rjcooper.com
RJ Cooper makes special-needs instructional software, access software, switch interfaces, and adapted trackballs and joysticks. RJ produces everything he makes for Mac and Windows, as well as his "old" library of Apple II software. Free demos are available. RJ has what may be the only online interactive, real-time, single-switch arcade game. Download his Movie Viewer to be able to play the games at his Web site.

Sunburst Communications
Web site: www.sunburst.com
Sunburst produces quality educational software in nearly all curriculum areas, for all grade levels, for Macintosh and PC-compatible platforms.

The Spinoza Company
Web site: www.spinozabear.com
Spinoza, the bear who speaks from the heart, was developed by a communications specialist and a special education teacher. The 17 inch teddy bear has a cassette player inside and comes with a collection of nine tapes designed to build a positive self-concept. Spinoza is used effectively by parents, teachers, and health-care professionals to promote literacy, emotional health, and social skills. Also available with a Talking Book player (to play four-track tapes as used by people with visual impairments).

TeleSensory
Web site: www.telesensory.com
TeleSensory manufactures and distributes a wide variety of products for blind and visually impaired children and adults. These products include low-vision reading aids and access peripherals that include speech access devices, computer screen enlargers, Optacon print reading aids, Braille printers, OCR devices, and refreshable Braille display.

William K. Bradford Publishing Company
Web site: www.wkbradford.com
William K. Bradford Publishing Company produces K–12 educational software. They carry the school versions of product lines such as Explore-A-Story and Explore-A-Science. Additionally, William K. Bradford Publishing Company produces home versions of certain D.C. Heath titles, as well as many other titles from a variety of developers. Home versions are configured with brief user instructions, appropriate disks, and any other support materials needed for operation.

INDEX

A

B

V

W

Y

Z